T0365563

Appraisal of the Growth of the Christian Faith in Igboland

A Psychological and Pastoral Perspective

Bartholomew N. Okere

iUniverse, Inc.
Bloomington

Appraisal of the Growth of the Christian Faith in Igboland
A Psychological and Pastoral Perspective

iUniverse books may be ordered through booksellers or by contacting:

iUniverse
1663 Liberty Drive
Bloomington, IN 47403
www.iuniverse.com
1-800-Authors (1-800-288-4677)

ISBN: 978-1-4759-1109-1 (sc)
ISBN: 978-1-4759-1110-7 (hc)
ISBN: 978-1-4759-1111-4 (e)

Library of Congress Control Number: 2012906625

Printed in the United States of America

iUniverse rev. date: 6/20/2012

DEDICATION

This book is dedicated to all Advocates of Inculturation and Flexibility in their religious sensitivities bearing in mind that all religions are God's religion and no specific one is His – "We live lives forward but we can only understand them by looking backwards" – Jon Overvold (Director of Pastoral Care, NSUH).

PROMOTIONAL BLURBS

Rev. Fr. Bartho Okere's research into the appraisal or 'dilemma' of slow growth in Christianity is a rewarding academic excursion into the existence of a conflicting duality of beliefs and practices between the traditional religion and the Christian faith among Ngor Okpala and Igbo people of Nigeria in West Africa. The author concedes and in fact emphasizes that the malady is not unique to Igbo people alone, but is a universal phenomenon all over the world where Christianity was introduced by missionaries and practiced till date. After describing the various aspects and manifestations of the dilemma, Fr. Okere proposes a structured approach to pastoral care, through which a non-prejudiced understanding and incorporation of the people's culture with Christian theology could become the long desired panacea to the problem that had hitherto militated against the growth of Christian religion. The research is exciting and desires careful study by all people who want meaningful and more successful re-evangelization of the world.

Mazi Amam A. Acholonu
Writer and commentator on Igbo cultural studies
Consultant-Urban & Regional Planning AND Behavior
Rehabilitation,
USA.

After reading Dr. Okere's book on the appraisal of the Christian faith in Igbo land, I wondered why the same Christian message has not produced positive results in many parts of the globe. The book has revealed a striking point in the sense that many people have simply presented Christianity as a certificate of "do what you like", while their lives are abhorred from the truth of the person of Jesus. Read this book and evaluate your life within the divine equation.

Dr. Sebastian Obioma Gubor
General Educational Development
Instructor,
New Haven Correctional Center
Connecticut, USA.

I congratulate You, Rev. Dr. Barth Okere for your courage to delve into the most sensitive issue that involves eternal life in heaven or hell. Your disagreement with me in some of my views on the reasons for the dilemma is the height of scholarship. I hope society will learn much from your academic contributions and heal herself from possible complexities or dilemmas in the growth of faith.

Anthony O. Nwachukwu, PhD, Psy.D.
Prof. of Counseling Psychology and West African Studies,
Chair, PhD Defense Panel, NY.

As long as Christ was introduced to Igboland in a borrowed robe with a western face, the Christian faith will not deeply grow there, unless the truth of the person of Christ and his mission are well introduced and explained to the people. The missionaries alerted the Africans of the presence of Christ in their midst, the people have come to encounter him in their ways of life. As the Author said, "Christianity in a foreign face is dangerous". In this book, Fr. Okere is calling us to avoid further complexities or dilemma and embrace Jesus as our brother and savior.

Dr. Christiana C. Onu (Nee Ekeh), RN, BSN, MA, PhD
President, Messiah Pharmacy Inc, PA, USA.

Foreword

Emile Louis writes, "If life is meaningful, it has to be purposeful, focused and admired...If Christianity is necessary for the Igbo people; it must have effects in their lives. A Christian should exhibit certain attitudes that distinguish him or her from the rest of others" (Emile Louis, 1965:55), irrespective of culture, race or status. The question then focuses upon the meaning of life, why faith is essential in any life aspiration or goal, and more importantly, the nature of our relationship with and worship of God. Indeed, many philosophers have defined the meaning of life in different ways by how they named our species. The Scholastics referred to homo sapiens, that is, 'knowing man. Jean-Paul Sartre referred to the homosexual, a being realized by sex drives. Others have spoken of man as religious and political beings. As Darrell Cole writes in the Spring, 1999 ISSUE of the Journal of Religious Ethics, and I quote, "For Aquinas, the ultimate end of human life is otherworldly. Nothing can be the final end for human beings except that perfect state of happiness found in the beatific vision of God, which can take place only in the afterlife". I personally believe that man is able to make his or her life meaningful amidst the struggles of today's world. Human beings are able to lead their entire lives as referring to God, reflecting on human excellence, virtues of faith, hope and charity. Human beings can choose to direct their lives in conformity with God and live the right view of life, facing and controlling their emotions and above all, being happy. By the gift of freedom, they can also choose to do otherwise.

In fact happiness is the goal of human life, and every human being must strive towards achieving happiness, identifying with the meaning and essence of life. These are the main thrusts of religion. When religion ceases to guarantee hope and reinforcement that energize and motivate the worship of God, it loses its credibility. My point here is that each individual must determine his or her own meaning of life in a loving and caring way. Though this is quite difficult in a world of today, yet we need to struggle to discover the important aspects of life and avoid the distractions in order to achieve a meaningful life.

Consequently, one may begin to ask, "What is the meaning of life, what is our relationship with God?" I believe that through our relationship with Jesus we can find the meaning of life. Jesus Himself claimed to be the way, the truth and the life. (John 14:6). Jesus said, "I am the bread of life, he who comes to me shall not hunger" (John 6:35), yet many are hungry of unsatisfying urges and desires. "I have come that they may have life, and have it to the full" (John 10:10), yet many are still confused in their lives. Jesus went further to say, "Come to me, all you who are weary and burdened, and I will give you rest. Take my yoke upon you and learn from me, for I am gentle and humble in heart, and you will find rest for your souls. For my yoke is easy and my burden is light" (Matthew 11:28-30). Still many are afraid to come to life; instead they prefer darkness to light or learn from Him. "If anyone would come after me, he must deny himself and take up his cross and follow me. For whoever wants to save his life will lose it, but whoever loses his life for me will find it" (Matthew 16:24-25). This is the crux of the matter; many would want to save their lives without carrying any cross. Eternity without a cross is a contradiction and impossible. To avoid dilemma of the growth of the Christian faith, whether in Africa or elsewhere in the world, the cross is inescapable. Intrinsically, he or she who follows

Jesus shall not walk in darkness. As Jesus lays his own life for his people, so too Christians must lay down their lives in order to find meaning and happiness in life by the little things they do for each other on daily basis.

Therefore, Rev. Dr. Bartholomew Okere has challenged each of us in this book to discover the true meaning of life by following the footsteps of Jesus, the Eternal Savior. The Appraisal or 'Dilemma' as conceived in the African culture and which featured predominantly in this book could not have arisen if the Christian message was introduced in the spirit of the Founder, especially to a people who had not doubted their relationship with their God. The Igbo people are so religious to the core. The Christian message is not incompatible with their values of honesty, holiness, truth, justice and peace etc. The dilemma in question surfaced as a result of hypocritical attitudes of some Christians whose styles of life are in opposition to the cherished and long-practised values of the Igbo people. Significantly, Okere's book has called our attention to imbibe the good qualities of truth, hospitality, openness, love and oneness that are inherent in both religions and give dilemma of the growth of the Christian faith in Igbo land a mortal blow. I encourage everyone to grab his or her own copy today and discover why religion should be taken more seriously in these days of materialism by our values of right choices and behaviors.

Sr. Joanna Okereke, HHCJ
A PhD Candidate
Program Coordinator
Cultural Diversity in the Church
United States Conference of Catholic Bishops
3211 4th Street NE
Washington D.C. 20017

ACKNOWLEDGMENTS

The realization of this book has made it expedient to thank the various professionals and experts who assisted me in its development. To God be the Glory, honor and praise, the source of all wisdom, insight and knowledge, for enlightening me to the achievement of my dream to make a substantial contribution to society to grow in the peace and love of God and neighbor. I also thank all of you, whose materials were incorporated into this book and the various professionals, especially the teachers from Ngor Okpala, who assisted me in the data collection and validation of this academic manual/ book.

My greatest appreciation goes to my Professors, Staff and Alumni of Graduate Theological Foundation [GTF], affiliate of Oxford University, London and Centro Pro Unione, Rome, who in many ways rendered invaluable help to the progress and publication of the masterpiece. On this note, I am most indebted to the Administration of GTF, Dr. Kendra E. Clayton, The Director of Academic Affairs Committee, Dr. Linda G. Morgan, Provost, The Registrar and Special Project Coordinator, Bethany C. Morgan, Director of Management Systems, Dr. Russell Neitzke and Director of Student Services, Luann Falkowski, to mention but these few.

On the same par, I am indebted to my PhD Defense Panelists, especially the Head of Panel, Prof. Anthony O. Nwachukwu, External Examiners, Prof. Christian Anyanwu and Dr. Edward Duffy, and the rest of the Panel members who bombarded me with innumerable questions on that very heroic day I changed my academic status. All you did that day was to prepare me for the tough job ahead, the publication of this book.

I am singularly grateful to Dr. John Morgan, The President of GTF for his orderly and well-articulated research books that guided me in putting together my materials to a researchable and publishable perspective. His encouragement and support to me throughout the course of my academic research at GTF were instrumental to the publication of this book.

To you, Sr. Joanna Okereke, HHCJ (PhD Candidate), I sincerely thank for accepting to write the preface to this book and your technical advice to me during the course of writing this work.

In a very special way, I most sincerely thank my Sponsor and Ordinary, Most Rev. Dr. Anthony J.V. Obinna, the Archbishop of Owerri Archdiocese for his permission and encouragement to engage in a PhD Program with Graduate Theological Foundation. Many thanks for being there for me.

More importantly, my filial recognition and immense gratitude go to my dynamic and dedicated Supervisor, Prof. Anthony O. Nwachukwu, whom I will call an icon of African literary scholar, who accepted to guide my Dissertation process. He was good to a fault. He actually inspired me with provoking ideas for human growth, religious advancement, the shaping of our destinies and for the pastoral practice of justice and the application of the principles of equality, probity and integrity. Prof. Nwachukwu painstakingly supervised this work/book to its completion. He equally provided me with some academic instructional materials, support and valuable resources, especially his text books on *"Salvation in African Context"* and *"Keeping Human Relationships Together ..."* as powerful tools for making this venture a reality.

In the same vein, my heart goes for my Professors at St. Joseph Major Seminary Ikot Ekpene (Akwa Ibom State), and Bigard Memorial Seminary Enugu in Nigeria, where I previously studied. These formative Institutions gave me a head start and prepared me for the rigorous studies at the Graduate Theological Foundation.

I equally express my unalloyed and unflinching gratitude to Prof. A.E. Onyocha, Prof G.G Agulanna, Mr Vitalis Nwaneri, Sir E.A.C Orji, KSJ for their unique and dependable advices and encouragement towards the realization of this book. In fact, I am thankful to them for standing by me throughout my academic journey at GTF

I particularly owe huge indebtedness to my brothers and sister- in law, Dr. T. C. Okere, Barrister Nze Felix, and Julie Okere, who helped me in organizing some relevant textbooks and articles from Nigeria. Thank you all.

It is my sincere wish to express immense thanks to the University of Arkansas in Little Rock, Library staff, for making their Library accessible to me for most of the books and articles I integrated in the development of my monograph, leading to the publication of this book.

Also, I am indebted to my bosom friends for their financial and moral support toward the realization of this book.

My profound gratitude goes to my Professional colleagues at St. Vincent Infirmary Medical Center, Little Rock, Arkansas for their fraternal understanding and assistance to me during the writing of this book.

To you, my beloved family members, both at home and in the United States, I am grateful for inspiring; encouraging and supporting me in ways I can never adequately express. Pa Benedict and Ma Esther Okere, my cherished parents, you are most certainly enjoying heavenly rewards for lives well spelt on earth. I have no doubt you are smiling over there, especially to see me achieve my dreams and academic goal.

Rev. Dr. Nwaofoani and other contributors to the success of this book, I say: "Bravo and remain blessed".

Finally, there are so many experts and professionals who made substantial contributions to the development of this book. I owe you huge appreciations. Even though I did not mention your names, I really appreciated your immense contributions and supportive presence throughout the course of my studies. While I do know that some of you would prefer to be anonymous, I still feel obliged to express my sincere gratitude to you for enriching my dissertation with the generous gift of your time, talent and wisdom. May God enlighten our minds to appreciate religious values that are on the path of justice and truth.

You are all in my daily prayers.

Rev. Fr. Batholomew Nneji Okere, (Ph.D)

CONTENTS

INTRODUCTION

If Christianity were taught and understood comfortable to the spirit of its Founder, the existing social organism could not exist a day - Emile Louis (1965:55).

To the question: "Why was Christianity not taught and understood to the spirit of its founder", this book serves as an antidote. Yet, on the side of "the existing social organism could not exist a day", I invite you to take a guess. The message the book has put across here points to a dilemma in a sense that most of the people of Igboland today are confused as regards what to believe in or not. It was precisely and due mainly to these conflicting faith crises that the author ventured into this sensitive area. But for the interest of those who seem to have accepted the faith or made up their minds, the word "dilemma" as used in this book needs to be understood within the context of 'complexity', or simply put, "APPRAISAL" of the growth of the faith in Igboland. To this effect, is it not possible that, as Nwachukwu noted in his book that "most often, something is keeping you uncomfortable, and at times, that something is you, your unhealthy choice patterns, bad life styles and insatiability" (Nwachukwu, 2010:9). Does it not sound funny that Christianity

1

was not taught and understood comfortable to the spirit of the founder but taught and understood comfortable to our own decisions and choices? What is it that is critical and counterproductive in Christianity that cannot be integrated in the Traditional religion of the Ngor Okpala people? Could the Christian principles be misleading or offensive? Whether we accept it or not, religion is part and parcel of us. We are religious people and there is 'dilemma' when people are brought to the crossroad of unacceptable faith options or confusion.

Even those we call Atheists, are equally religious as long as they are in search for meaning, the purpose of their lives. Is it better we accept to live a meaningless life, without any purpose, beginning and end? Or, do we exclude the Atheists because they do not profess any belief in God? What is belief in God when an Atheist does everything humanly possible to live at peace with one another and a Christian who continually nurses animosity for his neighbors? By "continually", I mean that research has shown that most people who claim to be religious are the perpetrators of evils in society today. Take the census of the crimes that are committed on daily basis, higher percentage falls on the Christians than some of those we regard as non-believers. We need to understand the primary aim of Christianity and decide whether or not it is suitable for us. Most people are in haste when challenged by Christian principles that guarantee lives but seem to crave, relax and feel comfortable in transient matters that satisfy only earthly appetites.

Wait a minute; can there be a true believer in God when most people seem to indulge in high level of hypocrisy? We are our own religions in the sense that whatever we project as our own religion – materialism, inordinate desire for sex, affluence, fame, God, sound moral life, etc, manifests itself in our behaviors and actions. It is only when others validate our actions and assign marks to them that it dawns on us the force, being or God we believe and worship in our everyday lives. We deceive ourselves in deceiving others but it does not last forever. Faith only works in action and not in kneeling for many hours in the church, speaking in such tongues that aim at immediate profit or gain. In other words, while so many people may be pointing accusing fingers on the Church and her Ministers, Government, or Parents, etc as regards the dilemma of the growth of the Christian religion in Igboland, this book invites you to look into yourself first. At this juncture, I invite you to join me to investigate why we cannot accept the values of Jesus Christ – Christianity. Have we ever resolved to accept them at all? We are equally our own choices.

However, an introduction to any scientific endeavor or book provides readers with the necessary background and over view of the entire message the author has in stock for the individual in particular and society at large. As an avid reader of works on the Christian faith, coupled with my personal and professional experiences as a minister, I have always felt disappointed whenever questions on faith arises among my people, especially considering the enormous sacrifice Jesus made on the cross for our salvation. In Nwachukwu's words, "It was not the nail that kept Jesus on the Cross, but His love for us" (Homily, Easter Sunday, 2012). One question that surfaces in my mind bothers on two fundamental concerns, namely: Did Jesus actually fail to accomplish his salvific work or was the problem from man's unmanageable and corrupt nature? We are bound to accept one option. Within my area of research, Pastoral Psychology, which involves psychological practice, I am compelled to apply the findings in psychology to the advancement of faith. Faith works in action and the best way to prove it is to make Christian practices relevant in human activities. That is why our findings in pastoral psychology place much premium in the marriage of religion to psychology. In a sense, according to Nwachukwu: "There can be psychology without religion but it is inconceivable to practice religion without psychology" (Nwachukwu, 2011:194). A closer examination of what Nwachukwu has noted reveals that the problems and dilemma we encounter in the growth of religion today stem from the ways people get about practicing their religion and not necessarily from religious obligations themselves. It is one thing to recite the creed and another to put it into action. Time of kneeling or ambush theology is over. God always loves and wants us to remain with him in our actions.

As it were, the need to study the dilemma of the growth of Christian faith in Igbo land becomes expedient. Again, issues of faith can be approached socially, politically, economically, religiously and so on. But in this very book, I deemed it classic to approach it from pastoral and psychological points of view. The pastoral implication is that those who belong to one faith tradition or the other want to know how their efforts impact their lives generally. Is it possible for one to believe in a supernatural being who has no effect in one's life? Can the notion of God be therapeutic in any sense, especially when people face different life threatening situations? On the economic perspective, does poverty affect one's belief system in any form? Can a hungry person sing and praise God on empty stomach? On a different note, to what extent can the name of God be employed for political gains? We see it happen every day on political spectra. Many have used God's name to win elections only to turn around to attack God, his people and values. Yet some others have religiously carried out and perpetuated their evil intentions in their everyday lives. Religious values cannot be equip-rated with every social life. On the other hand, religion is meant to guide and elevate society to appreciate ideals that respect individual freedom, sacredness of life and the dignity of the human person. This is where pastoral psychology takes its foundation and function. If life is meaningful, it has to be purposeful, focused and admired. Religion should not dichotomize between human actions that advance peace and progress of society but rather encourages them. In this way, to practice religion is to optimize the various values of society and channel them to avenues that reflect the dignity of the human person, created in the image of God who is truth and peace.

Dimensionally, the Igbo of Nigeria had practiced their religion and faith before the advent of Christianity and they were very confident in the God they worshipped. The African traditional religion is holistic and all embracing. In today's terminology it is "Catholic". Therefore, the issue of dilemma is traceable to factors outside the confines of African or Igbo land. This is what makes this book interesting. For instance, if the Igbo people have enjoyed a lively faith and communal spirits of oneness, truth and peace, what then brought about the dilemma we are talking about here? What was actually the psychology of the African religious and belief systems or faith before the coming of Christianity? How can such faith level be evaluated in the light of what is happening in Igbo land today? In short, what brought about the dilemma in question? How and why did elements of syncretism infiltrate into their religious system? There are thousand and one questions and concerns one can raise considering what happened and at what point did it happen. Faith is essential in any life aspiration or goal, and more importantly in our relationship with and worship of God. If Christianity is necessary for the Igbo people, it must have effects in their lives. A Christian should exhibit certain attitudes that distinguish him from the rest of others. An African Christianity with a foreign face is dangerous and complicates its acceptance among a people who have no doubt in their God. That was precisely what gave the Igbo people their name in religious circles. An African or traditional religionist is easily spotted out from those who are not. In this context, a religious person is seen as an embodiment of truth and justice. In other words, truth is the main ingredient that propels the engine of religion and ultimately binds the Igbo adherent to God. Then, once this number one unifying factor of heart and body is lacking in a person, a pastoral psychologist is compelled to raise questions as how to fix the anomalies created thereupon.

Eventually, after reading Dr. Nwachukwu's books entitled "Salvation in African Context" and "Keeping Human Relationships Together", I was moved to the choice of this research topic: "The Dilemma of the growth of the Christian Faith in Igboland of Nigeria: A Psycho-Pastoral Perspective". While Nwachukwu delved into and dwelt extensively on the socio-cultural aspects of the dilemma, the various instances and salvation opportunities in the African context, I appreciated and appropriated them as important values that could be incorporated into the enhancement of the faith of the Igbo Christian and a way of resolving the impending religious and Christian dilemma thereof. In other words, Nwachukwu's work in the life of the African experience is going to be appropriated, in a large extent, adopted and applied specifically for the Ibos from the point of view of the people of Ngor Okpala, Imo State Nigeria. Call my book an indirect critique or review of Nwachukwu's indebt insight on psychology and religion; its originality explicitly spells out in the very approach I have adopted here.

Obviously, this is not to say that I agreed with all the Nwachukwu's views and arguments. We have areas of agreements and disagreements. However, the need to develop the thoughts and sentiments of some Nigerian erudite scholars is timely and necessary at this 21st Century when Christianity seems to have become a child's play at the hands of individuals who consider themselves equal to God, not only in

Nigeria but also in most parts of the world. The work is going to be substantiated by the findings of teachers who are deeply committed with the education of the mind and body, and particularly, involved in the predicaments of religious practices among the Ibos at large. Teachers are equally considered as important figures in decision-making and evaluation of the dilemma of the growth of the Christian faith in Igboland. Therefore, any piece of information we gathered from them was considered vital in the conclusion of our findings in this work. Besides, the work is a case study of how the Christian religion has impacted and informed the consciousness of an average Igbo man or woman. As a case study, it will be analytic as well as narrative.

Generally speaking, 'the dilemma or hindrance of the growth of the Christian faith in Igboland of Nigeria: A psycho- pastoral perspective' is the main thrust of this book. Man by nature is "homo religiousus" – a religious animal. There is no epoch in the history of mankind, including that of the people of Igboland that seems to have passed without raising questions concerning the ultimate end and nature of man. Still, man is continually in a struggle for a lasting security, his faith, belief and search for the meaning of his existence. This search, call it man's religious affiliation, is sought, interpreted and understood in different dimensions. The word "Christian Faith" means a lot of things and differently too, to a lot of people. In fact, the people's religion, culture, tradition, social- political systems, their ritual observances, and whatever defines them as such, point to the different notions and understanding of the concept of Christian Faith. Serious efforts were made in this book to x-ray the meaning of the Christian faith, its growth and hindrance in Igboland of Nigeria. For instance, when an Igbo man or woman says: "I am religious", does this mean the same thing as being spiritual (Nwachukwu, 2010). Are there different types of faith and religion or do they generally have the same meaning, especially for an Igbo man (Christian) and other people, non-Christians and in various places? The word 'faith' biblically speaking is a supernatural virtue by which, through the help of God and through the assistance of His grace, we believe what He has revealed to be. In a way, faith is accepting as objective and true what is yet to happen or believed to be the case. For many people, faith is a risky game but for real believers, there is no ambiguity or contradiction in accepting as realized by one's belief system. Faith is life, the very belief or way one lives out.

Believing as truth what one has not seen or received is therefore described as an act of faith. In this perspective, it is easy to discover that faith does not necessarily depend on intellectual capabilities or wisdom, but total conviction on the part of God and destiny. How do the Igbo people of Nigeria see this approach on faith from the context of their belief systems? The Igbo people see faith as a matter of one's own choice, filling oneself with hopes and trust. The Igbo people believe in other persons, institutions, in values and causes of this physical world and created order. These institutions and persons can fail but faith in ones God is unshakeable and absolute. As it were, the people's remarkable relationships and commitments with each other and their God arise out of such choices that have their bearing with the supernatural being.

To believe in nothing for the Igbo man or woman is a form of death. It is their faith that sustains them in whatever they do or intend to carry out in their lives. Joshua seriously advocated for faith and self-commitment to God for the Israelites as evidenced in the Bible so the Igbos through their monotheistic belief and phenomenological tendencies to their religion clearly identify God as the Supreme Being in African Traditional Religion. In Igbo Traditional Religion, Chi or Chi-ukwu or Chukwu is the Supreme Being and He is known by many other names as in Judaism. Early European missionaries, who came to Igboland, and could not understand the Igbo religion due to language barrier encountered many problems, as we shall see in this book. Monotheism was ubiquitous in Igbo Traditional Religion before the advent of the Europeans around 1885. Igbo Traditional Religion is not essentially polytheistic, but monotheistic.

Therefore, owing to the contextual nature of our enquiry, this book is limited mainly to the discussions and deliberations as they concern the concept "dilemma or hindrance to the growth of Christian faith in Igboland of Nigeria". Although the issue of faith is important in all the religions of the world, we shall carefully examine the two religious traditions, hand in hand in order to strike a balance - Christianity and the traditional religions as they affect the people of Igboland in their perception of the Christian faith.

Besides, some paradigmatic or model examples will be taken from particular cultures. We must accept that Nigeria, West Africa in the continent of Africa, is not totally homogenous in culture. Thus, there will be areas of agreements and conflicts. As we know, there is no researcher who can presume to cover every detail of all Igbo religious traditions. We intend to dwell or take most of our bearing and analysis from the culture, tradition, customs and religious practices of the Igbo people of Nigeria, especially from Ngor Okpala Local Government Area, Imo State. Based on the diversified nature of the various Christian denominations today, "electronic churches", notwithstanding, our bearing is mostly taken from the Catholic traditions and also from the institutionalized Churches as Protestant Christian traditions.

Eventually, the need for a distant author-reader dialogue cannot be over- emphasized in any scientific investigation or book of this nature. In our context, the basic motivation behind the writing of this book is primarily to provide society in general and the Igbo people in particular, with a document that has the potential to offer some explanations to the Igbo people's quest for the reason why the Christian faith or religion is not striving ever since its foundation around 1885. A couple of information embedded in this introductory page will enable the reader to know at a glance the purpose of the topic, its content, as well as a scratch-surface information on the author which provides the necessary insights into his qualitative academic orientation and interests that are incontrovertibly brought to bear on the quality of the researcher's contributions to the chosen topic. In effect, this introduction supports, not only, any form of the abstract of the book in general, but to a larger proportion, constitutes the summary of research, which chapter five of this book addresses also.

Besides, to provide information that gives meaning to people's existence here as well as helps them to appreciate the values, which their religions hold for them, are the prime targets of this book. The Igbo man of today is exposed to the cosmological implications of two religious traditions, one by heritage and the other by missionary or colonial influences. The Igbo man's world- view, his idea of divisions, heaven and earth, land, water and trees, custom and tradition, the powers that influence human activities, man's spiritual enemies, who inhabit where, affect his religion as well. The religious sensibilities of man reveal an inner urge for man to satisfy his spiritual aspirations. Yet, the stark reality of the great beyond inescapably lies before his consciousness. At times, man finds answers to his problems, and at some others, he is left in a dilemma of what tomorrow holds in stock for him. Besides, we know too well that the ineffective practice of the Christian religion by the Igbo Christians of Nigeria has much to do with its backwardness. Too many ugly influences ranging from materialism, secularism and the loss of the sense of the sacred have made it imperative for the Igbo Church or Christian religion not to grow in Igboland of Nigeria. On this note I welcome you to the world of the various dilemma of the growth of the Christian faith in Igboland of Nigeria: A psycho-pastoral perspective.

By "dilemma" in this context, we mean that the nature, confidence, purpose and therapeutic guidelines the Christian religion should have provided the people have failed in a large proportion. There is dilemma because the honest lives the people would have lived and enjoyed today due to the claims of the Christian religion are not there. There is confusion. People are asking questions as whether Christianity has served its purpose or are they going to anticipate another form of foreign religion that would assist them appreciate themselves in the light of truth, justice and peace? Can there be peace without justice or justice without truth? These are the truths of the matter. There is dilemma in most of the things the people do today. Even in Christian marriage circles, unlike in the African traditional religion, where fidelity is revered as sacred, things have fallen apart. With Christianity, cases of infidelity have crept up in many respected quarters of society even among religious leaders themselves. Therefore, this research or book is asking a pertinent and theological question: "What do we do?"

In order to address the matter scientifically, the research adopted serious fieldwork, library resources, interviews, and Internet consultations to suggest some possible ways the people can contend with the situation. The book is not going to offer any absolute solution to the failure of the Christian faith in Igboland because people behave differently even to constitutional and conventional matters. However, as already hinted, the book attempts to raise practical concerns that can assist society and individuals think of the best ways they can live their lives as authentic and reliable children of God and rational human beings.

Consequently, the need to approach the matter from psychological and pastoral perspectives becomes necessary. The impression the Christian religion impacts on the people equally determines the manner they approach and relate to God and neighbor. For instance, if a minister of the Gospel cannot be trusted in matters of public fund, faithfulness, holiness, truth and justice, and the people know it is true, obviously, belief in God will only depend on individual efforts. Society wants to see God reflected in the practice of religion and lives of their ministers, in their words and actions. Anything short of this basic expectation and confidence frustrates the growth of the Christian faith. That is the climax, height and apogee of the dilemma. By the time we have finished this enquiry; it would be evident that this ugly monster of secularism is not only limited to the people of Igboland but also to many cultures of the world.

Therefore, the justification of our approach in this book hinges on its strength to offer some explanations and healings to the Igbo man's quest for his spiritual satisfaction and security. This will lead to a new fruitful and spiritual rearmament, and the ability to accept religious revolutions from inside. Any assistance, whether spiritual or material, which gives meaning to man's existence here on earth especially to Igbo person equally goes to support the need for this scientific undertaking.

At this point, I am bound to give the organizational outlook of this book. The book consists of eight chapters, which aim at giving a selective but comprehensive coverage of the dilemma of the growth of the Christian faith in Igboland of Nigeria from psychological and pastoral perspectives. Each chapter has been organized, developed and written carefully to address the topic as specified. It is important to note also that each chapter is a current reflection of the author's thoughts and feelings, based on his professional experience, research and interpretation of the works of others as we shall see in our chapter two. Indentations are equally employed here to emphasize the points raised and for easy accessement and digestion of the therapeutic guidelines offered.

The introduction of a book is an icon, a road map that directs and guides people to their destinations. As earlier on noted at the beginning of this project, the introduction opens the door for the reader to enter the various rooms of the house. In this light, the noun "Introduction" has 7 senses:

1. The first section of a communication
2. The act of beginning something new
3. Formally making a person known to another or to the public
4. A basic or elementary instructional text
5. A new proposal
6. The act of putting one thing into another
7. The act of starting for the first time; introducing something new (AudioEnglish.net).

At times we take certain things for granted. There is no uniformity or consensus as regards where some authors decide to place their introduction. Some authors may choose to present the body or content of their book or the message they have for their readers right away and conclude with the same story. On the other hand, this book is the fruit of research, carried out specifically for those who value their religions to keep their hearts in their faith and to avoid whatever might lead to the decline of the growth of faith in their religions. It is our utmost desire that students of religion, psychology, theology and pastoral care will find this 'basic instructional text' very helpful in their research assignments. Hence, we have no option than to follow a design of work that is acceptable in most academic research works. As such, the highlights of our introduction will take the following steps and procedures:

Chapter One: The chapter addresses the statement of problem, which this book is going to investigate. As already noted, the problems hinge on the dilemma or the predicaments, which have hindered the practice of the Christian faith properly. In a general sense, before a person begins to seek for a doctor at the hospital, he might have suspected and experienced some discomfort with his somatic systems and feels the need to check them up. In this instance, the background and reasons for such discomforts and somatic problems give clues to reasons for the doctor. In scientific investigation, we refer to this as statement of the problem or the reasons for the sickness or need for seeking medical attention. As it were, the chapter one of every research work gives a comprehensive background of the problem as such. In our context, we are looking for the background, especially as regards the religion of the Igbo people of Nigeria before the advent of Christianity and how it has metamorphosed into a dilemma or predicament. In order to tackle the statement of the problems, there are certain parameters that must guide the investigation. They include: the background as noted above, the purpose of this study, its scope, and significance. The perimeters will be clarified in the main chapter of the book.

Chapter Two: This chapter is going to focus on the related literature. It engages more on the review of related materials on the dilemma of the growth of the Christian faith in Igboland of Nigeria, substantially adopting some of those literatures that are written by indigenous professionals. Various authors have aired their views on the impacts of the Christian religion and faith in many cultures and traditions. In this chapter, we shall examine those views as to ascertain which ones may assist us accomplish our set objectives in this academic endeavor. We have to explain the different meanings of the words employed in the work in comparisons with related concepts and meanings in other people's works. We shall try as much as possible to avoid serious academic limitations by giving definitions of terms. Rather, we shall incorporate Gabriel Marcel's phenomenological approach by allowing the reality and meanings of those words manifest themselves within the context they are applied. For instance, the different Christian traditional beliefs are appropriated in their application to concrete human situations and not presented here as theological reflections and enquiry.

The book is more of a praxis, pragmatic and demands immediate transformation of individual hearts to the signs of the time. Days are gone when teachers stood in the classrooms and dished out principles that would guide actions without specific manners how those principles could be actualized. The age of theorization has overlapped with needs and actions. Theory is considered adequate in every academic enquiry as the springboard to discoveries. Any academic endeavor aimed at theories alone is bound to fail. The main thrust of the book has gone beyond theorizing issues of faith. Not even in Platonic world of ideas can works of this nature be acceptable any longer. We need application and integration of values that might clear doubts and dilemma in the practice of both Christian and Traditional religions. It is only proper that parents, for instance, anticipate the fruit of the labor of training and spending for their children. Life works that way because it is both paradoxical and cyclical.

The chapter two of any research work is always relatively voluminous due mainly to the nature of the enquiry. Like the case at hand, this chapter deals with the people's culture, custom and tradition in the light of how the Christian faith informs and impacts them as a people of Igboland of Nigeria. Whatever affects a peoples' belief equally touches their lives in an intrinsic degree and magnitude. This is precisely why the psychological and pastoral dimensions of the impact of the Christian religious practices on the people's belief systems, socio-religious, economic, cultural and political are extensively discussed in this chapter. The body and soul are closely knit together. Discussions about a peoples' religion or faith cannot be isolated from the basis of their lives as such.

Although, the chapter two of any research work is one where nobody claims to have exclusive right as who has the final say on the matter, yet the kernel of the matter remains unalterable. The chapter is always a comparative and configuration one where professional ideas are weighed and considered for the scientific alignment of the entire work. As I noted earlier in my introductory remarks which I planned to discuss in details in chapter two, the dilemma in question has raised a danger signal or revealed that something has gone wrong somewhere; either with the Christian religion in Igboland of Nigeria or the people have misunderstood it all together. This is why the need to consult the views of other experts for a valid conclusion is a matter of necessity. I may agree or disagree with some authors, but I own the originality, authenticity and likelihood of criticisms to the position I have adopted in this book. This is an incorporation of united efforts to fight a common universal problem that affects the practice of the Christian faith in society, particularly in Igboland of Nigeria.

Eventually, we have not only decided but also attempted to be exhaustive in this subject, call this an enculturation of the Christian faith into the traditional cultures of the Igbo people of Nigeria, with particular reference to Ngor Okpala people of Igboland and vice versa. This chapter critically studies the people's response to the Christian religion and their practice of the faith thereof. It studies the principles for fruitful and spiritual rearmament, and the sense of religious revolutions among the Igbo people from within, particularly the people of Ngor Okpala. The chapter also deals with the emergency of Igbo Catholic Christianity, through the use of images, symbols and stories. Some religious values and concepts are being examined in this chapter as a way to bring to the limelight the problems at stake and their possible solutions as well. The chapter attempts to explore the synthesis and antithesis of the various responses of both religious traditions whose basic values seem to have been violated. Here, the Christian ministers are called to an authentic proclamation of the word of God without any fear of contraction or favor. The avoidance of religious bigotry, ethnic prejudices and the global syndrome of "abrakataba" or magical forms of religious practices and fictitious healers are equally given serious attention in this chapter.

Chapter Three: This is the key or soul of any scientific enquiry – the methodology. Volumes are not as important as the design expected in this chapter. Yet, it is more important and expedient to specify how one arrived at one's conclusions. Writing can be an art which posses a riddle for readers to interpret. On the other hand, a research work of this magnitude requires a method through which the various findings were made, analyzed, interpreted and presented to public. Therefore, in this chapter, we shall justify and defend our thesis statement and topic. Any research work that lacks valid methodology is like an automobile or motorcar that has no horn and brake. In other words, to have a scientific work that lacks a method is more of a disaster that brings no progress. The chapter three of every research work is the ladder through which readers climb the bulk, content of the work and understand the mind of the author or researcher. Specifically, it is important to note that chapter three of a research work traces its development and how the researcher arrives at any acceptable and valid conclusion.

Chapter Four: This chapter mainly examines the various data gathered from different perspectives as presented from chapter three. It raises the basic questions as how the dilemma of the Christian faith initially came about and underscores the efforts made to study them for possible interpretations. It is true that the Christian religion in Nigeria, and its influence have affected the people of Igboland in a dramatic way. In this chapter, it becomes necessary to underscore some dimensional testimonies and evidences of the crux of the matter. For instance, after chapter three has outlined the areas of study and instruments employed in the research, this chapter analyzes and interprets the results of the various findings that justify the statement of problem as such. This chapter is so important in that it furnishes the readers what the facts are and goes to validate the work as a scientific undertaking. There is no guesswork in a scientific work that will not be investigated or proved, especially when it involves experts and professional minds, field works and systematic enquiries. The motives of the early Christian missionaries in Igboland and how their activities impacted the people have to be clearly interpreted and comprehended. It is only within these confines that a solution can feasibly be proffered.

Chapter Five: This chapter handles the summary of the work. It gives an overview of the entire writing and presentation. In many research works, a lot of readers consult this chapter for a quick update of the topic at hand. This is a comprehensive chapter in that it articulates the various items, scope and contents of the entire research work or book. In this case, one may wonder whether or not, our introduction here has served the same purpose as chapter five. There is an ocean of difference in that chapter five is an in-depth and comprehensive analysis of the whole book at a glance. The language is always in the past, which indicates an investigation already concluded whereas our introduction serves as guide to what the reader expects in a book of this magnitude.

The issue of "The dilemma of the growth of the Christian faith in Igboland of Nigeria: A psycho-pastoral perspective" is presented here in a glance. It gives a detailed account of the work and severs as a catalyst for exploring the output of the work. This is a summary chapter that provides the mirror through which the work is perceived, studied, digested and appreciated as such. However, research has proved that this is the most difficult chapter because, to summarize a work that runs into volumes in one chapter has always constituted a tough procedure or been an uphill task. To deal with the general summary of the entire work, conclusion and some recommendations are not easy. As a summary chapter also, it attempts to suggest possible avenues that could help the readers particularly the Igbo people to traditionalize and Christianize the true Gospel message of Jesus Christ in their lives unadulterated. For Christianity to succeed or serve its purpose among the Igbo, it has to be presented within the cultural values of the people. It was precisely on account of this irreplaceable tool that we substantially incorporated the work of Nwachukwu on the cultural values of the people to buttress our position.

Chapter Six: This chapter is an elaboration of the scope of the book. In this section, the researcher is bound to furnish his readers with the strength and weakness of his work. Chapter six of any serious academic or research work is often divided into three sections, dealing with the limitation of the study, its educational implications, and the recommendations for further studies on the related topic. It is always referred to, as "work yet to be done". In effect, it has been proved that no researcher can claim to have exhausted his or her topic at hand. Therefore, every deliberate researcher is bound to identify the areas where he failed to emphasize, handle or treat. That is what it means to be scientific. Such limitations should consider the content of work, scope, population, instrument for data collections, sources of work, language of the work, etc. This is the only chapter where the researcher acknowledges his or her shortcomings, omissions, and criticizes himself in a manner he could not have ordinarily accepted or admitted. These procedures make every research work scientific and a systematic enquiry.

Chapter Seven: This chapter is largely designed to acknowledge the various resources and Bibliography employed in the work or book. The importance of specifying one's resources is not only helpful in terms of being honest and objective but also guides other researchers in understanding the reasons for certain points of view.

Chapter eight: In research work, this is mainly the last chapter of the work. It deals with the appendices and Glossary of terms. The need for this chapter is essential because there might be maps and instructional materials employed in the development of the work. This is the right place to display them. Besides, in many serious research works like this one, foreign and native words are inevitable. The glossary of terms is necessarily explained here in order to make the work more accessible to readers and subsequent researchers.

CHAPTER ONE

꒳

THE STATEMENT OF THE PROBLEM

This chapter deals with the statement of the problem this book will tackle. Just as the heading suggests, the statement of problem brings to the public the nature and magnitude of the instances that have created problem in the growth of the Christian faith in Nigeria. It raises concerns about what gave rise to the problem in the first place. For instance, has there been growth of the Christian faith in Igboland of Nigeria at any period since its inception? If there was growth, what brought about the changes in question? Also, handling these problems from psychological and pastoral perspectives, from my expertise as a Psychologist, practically presupposes two basic facts, which the book has to address. They include:

1. To what extent has the problem escalated as to affect the growth of Christian faith of the average Igbo man or woman in his or her behaviors and life patterns? Does the dilemma in question extend to the areas of decision - and choice -making? This is the psychological aspect of the problem to be addressed, the problem that affects the entire person

as a human being. In this instance, the role human nature, personality types or selfish inclination plays in the practice of the Christian faith has to be handled here also as a major contributor to the dilemma of the growth of faith in Igboland.

2. From the pastoral perspective, to what extent has the dilemma of the growth of the Christian faith in Igboland assisted or hampered the collegiality and solidarity of the people with one another? In a situation where people become less sensitive to the sufferings and problems of other people, the matter can also be described as a dilemma. In effect, how has the dilemma in question affected the religious consciousness of adherents to the Christian faith?

This chapter, therefore, will lead us to the holistic understanding of the Igbo people of Nigeria, with particular reference to the people of Ngor Okpala, of their cosmological perspectives and worldviews, their religion, cultural, political, social and economic situations. The goal of this understanding is to know why the dilemma originated. At the same time, it will lead us to examine their psychological life patterns, organizational strategies, and community compositions, laws, features, and occupations, style of interactions within their community and outsiders.

As already noted, chapter one of any research work is the thesis statement or the hypothetical and analytical exposition of the matter to be discussed and approached scientifically. In this book therefore, the highlights will touch every strata of the people under investigation as a recipe for comparisons with other nations or cultures of the world. It is an invitation chapter in the sense that each reader is at liberty to evaluate the factors that created the dilemma in the growth of Christian faith in Igboland and how such similar factors could create problems in one's own cultural milieu. Considering the parameters that can highlight or assist us in examining the various problems in question, we are going to treat them under several headings.

1. Background of the Study

According to Dr Morgan, quoted in Nwachukwu (GTF 2008), "Attrition does not just happen; it happens because something went wrong" (Morgan, H. John. 2003:62). When something goes wrong, an alarm is raised as what brought on the problem in the first place. For instance, when a child sees its parents and runs away, it often indicates that the child has done something wrong. Likewise, when something goes right, it extends to different angles, humans, vegetations and what have you. Thus, in this book, we considered it appropriate to find out what has gone wrong among the practice of the Christian faith in Igboland from its psychological and pastoral perspectives. By psychological perspective, we mean that the joy of life has been limited; from a pastoral perspective, we see that people have encouragement to practice syncretism. With each of these factors, the mind and body appear dichotomized and need to be aligned once more for an individual to function holistically as a human being. Within this background, the historical, religious, especially the cultural aspects of the problems are involved. They need to be examined also for a possible reinvigoration. We are forced to raise a lot of questions as whether the problem of the Christian faith in Igboland is individual, group, communitarian or societal? These are the areas to which we must pay attention in the course of the investigation. It is possible that misplacement of priorities could be responsible for the decline of the Christian faith among the people. Problems ranging from economic, social, religious, political, cultural could be the case as well. Most importantly, we are constrained to ask this fundamental question: "Has the Christian faith ever been solidly planted in Igbo land before we can speak of the dilemma? What form of faith is involved in this discussion or are we talking about since the Igbo people strongly maintain a belief system in their ancestors and God.

In the light of what Morgan has noted above, Sheffield, following the same line of argument, reiterated that nobody deliberately goes out to look for trouble, to mire oneself in problems, or sabotage one's own spirit and courage. If such happens, it simply means: "Someone else has initiated the process" (Sheffield, Anne. 2003: 144). Put differently, is it possible that someone can deliberately put himself into trouble for whatever reasons? Again, this is where we are faced with a lot of dilemmas. Judging from historical antecedents, the sophisticated nature of our world and what I consider a wrong application of freedom, many have gone to extremes to inflict injuries to themselves and others. For instance, issues of terrorism, secret societies, cultism, serial killers, and various forms of atrocities are not entertained or compatible with progress and peace among human society. Youthful age was seen as a blessing, especially among the Africans and some other countries of the world. A stage in human development universally regarded as a period of liminality in the pursuit of future, achievement and heroism has turned and metamorphosed into chaos, insecurities, injustice, immoralities and uncertainties because of bad lives.

Today we cannot deny that there is dilemma in most human organizations due to hypocrisy, let alone the growth of the Christian faith among the Igbo people. There are so many factors that could have been responsible for the dilemma. Unfortunately, in a society where every Dick and Harry claims to be right and just, it becomes practically impossible to have anything done appropriately. The metaphysical composition of man is rationality and animality, body and spirit, and each person needs the two to be human. According to Anyanwu in Nwachukwu: "To separate the physical from the spiritual creates a metaphysical quagmire because man is a composite of body and soul at least in the Aristotelian – Thomistic intellectual tradition" (Nwachukwu, xxi). I do not need any person to convince me that human beings are equally mysterious beings, created in the image of their God. This image is far from being wrong priorities, values of wrong choices and behaviors. In a sense, this is the spiritual source energy of humanity. Man cannot but exercise certain spiritual functions akin to his nature by living on the spiritual level of consciousness. It is only when man digresses or wanders away from this original and fundamental goal that dilemma becomes apparent.

In this research, it is our uttermost desire to dig the problem from the root. Obviously, the manner in which the Christian religion was presented to the Igbo people was a factor. The traditional values of the people got mixed up with those of Christianity. This is one of the major problems facing the work. It is not all. The role of the Christian ministers of religion appears to have worsened the situation. There is high sense of competition and rivalry between the traditionalists and the Christians as who are the embodiments of peace or true religion in the land. The people of Ngor Okpala are confused as why an ardent Christian, well known in the community and goes to church on daily basis could be the embodiment of crimes and all forms of atrocities.

Eventually, this book will essentially examine and integrate Nwachukwu's research on most of the traditional values of the Igbo people and how the western civilization or religion seems to have destroyed them today. This is a hydra-headed enquiry in that ministers of the Christian religion have a lot of questions to answer as what created the religious quagmire in the people's cherished religion and metamorphosed into the dilemma it faces today. Every culture is relevant for its own people and within the time of its existence. No wonder, so many authors in African traditional religion maintain that culture is both dynamic and progressive. What this means in effect is that, for any culture to serve society, it must have to be flexible, undergo certain series of changes to suit the present society for whom it is meaningful and necessary. We shall, therefore, give much attention to the culture of the Igbos and objectively weigh its relationship with Christianity and possible progresses made so far in this context. The dilemma of the growth of the Christian Faith in the life of the people of Igboland can be summarized from what an indigenous Igbo writer noted as cited in Nwachukwu (GTF, 2008, confer Salvation in African Context, 2008:11) in these words:

> *Why is it that the Igbo Christian today is prepared to give God*
> *his due at Mass and service on Sunday, and at the same time*
> *he gives Amadioha his due when he goes home*
> *(Ihuoma, O. Eugene, 1990:13).*

The statement just cited has a lot of implication for the surface religious atmosphere the westerners seem to have created in Igbo land of Nigeria. That statement may sound funny but goes to confirm to a large extent the mess the Christian religion has indirectly made in the peoples' religious consciousness. A closer look at what Ihuoma has noted will guide this discussion of dilemma in a substantial level towards proffering a solution that may bring the peoples' religion back on track and give a mortal blow to the dilemma in question. For instance, judging from the above statement, the following seemingly hypocritical and self-deceptional displays are easily deduced:

1. The Mass and service on Sunday are meant to be the highest form of the Christian worship to God for most Christians, especially the Catholics. The Mass is a Liturgical expression of the peoples' faith and trust to their God and fellowship – koinonia. For the Igbo Christian to attend Mass and Service on Sunday means he has fulfilled the obligation and worship expected of him from God and man. This is a free service one willingly feels committed to observe as a way of spiritual edification and rejuvenation and not necessarily compelled by any force or law. It is important to understand the aspect of this statement properly. The fact that one worships and attends Mass and services on Sunday implies that one has embarked on a serious spiritual function one considers irreplaceably meaningful in one's life. As earlier observed, even though it is an obligation to do so, one is still free to worship or not. Yet, to double-deal in matters of religion for the Igbos is to attack one's life and source of being. Then, the question is: "Why should the Igbo Christian be dubious in his religious acts and worships. What does he gain by paying double allegiance to God and Amadioha?" What does he gain by doing so?

2. On another note, the same Igbo Christian also gives "Amadioha" or the heathen god or man-made god his own due on equal capacity. This is the crux of the matter or the statement of problem, which this book has set out to address here, leading to such questions as: Why are there dual commitments in the service of the Igbo Christian? Who is an Igbo Christian? Is an Igbo Christian different from an Igbo traditionalist? Or, has this practice been associated with the Igbos in general or did it originate with the introduction of the Christian religion in their land? Again, assuming that the same Igbo Christian is the traditionalist, why must he practice syncretism and double-deal in matters of faith

and worship? More importantly, what is it in the Christian religion that is lacking, that the traditional religion must have to substitute for Christianity? The problem extends to asking if Christianity is real and meaningful for the Igbo Christian. We have to note that Igbo tradition religion is part of the cosmology of the people. This is the religion that has guided them for centuries as communities and peaceful people in the planet. Christianity is a latecomer in the annals of the history of their faith journey. If the Christian religion has lasted for more than 2000 years and the Igbo Christian still gives dual allegiance to both God and Mammon, then to what extent has the Christian religion succeeded in Igbo land? This is the dilemma. How can the Christian faith meaningfully grow when the people still resort to their traditional beliefs and values to solve their problems?

As Nwachukwu rightly observed in his published work on Spiritual Psychology, the emphasis on the above quotation is on the word "today". Ihuoma has directly or indirectly, not only lashed the Christian religion in a very general sense but also made a big distinction between the traditional and Christian religions and how the two have presently dichotomized the basic values of the Igbo people. In the understanding of the people, Amadioha has no footing or comparison with the Omnipotent and Omniscient God of Christianity, called "Chi-ukwu". The people worshipped him with their whole life. They had never doubted what their God could do or not do in their lives till the advent of Christianity. As it stands today, if the same Igbo Christian who worships his God on Sunday at a particular hour of the day, goes to worship the pagan god on the same day, it means he is not sure of the capability of the two gods to save him. Apparently, we can feel the struggle this worshipper is making to ensure he is attuned to his God.

Primarily, this is the background of the dilemma of the growth of the Christian faith in Igbo land. By "Faith" here, we mean religion also and its practice. The people's religious worlds have been divided and the center can no longer hold for the vulnerable and the sincere and honest people who are anxiously in search for meaning or to worship their God. Judging from the foregoing analysis and revelation, the principal reason for the dilemma of the growth of the faith in question is seen at a glance. Ihuoma has said it all. We can now deduce the role associations and environments play in our lives. Despite the fact that the Igbo people have tremendously benefited from the western civilization and education, their belief system, which is fundamental in one's life, appears affected in a drastic manner. Nothing is more important in one's life than belief, trust, and accepting one's life as it is. Belief system is basic and forms the foundation of one's life, past, present and future. To tamper with it is to tear the foundation on which one's life is built. There were various ways in which the Christian message could have been presented to the people without destroying their identity as a people. That was precisely why I appropriated Nwachukwu's research on the culture of the Igbo people.

As it were, syncretism has never been the child of healthy associations. In the light of our enquiry, the greatest problem we should tackle now is to find out why and how this ill wind of religious syncretism blew into Ngor Okpala of Igboland. To whom do we ascribe possible blames, the missionaries who brought the Christian religion to the people without proper catechesis or the peoples' lack of understanding of the new religion before they welcomed it? In either case, there is need to listen to both sides of the coin and stories. The Igbo people are called the Ireland of Nigeria both in faith and development. The belief systems of the Igbo have not been subjected to any scrutiny in their history. There is need to validate these claims in the light of likeable hypocritical behaviors today as the result of the new evangelism?

Consequently, the major problems the book handled hinge on these underlying factors:

> The problems that concern the incarnation of the Christian Message in Igboland and as received by the people of Ngor Okpala of Nigeria,
> The ones that arise from the culture of the people as such, And
> The ones arising from the activities of the Ministers of the Christian Message themselves.

These problems or concerns were carefully examined in this book. There are so many problems emanating from the implanting of the Christian message in Igboland. They are going to be juxtaposed with those of the culture of the people of Igboland in general as Nwachukwu has carefully outlined in his work. These problems are going to serve as the basic resource materials on the issue of religious predicaments or dilemma in this enquiry. We shall extensively present, study and elaborate them in the course of the research work, especially in chapter two of the book. Meanwhile, let us underscore the main purpose for this undertaking or study.

2. Purpose of the study

The purpose of any book reflects the mind and findings of the author, which he or she wishes to put across to his or her readers. The purpose takes into account the "Why" of the book. In many books this very aspect falls within the general sense of the writing. But in a research work such as this, the author is bound to specify the main objective or message he or she wishes to communicate that can be beneficial to the public. If a book or research work does not pin point the very line of argument that can guide prospective researchers and society to the right direction, it is generally considered incomplete. We have already looked into the background of this book, noting the failure of the Christian religion to deliver its message effectively. The purpose then directs us to the main reason for embarking on this project in the first place after the background has given us a big hint on the need to proceed with it.

This book is primarily aimed at assisting students and teachers of theology, individuals, evangelizers of the Christian Gospel in general and groups of researchers in African Studies and socio-religious aspects of Igbo culture and tradition become more conscious of themselves in the light of the need of societal crisis in particular. These groups of people are daily confronted with questions as regards why the Christian faith appears to produce no fruits because of hypocritical tendencies in society today. The first reaction as noted already is a call to the spiritual source energy of each individual adherent. People must have to trust their natures and themselves before they can aspire to advance to the supernatural hemisphere. The general reader who seeks an authentic panoramic view of a good number of issues that impede the growth of Christian religion in Igboland of Nigeria will definitely benefit from this book. It is no longer a guess that the Igbo of Nigeria have suffered from misrepresentations of the Christian faith in a large proportion. The matter has reached its climax to the point that a well-respected religious Christian could create unimaginable problems for the general public in the name of religion.

The net result is that the Christian faith seems to have failed to be bringing any spiritual energy to the people in many respects. In politics for example, most Christians occupy the leadership positions and yet crimes mount in thousands. In the religious circles, the ministers of the Christian message do not seem to agree among themselves as regards what the central kerygma – "the apostolic preaching of the life and teachings of Jesus Christ" (Webster's Dictionary Thesaurus) should be. For instance, the traditional religion of the Igbo of Nigeria has its focus on morality and meaning of life itself. This is a religion where faith in the ancestors influences the peoples' daily activities. In such practices, respect for the elderly is considered a spiritual function. Unlike the Christian faith that focuses on the principles and legacies laid down by the Founder, Jesus Christ, the traditional religion of the people is life itself and demands a general conformity. It is evident on what is happening today, where a Christian could give God his due on Sunday and turns back to offer sacrifices to the evil one on the same day.

To say the least, this ugly attitude has led to a strong sense of religious bigotry among the various religious groups. In one hand, the Catholics seem to claim authenticity in their Christian practices and on the other; the Protestants claim to control the government or power, while the Pentecostal claim to have the Holy Spirit. Even among the Christians themselves issues of the Holy Spirit and speaking in tongues are being misunderstood. For instance, the Lucan account of the Christian message includes the Pentecostal perspective of Christianity while the Pentecostals themselves claim to speak in tongues. These are confusions that need to be solved technically. When St. Paul spoke of Charismatic dimension of speaking in tongues, he made it clear that "glossalolia" – speaking in tongues demands an interpretation because of the unintelligible words being uttered. Yet, among the Igbo Pentecostals, they go into strict trainings regarding the various sounds their utterances could produce as speaking in tongues. But is it necessary? This is part of the cause of the dilemma. On the day of Pentecost, when the Galileans spoke, everybody heard and understood what they said without the assistance of any interpreter. This is Christianity in its unadulterated form. The Christian religion is Pentecostal and charismatic because it is pneumatological – a religion characterized by the Holy Spirit, eschatological – a hopeful religion, a fellowship (koinonia) a celebrating religion and parousia – expecting the second coming of Christ.

From its etymological standpoint, the phrase "speaking in tongue" derives from two Greek words: 'glossa' – tongue or language and 'lalein' to speak. Therefore, speaking in tongue in Christendom is part and parcel of its prophetic package. It is not exclusive of any Christian sect. Pentecostalism is Christianity because on the day of Pentecost, the Holy Spirit descended on those present – including the apostles and women. It was on that day that the Church was born. Learning to speak in tongue as a group or an individual is not as important as trying to live good lives. There should be no confusion as who has the authentic Christian message or which group of the Christian faith has any message that can assist people deal with the problems confronting them on daily basis – economic, social and spiritual. The gift of the Spirit is equal in magnitude and function. There should be no dichotomy or autonomy of the Spirit.

Each individual has equal amount of the Spirit, the difference lies on one's ability to manifest the Spirit in one's daily activities. Just as in the case of the sowing of the seed, equal amount of seed was sown in each soil; the difference was based on the various soils that received the seed. Those who try to tap their strength from their spiritual source energy tend to produce more fruits in abundance than those who tap from material source energy. The ability to address the dilemma in question depends on individuals and their choice points and levels. It is necessary to note that without the advent of Christianity, the traditional religion of the Igbo people could not have faced any dilemma. There is dilemma today because of the inroad of the Christian religion to the Igbo land of Nigeria.

On this note, the work on the dilemma of the growth of the Christian faith is set to contend with the various psychological and pastoral problems the people are having today. There is need to identify what makes a person a Christian and reasonable. The Igbos themselves have to claim their own identity as a people irrespective of the inroad of the Christian religion in their land. This work calls for enculturation in which those traditional values, which are in alignment with the Christian religion, have to be integrated, practiced and emphasized. Until we come to this conclusion, the Christian religion in Igboland will remain a surface one without any in-depth signification. That is why the book is poised to underscore the differences between the traditional values and those of the Christians as to bring or suggest a synthesis of the two worlds. When the Christian religion is properly understood in the context of its founder, the dilemma in question will begin to pave way to tolerance, more understanding, openness, unity and peace.

The people of Igboland deserve the best from their religion, make themselves worthy of their being, their communal ancestry respected, and in that way, they can easily fulfill their destiny. But with the problem at hand, when their religious values and destinies have been mixed up, they may remain in a cross road of cultural transference and shock for life. The book therefore offers to assist the people come to terms with their cherished values and those of Christianity.

Therefore, the book specifically seeks to achieve the following:

❖ To identify the nature and enormity of the religious dilemma and confusion the Christian religion has created in Igboland of Nigeria.

❖ To extensively examine the sources (causes) of such religious dilemma and to what extent it has affected the behaviors of an average Ngor Okpala man or woman in particular and the Igbo people at large.

❖ To determine and ascertain the best methods and measures the research could assist to bring authenticity of religious faith and practice among the people.

❖ To determine to what magnitude this religious dilemma has damaged the spiritual consciousness of the people in question.

The book, according to the Catholic Bishop's Conference of Nigeria, as cited in Nwachukwu, is aimed at:

A total transformation of primordial values, which shape the individual attitudes and judgments, decisions and choices, behaviors and relationships (CBCN, 2004:5).

The Catholic Bishops Conference of Nigeria has noted an important factor that could assist the Igbo people, especially in Ngor Okpala understand the need to keep to what works well with them in their religion. Any Christian religion that violates those fundamental values of respect for the elderly, hospitality, traditional laws and customs, social systems that bring the people together etc, has to be dropped. Similarly, traditional customs that militate against the basic tenets of Christianity, such as love of one's enemies, forgiveness, and reconciliation have to be questioned and revisited if not discarded out-rightly. As already suggested by the Catholic Bishops Conference of Nigeria, the transformation of the individual primordial values is expedient. This boils down to what we have suggested earlier that the ability to reason properly, comply with the norms and mannerisms of the people is an important factor in any decision-making, choice of right steps and formation of quality character, irrespective of religion itself. For the missionaries to have embarked on a wasteful mission in Igboland of Nigeria without achieving the targeted results if any, tantamounts to a serious violation of the integrity and identity of the people. I strongly believe that the worst thing in life is to waste one's talents and the happiest thing being the right choices one makes. The book intends to set the clock right again.

3. The Scope of the study

The dilemma of the growth of the Christian faith, whether it is in Igboland or elsewhere, is a matter of great concern experienced in every part of the globe today. For instance, in the western world, science and technology seem to have created the atmosphere of secularism, modernity, and the rejection of the supernatural as being instrumental to solving people's problem. Today, religion is de-emphasized in many quarters because of its seeming non-practical effects as medicine or food. Contradistinctively, those who have strong faith in their God claim to have everything. This is the situation with the people of Ngor Okpala. These are people who put smiles in their faces despite the vicissitudes of life. Their steadfastness amidst suffering and diseases underlies their level of spirituality. As observed earlier, their religion, psychology, worldview or cosmology, socio-political life styles are inseparably one and the same thing.

However, this work has significant universal application, cutting across gender, class and ethnic groups. But the main emphasis is laid on the Igbo of Nigeria with particular reference to the people of Ngor

Okpala community. Despite the damage the western civilization seems to have made on the religious consciousness of the people of Ngor Okpala today, high level of dilemma is more recorded on developed countries like America and Europe. By limiting our discussion on the Igboland of Nigeria with particular emphasis on the people of Ngor Okpala, we politely invite all nations of the world to address the decline of religious growth in their own countries as well. In this sense, we are at liberty to investigate religious dilemma from different parts of the globe or from other cultures, our scope is limited to the Christian and Igbo culture of Nigeria, as lived, practiced and experienced by the people of Ngor Okpala.

Therefore, the work is limited to and concerned with the various religious atmospheres that seem to have brought or created dilemma in the individual, religious and ethical, social, cultural, personal and interpersonal relationships and perspectives of the people under investigation. We necessarily deemed this work consequential in dealing with the problem of religious dilemma particularly in this part of the world because of what is happening there today. In this sense, the book is not going to claim to have exhausted all the issues that pertain to religious dilemma in all cultures and countries of the world. Rather, it is credited for creating the consciousness among the Igbo people and the future generations so that they can begin to fight those factors that militate against the real practice of their faith in the right direction. This mission goes to confirm one Igbo aphorism that says: "If a child does not take time to find out what killed his father, his own safety is at risk because he might end up the same way his father did". No wonder some experts of medicine hold that prevention is better than cure. The earlier the people of Ngor Okpala take cognizance of the major factors that erode their religion and belief systems, the better they are prepared to deal with it, hence the psychological and pastoral perspectives of this work.

On a broader perspective, the book is designed to address a global concern and application in order that those cultures such as the one under review, that have similar religious attacks might be equipped to fight for their faith and religion. It is important to note that every scientific or research work carries along with it the cultural melieu, perspective, psychology and people that lived within the period or time of discussion. As it were, this book, to a great extent, is largely punctuated by the African traditional religion, culture and those of the westerners especially as regards their attitude to the Christian religion in Igboland of Nigeria. A lot of questions have been raised as whether the missionaries deliberately eschewed their attention from studying the peoples' culture and mannerism before they embarked on their evangelical mission. It is within this wider perspective and horizons that the cause of the dilemma in question will be expounded and best understood.

Generally, the book studies the causes, effects and conflicts, which the Christian religion seems to have brought to the people of Ngor Okpala and the best ways the people themselves can find a meaningful balance in the face of the dilemma. The case study or fieldwork of this book as noted in the statement of problem is chiefly limited to the Christian religion, Western and Traditional cultures of Igboland of Nigeria, with particular reference to the people of Ngor Okpala in Imo State. Consequently, our population is largely going to be drawn from the Questionnaires, which some enlightened people, mainly the teachers, from Igboland of Nigeria, precisely, Ngor Okpala people furnished us as regards the reasons for the religious dilemma in their land. Our population could have included more groups than the teachers alone such as the ministers of the word of God in Ngor Okpala, the various sodalities, religious societies, youths and other organizations in the churches. Our choice of teachers alone in this survey was intentional and targeted because they are daily involved in the teaching of religious knowledge in both secondary and tertiary institutions. Besides, this group has encountered first hand cases of the dilemma in their various teaching professions.

4. The Significance of the Book/Study

The significance of any book conveys its relevance to the reader. There are so many books written under the sun. Some hold important message for the general public and individuals while some appear to hold nothing of worth. There are various ways one can find the significance of any book. There is a popular adage among the Ngor Okpala people that says: "Nobody tells a blind man there is salt in the soup". The fact is that, even though the blind man does not see, but he enjoys his sense of taste and does not need an interpreter to know that. Thus, the significance of this work hinges on the question: "What contribution is this book going to offer to individuals, groups, ministries, society at large and the people of Igboland in particular after they have read it". The book becomes relevant or significant when it squarely addresses the problems enumerated here, especially with the dilemma of the growth of Christian faith in manners that are accessible to the people. In other words, assuming that this book is made available to the people of Ngor Okpala, is it going to assist them understand the need to appreciate the Christian religion the more and integrate the traditional values in their lives as recipes for evangelization or is it going to create confusion for them?

However, it is hoped that after individuals have read this work, it will lead them to appreciate the following changes in their lives:

1. The need to understand and appreciate the Christian religion in the light of progresses and values that may assist them to strongly believe in their God the better.

2. The importance of the Christian religion in the enhancement of the traditional religion.

3. The issue of belief systems as transformable forces for flexibility, tolerance and openness.

4. The integration of the traditional values into other religions that focus on truth, justice, peace and solidarity of the Umunna or community.

5. The need for religion in personal lives and experiences that do not contradict or constitute obstacles to other people's practice of their own religions.

6. That man is naturally a religious animal whether he believes or has any religion or not. The major difference between humans and brutes points to the spiritual and religious consciousness, which is not ascribed to other animals. In this sense, what Henri Matisse once noted as cited in Nwachukwu becomes necessary here. In his own words, we read:

When we speak of nature, it is wrong to forget that we are ourselves a part of Nature. We ought to view ourselves with the same curiosity and openness with which we study a tree, the sky or a thought because we too are linked to the entire universe (Henri Matisse, Internet Resource).

Henri has pointed out an important factor that involves each of us as human beings. Consequently, we all are, in one way or the other, part and parcel of the created order in which there is harmony. It is only when humanity realizes this uniqueness in her being-ness that hypocrisy which is another factor that leads to the dilemma of the growth of the Christian religion today can substantially be uprooted. Having briefly examined the parameters that would shape our investigation in this matter - the dilemma in question, we are better disposed and prepared to critically evaluate the culture of the Igbos that seems to have conflicted with the Christian faith or religion. This is going to take us to chapter two of the book, the most voluminous of all other chapters. In this chapter two, we shall consult and study the various thoughts and minds of other professionals and experts on the subject at hand. This is where we normally agree and disagree especially when authors raise issues and concerns that are unacceptable as ways of arriving at a conclusion that validates our hypothesis and objective or goal. The justification of the book lies on it's ability to offer the expected therapeutic guidelines that will assist the Igbo people of Nigeria self-supervise themselves on the need to practise and live out their faith concretely and meaningfully.

CHAPTER TWO

m

REVIEW OF RELATED LITERATURE

There are some related literatures on religious dilemma in some parts of the globe. As already noted from our introduction and chapter one, our emphasis here is on the people of Igboland, with special reference to Ngor Okpala of Imo State. The media is never silent over different developed countries of the world that have eschewed religion from the school system. Individuals and some 'end-time preachers' equally emphasize the need to have religion for whatever reasons, personal or otherwise. At times when such discussions are held over the wireless, radios, TV without a concrete text one can lay one's hands on, we cannot strictly include such pieces of information as literature. Conventionally, literature refers to "imaginative or creative writing, the body of written works of a particular language, period, or culture, printed material of any kind, as a political campaign" (The American Heritage Dictionary). Succinctly, by 'literature review' we mean to examine works and materials that have been written on the subject of discussion.

Unfortunately, based on the nature of our enquiry, literature on religious crisis in Igboland, especially in Ngor Okpala people is not as numerous as one would expect. This writing might be one of the scientific products or reliable manuals on the issue at hand. That is precisely why we have taken time to carry out serious field--work on it. However, some indigenous writers have attempted to give their own opinions on the subject matter in one form or the other as such. That is not enough. We need a reference book on this all important matter that might extinguish the light of faith of our future generation if not well taken care of at this pre-liminal stage. Therefore, we are compelled to seek resources from different authors that can assist us reach our desired educational objectives in this book. Besides, most of the views and opinions some authors have attempted to give on this subject are varied and need to be validated or proved by a scientific process. This is what it means to stand aside and examine the enormity of work involved and decide if we can do it or not. However, every repetition in this chapter is intentional.

Practically, from fieldwork, library and Internet resources we can formidably agree and objectively claim our stand. That was the point William J. Grace meant when he noted the following:

> Before one embarks on a serious study of a subject, it is helpful to stand aside and get the long view of it, to see it in perspective-in its largest terms as well as in its details...the material out of which the human artist creates is experience of life (William, J. Grace. 1965:5-6).

The author being aware of the invaluable remarks William has made here did not opt to navigate the search alone. He employed experts, professionals on the related fields, developed an incredible instrument to measure his findings, resorted to library and Internet resources as ways of authenticating his research. Again, in other to create the context for shared thoughts and views, this book examined the phenomenological descriptions of the Igbos in Nigeria and the consequences that have led to the decline of the Christian faith from its psycho-pastoral perspectives. The 'psycho-pastoral' dimension of this book has to be understood within the context of human needs that demand instantaneous attention. For instance, what could be the prompt means of addressing the situation of Mrs. B who is being deceived or cheated by her husband? In such a scenario, while the word 'cheating' appears to enjoy a general connotation especially in marriage life or partnership, does it mean the same thing in the case of Mrs. B? The Pastoral Psychologist or Counselor has to examine his management strategies within a wider perspective as to decipher how the present Client feels about her situation. In counseling generally, every situation is different and demands a process appropriate and unique to it. In counseling, emphasis is laid more on the welfare of the client or counselee than on the comfort of the counselor.

In a nutshell, I deem it necessary to review "The Missionary's Role in the Indigenous Church" posted on AllerNet.com by Jamaal Bell (May 25, 2011). This very review or analysis places us on a better perspective to comprehend the situation of the Igbo people to whom the Christian message was presented by the missionary. Had I known always comes at last. Had the missionaries who brought the Christian faith in Igboland had the time and disposition to examine what Jamaal Bell observed here, the faith could have grown more than it did today. Jamaal's points are worth considering here. They include:

In Creating Churches

According to Jamaal Bell: "Foreign missionaries do not create churches, but simply help local converts develop their own spiritual gifts and leadership abilities and gradually develop their own churches" (Jamaal Bell, May 25, 2011). The missionaries simply provided teaching and pastoral frame work on a church that had always been indigenous from the beginning. It has to be noted that the indigenous church has always been self-supporting, self-propagating and self-governing. Though, the Africans had no established Churches as we have them today, their religion 'is indigenous from the start or beginning'. In the case of the Africans, the missionaries came and created new religions. If we should take the sayings of Jamaal seriously, the people were not assisted 'to develop their own spiritual gifts and leadership abilities and gradually develop their own churches' as such. In creating churches or new religion, the missionaries did not examine what the people had already, hence the dilemma of the growth of the Christian religion in Igboland of Nigeria.

Meaning of "Indigenous Church"

It was William A. Smalley in Jamaal who defined an indigenous church as: "A group of believers who live out their life, including their socialized Christian activity, in the patterns of the local society, and for whom any transformation of the society comes out of their felt needs under the guidance of the Holy Spirit and the Scriptures" (William A. Smalley, Ibid). On the same note, Jamaal Bell insists that: "This definition communicates that the church-planting missionary must be willing to allow the indigenous church to have different manifestations of Christianity rather than export their denominational or personal patterns that are rooted in the missionary's history and culture" (Ibid). Things have fallen apart within the peoples' religious consciousness, and to heal the division will take time. The missionaries did not allow the people to approach the Christian faith from their culture; rather, they simply exported their denominational and personal patterns that were rooted in their history and own culture. Suppressing the peoples' culture in the name of religion is the beginning of religious fatalism.

In a way, the missionary felt it was his prerogative to make cultural decisions for the people. In his own words: "The missionaries can be valued advisers with their knowledge of scripture and history. In fact, it is the missionary's responsibility to be a source for cultural alternatives for people to select if they want and need them" or not (Ibid). But the matter was presented differently. The Igbo people were not given the options to make choices, but gradually meant to accept the options the missionaries had set for them. The dilemma in question today could have been avoided if the elders of the people had made 'cultural decisions based on their needs, problems, values and outlooks'.

'God Relates to Humanity in Culture'

Jamaal Bell has raised serious theological issues here that could guide not only the people of Igboland, but also the general public who care about God in their lives. I have always said it; we worship God the way we are. That means, we worship and encounter God in our culture and lifestyles. According to Jamaal, "The Bible reveals that God has always dealt with people in terms of their culture. God intentionally worked his law, spirit and relationship with humanity within a particular culture. The missionary must act the same" (Ibid). Even though the people had no bible as of the time of the missionary activities, God was not presented to them as one who could condescend to peoples' cultures and respond to their needs there. What of today when the bible has been made available to them, no reference is being made in connection with the culture of the people. As long as the people were not prepared to encounter God in their every day living, in their culture, most of them still have recourse to their traditional religion where God is ever present to assist in their needs and trials. It was on account of the failure of missionary Churches to appreciate indigenous culture that Jamaal remarkably lamented: "The missionary must be careful not to impose and decide what course a new church should follow, with having little to no knowledge of the cultural background of the people" (Ibid). Continuing, he noted that "the primary mission should not be to corporatize Christianity on people nor should it be to impose Western cultural norms on them" (Ibid). In other words, both the mission bodies and indigenous churches should have their own distinctive objectives to avoid the indigenous culture to embarrass the missionaries.

The matter appears momentous and critical here based on the observation Jamaal has made. It is sad to hear that those mission bodies that imposed their western culture and norms did not like indigenous culture because of its peculiarities. The question is: "Why should the mission body be embarrassed in the first place if she meant to bring good news to the indigenous culture?" This review is very essential in understanding the main objective of this book. There is dilemma of the growth of the Christian religion in Igboland of Nigeria due to wrong ideologies and unpreparedness to call a spade a spade. Before we examine the goal of the missionaries, I would like to treat the Heraclitian philosophy that could have assisted to shape the implanting of the Gospel message among the people of Igboland in general and Ngor Okpala in particular.

The Application of the Philosophy of Heraclitus on the Bible and Western Culture: Implication for society and Ngor Okpala people

Philosophy as a scientific discipline incorporates every level of knowledge and cultural milieu of each person. Every person, culture, issue has its own philosophy. The bible is a product of its own culture just as the western culture or Ngor Okpala represents the mentality and life of its own people. In this light I have treated Heraclitus' philosophy as it relates to the bible, the product of the Western culture and how it applies to the people of Ngor Okpala. Examining what Ford said here, that the "bible is a historical work in several senses" (Ford, Part 1, 1999, p. 9). If the bible is a historical work in several senses, do these senses include the people of Ngor Okpala? To what extent do they need the bible in the first place? What has the bible got to do with their day-to-day affairs?

One of the senses includes its role in the western culture and individual lives. Of what significance is the bible to any culture that has no regard for it or does not understand what it is? In the light of Heraclitus, what role does the bible play in the growth of the Christian religion in Igboland of Nigeria or Ngor Okpala? We need to understand these basic questions in order to ascertain why there is dilemma in the growth of the Christian faith in Ngor Okpala. Is the Nigerian understanding of the bible different from that of the westerners that brought the Christian culture to Igboland? Is the bible a cultural phenomenon, relative or exclusive of any culture? As it stands, for us to achieve our prime target in this book, there is need to study the philosophy of Heraclitus more closely as to know how it has shaped the understanding of both the Bible and western culture in guiding the lives of the people of Ngor Okpala. We have come to the crux of this matter – dilemma.

The Philosophy of Heraclitus, the Bible and western culture

Heraclitus, a Greek Philosopher of the late 6th century BC has scientifically offered society the various resources and values necessary for her to achieve religious growth, peace and harmony in life. In this sense, we are going to study and examine this great philosopher on certain basic categories of his teaching. According to Heraclitus:

- ❖ Opposites do exist in nature
- ❖ There is unity and diversity in creation
- ❖ Life has its basic and authentic existence
- ❖ Flexibility and Change are necessary for growth and progress

We noted earlier that each person is a product of his or her own age. Most often, what is applicable in one age may be old fashioned in another. There are differences in life, which the people of Nigeria must understand. Heraclitus, as an important figure in his own age, was greatly influenced by the works of such great philosophers such as these Greek philosophers, Thales and Parmenides. In this light, we can find a similarity with this age and that of the Igbo of Nigeria. The Greek philosophers were mainly concerned with the cosmos, cosmology, and the primary cause of things in the universe. The Igbo are not far from this belief. The Igbo of Nigeria, particularly the people of Ngor Okpala were so concerned about the cause of their existence that they did everything to worship God and his agents who were meant to be responsible for other happenings in the cosmos. However, as for the point at hand, Thales posited water as the cause or responsible for the physical world. Heraclitus, on his own side, posited fire as the cause of the universe.

From the ingenuity of these philosophers, the world came to the knowledge of the western culture. They shaped and gave it a name. Just like the Igbo of Nigeria, who believed on the permanence of reality as designed by their ancestors and God with the mentality of "things must be the ways they are handed over to us" and abhor change in a very serious manner. In this light, the philosophy of immutability of reality of Parmenides is readily welcomed in Ngor Okpala or Igboland of Nigeria. Yet, the principle does not encourage any growth, even in religion. On the other hand, Heraclitus maintained that nothing is permanent in life. For instance, what one considers wealth today may mean nothing tomorrow; a poor man today may be rich tomorrow. By this way, he encourages the unpredictability of life. The traditional religion of the Igbo which has served them for centuries may not have all the answers needed today to worship the Supernatural Being. Just as in the case of Christianity, there are certain principles in the Christian religion that will sound funny to practice today among some cultures.

The main reason is that the Bible was written within a particular culture to deal with the problem of the moment that may not be applicable to other cultures that do not have similar problems or issues being fought at that very time. In his observation, the only thing that may be permanent in life is change itself (Wikipedia, the free Encyclopedia). That means, change is continuous and does not need to stop at anything. That is to say in actuality, change is an irreplaceable value in the life history of any created order. We can gradually begin to surmise why we have dilemma of the growth of the Christian faith in Igboland of Nigeria today. Let us review the categories under which religion and its growth can be possible for the people of Ngor Okpala of Igboland of Nigeria. The first one I need to study and examine is:

Opposites do exist in nature

Practically speaking, Heraclitus maintains full support of the paradoxical co-existence of the good and bad of Paul Tillich, white and black, beauty and ugly etc. In this light, he maintains that opposites exist and they are necessary for life and change. This change includes, changing from one belief system to other or slightly done and not totally. In his belief, opposites are unified systems of balanced exchange in flexibility and practice. Nothing is actually permanent in life. For example, as noted before, a beggar at certain period of time may become a lender in another period. Even in the western world, things have happened that prove Heraclitus right. For instance, a black man has become the President of a nation that practiced racism in its highest level - the United State of America. Or, do we call this a myth that in a country like this, in which women were not allowed to vote at the elections, has turned out today to be such in which women run for presidency? That is why the teachings of Heraclitus have great implications for religious growth, unity, amicability and harmony in every aspect of human industry today. By not allowing the world to be identified with a particular substance, freedom has been given to individuals to make their choices and have or belong to any associations, churches, groups they want. In other words, change becomes the ruling principle that guides humanity and all exigencies of life.

Unity and diversity in life

The teaching of Heraclitus has much relevance for the Igbo people of Nigeria, particularly Ngor Okpala. Had the people known of this principle of change they could have adjusted easily to the message of the missionaries and accepted Christianity for what it really was? It was likely that the missionaries themselves did not understand this principle of change also. This is why unity is not the same thing as uniformity. An individual has different parts of the body, and each of these parts is unique in its way and important on its own merits and functions. Besides the unity of purpose, each of these parts functions for the whole system to achieve a common objective, the life of the human person. We need this awareness in human relationships too because, once individuals are able to underscore their differences and dissimilarities, they can work together for the benefits of each member. Had the missionaries and the people of Igboland come to this level of understanding, the dilemma of the growth of the Christian religion or faith could not have metamorphosed to the level we have it today.

Life has its basic and authentic existence

The unexpectedness of life is important for progress and unity. Expecting hundred percent of sound moral lives from others will always lead to disappointments. In the words of Heraclitus: "If you do not expect the unexpected, you will not find it" (Talk: Heraclitus – Wikiquote, July 2, 2009). We must give other people's behaviors a chance. Mistakes are not always intended. An honest act can turn around and produce evil effects. These are the major reasons people should be given opportunity to defend themselves in case something goes wrong in their actions. "Despite of" is an important disposition for interpersonal relationships. One has always to give the other what Tillich calls "despite of " or the benefit of doubts. Most often, we judge others based on our ignorance or limited knowledge of the real matter, when the case is otherwise.

Flexibility and Change are necessary for growth and progress

The philosophy of Heraclitus is human because of the changes we go through on daily occurrences. We are changeable beings, from infancy to adulthood. There are changes in our personality developments, educational level, social, economic, political et cetera.

We can change for the best. Though, some change for the worse, supporting Heraclitus in his philosophy of change. Even in religion, we change without knowing it. Modes of prayer and worship at times change. The recent "Questions and Answers about changes to the Mass" in the Catholic Church is a big change in her Liturgical life (Conf. Federation of Diocesan Liturgical Commissions, 2010, www.fdlc.org). Once the people of Ngor Okpala accept issue of change, though difficulty, there will be rapid growth in the Christian religion in that part of the globe. Change is an important value each individual person needs for adaptability to life changes. For instance, to say that somebody is hungry is because he or she has not been satisfied with what heals or removes the hunger. In the Catholic Church, one cannot remain a sinner after one has gone to Confession. In a very convinced fashion, Heraclitus presents the common-sense truth of change in these words: "Cold things warm up, the hot cools off, wet becomes dry, dry becomes wet (Nwachukwu, 2010:xxviii).

These principles, as noted above, are important for interpersonal relationships especially in a world that seems to have practically lost patience in everything. Eventually, since it is only change that is permanent, then it means every other thing changes. In his words: "You cannot step into the same river twice" (Ibid). In other words, everything is in a flux, nothing remains, or stationary. Once stepped into the river, the second cannot be the first water you stepped into. Even though, the river remains permanent, the same person stepping, the experience is always different from the other and must be recognized as such. Based on these principles and perspectives, we examined the Bible and western culture and their implication for the growth of the Christian religion in Ngor Okpala.

Undoubtedly, the Bible is the word of God, written and expressed in human writings. These expressions are done in the language and culture of the time. According to the Letter to the Hebrews: "At many moments in the past and by many means, God spoke to our ancestors through the prophet; but in our time, the final days, he has spoken to us in the person of his son…" (Hebrew.1: 1). The act of God speaking to humanity through his son made no distinctions. He spoke both to society as corporate body and individuals as recipients of the word. In this process, he equally spoke to the western culture and that of the Igboland of Nigeria. God's manifestations in the world have taken different turns in the course of history. Most of these manifestations are being misrepresented in many quarters. As we can see from today's events, there are as many religious bodies as there are human beings. It is the seed of faith sown in the hearts of everybody and each person perceives it differently, hence the dilemma in question. For instance, according to Matthew's Gospel:

> *Imagine a sower going out to sow. As he sowed, some seeds fell on the edge of the path, and the birds came and ate them up Others fell on patches of rock where they found little soil and sprang up straight away, because there was no depth of earth; but as soon as the sun came up they were scorched and, not having any roots, they withered away. Others fell among thorns, and the thorns grew up and choked them. Others fell on rich soil and produced their crop, some a hundredfold, some sixty, some thirty (Matthew 13:4-9).*

It is no longer a guess that the manner in which the seed is received in the soil of individual hearts determines whether the seed produces any fruit or not. This is the heart of the dilemma of the growth of the Christian faith in Igboland. Most often, there is no general consensus as what people do with their faith. Many people are free to approach religion the ways they want them. In the words of

Ford, it is undeniable that "the bible.... this venerated book must be introduced in the context of a number of problems and challenges" (Ford, 1999, 9).

The word "bible" has various derivations and is used in many senses as earlier noted. It is originally derived through Latin from the Greek neuter "Biblion" simply meaning "the Book". Its plural is "ta biblia" the books (New Bible Dictionary, 1992, p.137). But today, it is taken for a feminine singular 'the book' in which it refers to all the books of both Testaments. The bible has even remained the Book Par Excellence. It is an expression in writing of all the dealings of God with the people of Israel (O.T.), and the faith of the apostolic Church (NT), a genuine self-expression of the primitive Church. The Bible contains 73 books in which 46 were written before Christ (the O.T.), and 27 after Christ - the N.T., (New Bible Dictionary, 1992, pp.138-139). This account is an achievement for which the Church is laudable (Confer Nwachukwu, A. O. DLM, GTF 2006). The word has been preserved through the sacred Tradition. Eyewitnesses have tried to communicate their experiences from one generation to the other. The Tradition of each culture transmits this word of God originally entrusted to the Apostles by Christ the Lord and through the Holy Spirit. In this instance, we are not going to discuss the various books of the OT and NT, the Composition, Canonicity and Inspiration of the Bible. Rather, the discussion will be limited to how the idea of Heraclitus has influenced our knowledge of the Bible today and the western culture as the powerful tools for motivating the growth of Christian faith in Ngor Okpala, Igboland of Nigeria.

As noted already, the word of God has historically suffered some attacks, misrepresentation and mutilation in the hands of many cultures including those of the western world, and now, the Igbo of Nigeria. We can now recall why Luther broke from the Catholic faith and led to the revolt of "Sola Scriptura" ideology. By Luther's affirmation of his authority in the Bible, any word of God preached outside of the bible is baseless. It was unfortunate that the Church failed to hearken to Luther for the immediate reform he brought about. It was revolution in the right direction. Eventually, the Church went contradictorily to the philosophy of Heraclitus that nothing under the earth is permanent. That was the spirit with which the missionaries came to Africa – outside the Church there is no salvation (extra ecclesiam nulla salus). How can such assertions be acceptable today where Vatican II has opened the doors of the Church for fresh air to come in? Again, this is change and a clear proof of the position Heraclitus has held.

The Church failed to notice the positive change Luther was bringing because of its dogmatic mentality. The Bible is one and must be interpreted to suit various cultures of the world. What constitutes a moral issue in one culture may not be so in other cultures. This mentality suits Heraclitus's teaching or philosophy. There must be rooms for flexibilities even in the application of the word of God in the culture of the Igbo. As Sugrue would put it:

> *Luther did not originally intend to provoke great change; he was a conservative thinker. He wanted to cleanse the Church of accretions and doctrines for which there was no Scriptural justification (Sugrue, The Bible and Western Culture, Part 111, 1999, p. 4).*

While I do not believe or share completely Luther's position that everything has to be subjected to the Scripture, the paradoxical aspects of life have to be considered at all times. There are many good things we do in the name of Christianity which are not found in the bible. For instance, we do not consult the bible to go after our normal business in life, look for high paying jobs, aspire for leadership positions etc.

However, there are still problems, which the Church still faces today because of her refusal to hearken to Luther's reform. We do not mean to subject whatever we do to the Bible. There are physical life situations, as hinted above; we face on daily basis, which we do not refer to the bible to deal with. After all, people who have no religion equally belong to a culture of their own and must fight to make the best out of their existence without any reference to the bible or religion. This does not mean that they are dammed. Christianity is the basis for judging all the religions of the world. While there are so many opportunities for heaven in it, some other religions have theirs as well. What is important is keeping to the right directions and values. For instance, "our behavior is changed by the behavior of others....", (Romero & Kemp, 2007, p. 35). Many non-Christians challenge us on daily basis by their truthful and honest life-styles, while some of us are deceivers.

On a more striking manner, the western culture represents its life pattern, socio-religious systems, politics, beliefs and cosmology. By western culture, we are looking at those characteristics that make the western world different from the rest of humanity, especially those of Igboland of Nigeria. In fact, western culture includes the European origin, ancient Greece, the Roman Empire, United States, the Soviet Union, ethical values, religious, traditional customs, literary, scientific, philosophical principles and the identity. This is culture that stands differently from the cultures of the third world people of African, Asian and the Arab nations. Western culture is characterized and portrayed by elements of materialism, capitalism, commercialism, imperialism, industrialism, modernism, aesthetics, arts and literature et cetera. (Wikipedia Encyclopedia, Internet Resources).

This mentality seems to be leading society away from the supernatural and transcendence and creating dilemmas in the growth of the Christian religion worldwide. It was because of the spirit of the western culture that Dr. Cletus Imo argues and cites Berger in this context:

> *Theologians especially must not allow themselves to become conceptually or methodologically blinded to signals of transcendence. This is like an invitation to all of us involved in religious ministries- theologians, canonists and Church leaders to put into considerations the changes in human history (Berger, P.L. 1969:52 in Imo, Cletus, Foundation Theology, 2009: 52).*

The western culture is highly characterized by the spirit of anthropocentric, scientific and technological revivals and ideologies. These ideologies have led to the discovery of nuclear weapons that seem to threaten the global peace in general and the dilemma in question. Today, indiscipline seems to have become the order of the day. Most of our teenagers have turned into something else. There are no more respects for the elderly. Survival of the fittest seems to have dominated most of the mentality of the young ones. This does not mean that the tremendous advantages of the western culture can be denied in any form. But in the spirit of Heraclitus, there should be unity among people especially as regards the manner they look at the bible and the cultures. While there should be differences in approaching both, diversity of cultures and the word of God should form integral parts that guide the human race. If the early missionaries who came to Africa, precisely to the people of Igboland

and Ngor Okpala had taken note of these basic facts, the dilemma we are talking about today could not have been the case. There should be no dogmatism in any culture or religion/bible. People can still find reasonable values in the bible that encourage their culture while each respects each other's values or vice versa.

Implication for Society and Ngor Okpala People

The Bible and the western culture can complement each other. The bible is not limited to any culture. The word of God is meant to reach the ends of the world, including the westerners and the people of Ngor Okpala. God is one in every culture but understood differently. For instance, the God of the Bible is the Almighty Father of heaven and earth. The Igbo of Nigeria equally have him as "Chukwu/ Chineke" who is in charge of creation, the creator and controller of the whole universe. It means the same thing for the Christians too. Muslims call him Allah and the Jews, Yahweh. Among the Ngor Okpala people, as in many African cultures, there is a strong belief in Arch-deities. Even in Ghana, one of these deities is called "Tano". This is a god that is very good to people and answers their prayers without delay and blesses his worshippers (Ilega, D. I., (ed.) 2000:170).

In the spirit of Heraclitus, western culture is a development that could lead to unity. The bible itself is a product of its own culture as already noted. The bible and westerners are cultural documents that promote oneness. This oneness includes the people of Ngor Okpala in a very remarkable way. If there is a bible without a culture that interprets and uses it, it is of no use. On the other hand, a culture that has no moral principles that guide her equally heads to doom. This oneness calls for identification also. The bible, being the word of God cannot be applied in a way that condemns the culture but has to preserve it. Neither can any culture progress meaninglessly. Yet, our early missionaries failed to understand this. The Bible gives hope to the efforts individuals make in the realization of themselves. In other words, Heraclitus advocates a continuity in which the bible will always anticipate a change in the behavior of people irrespective of its primary goal or culture. A sinner today who contradicts every aspect of the bible may turn around tomorrow to promote it. Human life is always in the process of becoming, which may not be completed here on earth but in the world to come.

Each person is bound by the culture of his or her circumstances. There is no culture outside the individual environment. It is there for man and not the other way round. Therefore, while an Ngor Okpala person feels protected by God's words, he or she equally needs to feed well and remain alert for God's blessings. Nobody in society is excluded from God's favor. Just as the western culture has made it possible for me to enjoy global communication today, various media facilities, internet access, good health opportunities, easy transportations et cetera, so is the Bible guiding me to appreciate these amenities as God's blessings. The Bible could have become an archeology if western culture has not made it possible for people to read and write. Thus, both Bible and western culture are irreplaceable values in human life that can promote the growth of Christianity in Igboland of Nigeria.

However, there is need to appreciate both the Bible and western culture as God's own gifts to the Ngor Okpala people. The two have to co-exist to bring humanity to a fruitful end. While the bible is as cultural as the western culture, it is left to Ngor Okpala people to freely benefit from them. However, in a topic like this, where the researcher is meant to examine the implication of Heraclitus philosophy in the light of the bible and western culture, towards motivating the growth of the Christian religion among Ngor Okpala people, no researcher can exhaust it. We have fired the first shot with the hope that each person will appreciate the value of the Bible and the western culture and keep aside prejudices and all aspects that do not encourage effective and meaningful worship of God and growth of the Christian religion, particularly in Igboland of Nigeria. In other words, while society and Ngor Okpala people remain grateful for God's word, the bible, each of us has to be more grateful to the western culture that made it possible for us to have both, so that we can practise our religion more smoothly. Let us then investigate the goal of the missionary activity.

'The Goal of the Missionary Activity'

As Jamaal Bell titled it, what could we say was the goal of the missionary activities in Africa? If the people of Ngor Okpala were to be presented with this question, the answers will vary tremendously. From what the people know as religious activities, many will not accept or agree that the missionaries ever came to their land to evangelize them. They had different agenda besides preaching the word of God. In clear terms, Jamaal noted the following regarding what the goal of the missionary would be: "The missionary's goal is to preach that God, in Jesus, is reconciling the world unto Himself and the Kingdom of God is near. The goal is not to colonize or westernize indigenous populations into our worldview and culture" (Ibid). Therefore, in his own words, he added:

> *We must trust the Holy Spirit to grow and guide the indigenous church. An indigenous church is precisely one in which the cultural changes taking place under the guidance of the Holy Spirit meet the needs and fulfill the meaning of that society and not of any outside group (Ibid).*

It is left to the indigenous church leaders to decide for themselves if abstinence from sexual promiscuity until marriage, monogamy and putting on of clothes are real expressions of a Christian as such. As such, it will be ridiculous to hold that the missionaries can preach any Gospel that is not culture-bound without making some judgments. Preaching of the Gospel can only happen in cultural terms because God owns and lives in every culture. In this way, suggestions must focus on the Bible and supported by it. The indigenous church will never deny that the missionary equally assisted her with prayer in manners that are acceptable and welcomed by the people. The goal of the missionary in Igboland is difficult to achieve without the cooperation of the people. It is one thing to tell the people what the bible says and another for the people to do what the ancestors and God have commanded them to do. In Jamaal's view, the missionary activity was meant to reconcile the people unto Christ himself, but instead, most of the people lost their faith in the process of trying to believe the foreign religion. More essentially, the goal of the mission was not to colonize and westernize the people, but the opposite was the case. The people had certain laws and customs that have kept them united and strong for ages, but when the missionary established laws that abrogated the traditional ones, there was confusion all over. For instance, a man whose wife could not bear him any child or male one was susceptible to having a second wife. But the missionaries simply forbade it without understanding the implication of why the people resorted to that practice.

Hearing the voice of somebody in an issue is therapeutic itself. If the evangelizers knew the goal of their missionary activities well, they would have assisted to suggest to the people how to cope with their emotional problems and frustration in the face of certain eventualities. That is why preaching a non-cultural Gospel will not lead to conversion or faith because to do that in the first place is to annihilate the foundation upon which the people stand. In other words, using cultural terms according to Jamaal is very essential in driving home the Christian message. The people have to be involved in realizing the goal of the missionary because the salvation anticipated thereupon is their own. They would have been taken as important tools in implanting the message of the kingdom by allowing them play one substantial role or the other.

'The Danger of Syncretism'

We have already hinted the danger of syncretistic tendencies brought about by the missionary activities in Igboland, especially when we discussed the observations of Ihuoma. In this section, Jamaal has equally noted the danger of mixing up the new religion with the traditional one. Once the people have been brought to the cross road where they can no longer make decisions as regards where to go, problem must surely erupt. It was due to the same fear that Jamaal raised certain questions and made this long passage: "What is role of the missionary when the indigenous church blends incompatible aspects of their former religion into their newfound Christianity — for instance, other gods or rituals? There are few things the missionary could advise the new church to do" (Ibid). According to the Willow Bank Report, the missionary can advise the indigenous church:

1. To develop a leadership council to report heresy and errors in life and teaching.
2. To ensure all church customs and teachings are derived from Scripture.

3. To use visual or audible elements to illustrate biblical truths; for instance, architecture, worship and art (Willow Bank Report in Jamaal Bell).

These advices could have been possible if the missionaries have shown some interests in the culture of the people in the first place and move them from there to the new teachings. According to Jamaal: "The missionary must trust the indigenous church leaders with reflection on Scripture and culture" (Ibid) which the people know already. This is important because without involving the people and their leaders on how to interpret the scripture for edification purposes, so many others might capitalize on this loophole and make nonsense of the scripture as it is today in many quarters. Definitely, these were difficult tasks for the missionary. It was on this note that Jamaal had this to say:

> However, it is not in their place to be the CEO or lead pastor for the indigenous church. Their purpose as a church planter is not to create policy. The missionary must advise, guide and teach the indigenous church and give them the knowledge and tools they need to do the work of Christ in their village (Ibid).

In other words, the missionary must trust and believe that the Holy Spirit will be present and shape the new indigenous church to move on the direction. Unfortunately, contrary to the observations of Jamaal Bell, the missionaries assumed the position of lead pastor or CEO in the peoples' religion. They came to teach and direct the people to new way of worshipping God and not to be policy makers. From the manner the Gospel message was planted in Igboland, it appeared the missionary equally took the position of the Holy Spirit without giving the people the benefit of doubts that these people could, by the assistance of the Holy Spirit be at peace with God.

Having situated, sort of, the missionary activities in the context of our discussion, we are better prepared to appreciate the enormity and expectations of this chapter.

Therefore, this chapter is aimed at putting various minds together as ways of assisting both individuals and society to appreciate the diversities in human behaviors for a common understanding that may help curb the dearth of dilemma of religious progress in Igboland of Nigeria. If the Igbo adage that "a tree does not make a forest" is correct, then the need to have the cooperation of each other to build a manual for scholarship that may guide posterity is consequential. However, for us to enjoy the scholarship of this book, there are certain nuances that are typically African which we need to explore adequately. History has proven that the Igbos or Igbo are found in almost every part of the globe. They are known for their hard work and fidelity to what they believe in. These are people who will endure hardship of all sorts to make sure they put food on the table. Cases have not been known where the Igbo indulge in abortion for economic reasons. They treasure children as divine gifts, hence the saying: "Nwa bu Ugwu" meaning that children are the pride of life.

The issue of deceit was never found on their identity as a people, so generous, hospitable, accommodating, loving and ever smiling in the faces of sufferings and hardship. The Igbo of Nigeria before the advent of the western civilization were samples and symbols of unity and peace among humanity and created order. As we have severally eluded in this book, whatever that has brought a shift change in the ideologies and life patterns of a people who had been mirrored as true images of their creator must be traceable to the same infiltration of the western culture that came in the context of religion and development. In this light, it is important to study a bit of the history of the Igbo/s as a springboard to underscore and emphasize the major reasons why the growth of the Christian religion in Igboland of Nigeria has to be inspirited. In this light, we are going to examine the various factors that could lead to the dilemma of the growth of Christian religion in Igboland of Nigeria. To get started, there is need to situate the position of the Igbo in the context of our discussion.

Unique position of the Igbos of Nigeria

The Igbo are found mostly in the South Eastern and South- Central Nigeria called Igboland or Igbo society (Alaigbo or Anaigbo). The word "Ibo" can stand for the same thing as Igbo/s, singular or plural. By the late 20th Century, the population of the Igbos was about 27 million. The population of the Igbos is more than that of Norway, Switzerland, Denmark, and Luxembourg combined (Cf. Igbo Studies Association www.igbostudies.com/information.htm). The majority of the Igbo of Nigeria are Christians, but some of them practice the indigenous traditional religion, whose major tenets are shared by all Igbo speaking people of Nigeria (Uchendu, 1965). By "majority of the Igbo", we refer to the Igbo Nigeria of today after the incarnation of the Christian religion in their land. The traditional religion has been practiced and passed on to succeeding generations uninterruptedly before the advent of Christianity. Thus, this new way of life, called religion, in Igboland which came around "1885" has radical and tremendous effects and influences on the traditional beliefs of the Igbos (Talbot 1969) in general.

The Igbo are particularly known for their tenacious belief system. For them, to believe is to live and to live is to be in communication with their ancestors. Today, death is being associated with all kinds of feelings – fear, dreadfulness, annihilation, forgetfulness, end of life, an abandonment et cetera. Unlike the present day mentality, the Igbo celebrated death as a passage to the abode of the ancestors. Such vivacious beliefs guided the behaviors of the people. The consequences of losing the company and association of the ancestors whether alive or dead are enormous and no Igbo person ever dared to forfeit or exchange the hereafter with any gold or silver. We shall elaborate this point more in this book. What else could be the end of life when everything surrounding it is filled with hope and joy. Unlike today many people live unexamined lives and sheepishly as a general norm with no hope or future. The Igbo people have meaning for living and they embark on any project or undertaking purposefully.

Since the advent of the Christian religion, some divisions have come into their belief systems. In retrospect of the life of the Igbo people, there are no distinctions in their ways of life, culture, religion or cosmology. They are interwoven one and the same. It is because there is Christianity today; we can speak of the indigenous traditionalists as referring to those who practiced the traditional religion. Yet, the irony lies on what Ihuoma observed earlier on in this book. As long as there are Christians as well as Traditionalists, at times, it is questionably hard to differentiate them because of their dubious life systems. However, in everyday occurrences, certain levels of mannerisms seem to cloud or obscure the attitudes of Christians from the Traditionalists. For instance, Christians are easily spotted out among the people by the mere fact that such groups go to Church. In the light of what Ihuoma noted above, most of these people who go to Church on Sundays equally give 'Amadioha' – the pagan god, his due. The issue of being a Christian becomes a riddle that breeds a high sense of dilemma in the growth of the Christian religion among the people in question.

Hitherto, the indigenous traditionalists are well known by their not going to any church. These people believe in the vitality of God's creation and mode of governance. Such beings include: "Earth goddess, deities and ancestral spirits and in a creator - God, Chukwu, Obasi, Chi, or Chineke, the "Supreme God" (Achebe 1959), as shall be discussed in details in the course of this book. The good news about indigenous traditional beliefs is that everybody seems to know who the adherents are and the type of lives they lead. This is the height of the dilemma in question. We have no problem with those who officially decided not to go to Church based on a lot of issues as handled in this book. There is dilemme in the growth of the Christian religion in Igboland but there is no such a thing among the traditional religionists. As a matter of fact, while the Christians are susceptible and vulnerable to suspicion and scandal, the traditionalists hardly get involved in such ugly behaviors as deceit and immorality.

On a superficial level, traditionalists are open to conversions to the Christian religion for obvious reasons; economic or political, most Christians are neither intrinsically Christians nor instrumentally traditionalists. This appears to be a dangerous position in the sense that most of those who go to Church or claim to be Christians do not show any good examples in the community. Cases rarely abound where traditionalists create a serious scandal in the community. This fact goes to confirm our claim that belief system is foundational to the lives of the people. The Igbo traditional beliefs have some positive influence on the psychology and social lives of the people in general. There is no dichotomy between one's belief and one's actions. Unlike what is happening in the spectrum of Christianity today, a revered office holder in the Church may be responsible for the embezzlement of Church funds. Evidently, fraudulent activities occur more among Churchgoers than non-church goers.

From lots of historical antecedents, for instance, the forefathers or ancestors of the Igbos were known for their righteousness, honesty and hard work. As noted already, the issue of dilemma in their faith or belief system was never raised. They were highly respected as opinion leaders, impartial judges and people of impeccable character. In this instance, fear, oath-taking and orchestrated immediate justice in the worship of powerful gods like *Amadioha* played major roles in traditional religion. According to Amam A. Acholonu:

> *After an oath which was a common feature of traditional religion, the liar was expected to die within one year of the administration of the oath. To effect this, most often, the accusers may engage in spurious methods of poisoning the accused to cause his death. When such happens, it is credited to the power of the gods (Amam Acholonu, Interview, January 24, 2011).*

While I agree with what Acholonu noted above, the gods kill the liar eventually irrespective of the actions of the accusers. In Prof. Nwachukwu's own words: "Most often, humans help the spirits to accomplish their aims" (Nwachukwu, A. O. oral conversation on this subject, 2010). Regrettably, between 1885 and 1960, when Nigeria had her independence from Britain, the activities, cosmology, discipline and life style of the Igbo people drastically changed. This is the change that has led to the dilemma of the growth of the Christian religion among the people of Ngor Okpala. As it were, this book serves as an antidote to the dilemma and it's resuscitation to a reasonable degree, not that the problem will be healed from the root. The book is more of a breathing technique that is designed to offer some assistance to those who really wish to practice their religion and distinguish between life and belief. Religion becomes necessary to life only when it meaningfully guides the adherents to the path of integrity, peace, unity and love.

The growth of the Christian faith has dropped significantly in the recent years, and the issues militating against this backdrop is what we are going to ex-ray and tackle in this work. It would be very difficult, if not impossible to explain and analyze the terms related to the issue, discuss the individuals, have a comprehensive preview of the psycho-pastoral dimensions that are related with this dilemma of Christian growth in Igboland of Nigeria without an elucidation and explanation of the many labels describing the case/s of these fall outs. The book will further and critically examine the nature of Christianity in Igboland, with special reference to the Igbos of old Owerri province of Eastern Nigeria with a calculable table of analysis. It is my contention in this book that for the Igbos to understand Christianity properly, and its demands, the Christian message must be delivered to the Igbo in their socio- cultural context. The importance of enculturation at this level of the Christian growth cannot be overemphasized or underrated. We have come of age to understand when we need to consult medical personnel for health reasons, Christian ministers for religious matters, and the government for failing to provide infrastructures [the basic facilities needed for the functioning of a system] that keep society in alignment.

Invariably, this is not to lay blame on the missionaries who brought the good news here. Quite understood that the missionaries made fundamental mistakes by encroaching into the Igbo peoples' culture without proper catechesis, the people themselves needed to raise some questions. The overt possibility or the unconcealed nature of the matter is that due to the people's level of hospitality and friendship, they welcomed the missionaries with open hands. In this instance, the people are not blamable either. The thrust of this book is not to apportion blames, either to the missionaries or the Igbo people of Nigeria. The issue at ground zero is that there is dilemma of the growth of the Christian religion and nobody can deny it. Then, in order to fix the anomalies and irregularities, call the situation a misnomer of application, the Igbo people deserve to have their prime position in the annals of the history of religion. The people have to see and approach Christ in their culture and convincingly be able to relate and live him out on daily basis. The Igbo have no option because they do not have the essential prerequisite to accept Christianity in its 'wait till judgment time" for rewards and punishments? Therefore, it sounds difficult for the Igbo to accept Christ's panacea of allowing wheat and cockle to grow till harvest time. The only way the Igbo will appreciate Christianity is when they see the Christian adherents act and behave in accordance with the moral principles led down by the gods that protect and save lives. For the Igbo, heaven begins here.

Inevitably, we should accept the basic fact and see the Igbos as people who are inherently, naturally and eternally religious. In reference to their cosmology or the " Igbo cosmos" like that of other African peoples, there are no partitions between or that separate the sacred from the secular. This primary fact has to be understood. The life of the Igbos is one, inseparably whole in which God is believed to manifest and play essential roles in their activities, stand at the center of their being, immanent, immutable. By "activities" here, we refer to lives of proven moral character and objectivity. As already alluded in this book, before the inroad of Christianity into Igboland, the Igbos already had systems of clearly defined customs and practices in both the religious and secular arenas. But how these customs and cultures have changed the average Igbo person, and equally contributed to the decline of Christian faith in question and religion, is the main issue ultimately facing this book. In other words, we are not claiming that the Igbo/s are impeccable or having no flaws. As the rest of humanity, they have their own share of primordial lacks and defectiveness.

Elements of animalistic tendencies/indiscipline/ corruption

The issue of animism, paganism, fetishism, idolatry, magic, witchcraft, primitive religion, heathenism, juju and the like, were serious problems before the advent of Christianity. The Christian religion seemed to have given them mortal blows. But the fact remains that most aspects of these systems outlived the Christian message because of the reasons earlier stated – lack of proper catechesis and study of the peoples' culture. In other words, as systems they militate against the growth of Christian faith among the Igbo/s today. The Christian teaching did not espouse these traditional beliefs and suggested alternatives that could have assisted the people integrate their mission. I have always referred to this over sightedness as "an obscure or failed didactic". Any missionary activity that is not aimed at a specific goal is likely to fail and that was the case with the issue at hand. If animism is "a belief in primitive tribes" in which "natural objects and forces have souls" (Web. Definition), to what extent has science proved the dictum otherwise? Even in the field of medicine, drugs have no souls yet they are meant to give life or soul to the sick.

On the case of being primitives, who are the "primitive tribes" mentioned here except those who first embraced creation and its wonders, the founding fathers of human culture and identity? It is derogatory to speak of the Africans as being primitive without defining them in the context of the first human beings that ever existed. There is modernity today because there was primitive culture. Being primitive in one's attitudes is quite different from being traditional. Culture is as dynamic as human beings, and flexibility is the key, the ability to adapt to the changing events of life, which nobody has absolute control of. We cannot just veto ignorance on the table of light. We need to understand what animism means in our context as to figure out how it affected the growth of the Christian religion in Igboland. Apportioning blames on others due to one's own failures to properly comprehend the issues at hand is like asking a dump person to address the audience. There is limitation in everything. That was what Nwachukwu meant when he remarked that "the awareness of the obligation to do the good and avoid evil deeply points to the ability of the individual to weigh the consequences of his or her particular action". This is why consequential moral reasoning has to be weighed along with categorical, intrinsic moral reasoning.

We call this 'intellectual or moral virtue' because it perfects the intellect to reason correctly about particular actions to be done or avoided. This "intellectual virtue" or emotional intelligence is highly recommended in relationships" (Nwachukwu, 156). Animism and primitivity are human factors and they are not subject to any predication of a particular culture or people. Aristotle in his Nichomachean Ethics maintained: "virtue stands in the middle" (Nich. Ethics, 384-322 BCE, IEP – Internet Encyclopedia of Philosophy). By emphasizing the role of habit in conduct, no culture or country is excluded. In the same light according to Aristotle: "Virtue, therefore, manifests itself in action. More explicitly, an action counts as virtuous, when one holds oneself in a stable equilibrium of the soul, in order to choose the action knowingly and for its own sake. This stable equilibrium of the soul is what constitutes character" (Ibid).

Need for Ethics and Morality as ways out of the dilemma

Consequently, the issue of ethical principles and morality comes in here because dilemma of the growth of the Christian religion cannot be possible without some elements of indiscipline or immorality. The need to examine Aristotle's ethics and what he mentioned above is necessary in the book. After reading the ethics of Aristotle, I felt the need to integrate his message to this book as a way of suggesting factors that can help curb dilemma in the growth of Christian religion in general. I still remember, in the senior seminary formation, the seminarians were expected to have knowledge of Aristotle's ethics. In fact, till date, it is one of the compulsory courses taken in most houses of formation for future ministers and religious. On a more interesting note, as human beings, each person deserves some bit of moral principles to live with others. Once people understand themselves and the effects of their actions, surely they will make positive decisions either to have religion or remain without one. It is better to have no religion and behave well than having one and become a public nuisance.

Use of the term "Ethics"

Actually, it appears that certain issues are being repeated in this book. Yes, any repetition is done on purpose especially for the sake of emphasis and easy assimilation of the message communicated. Ethics is the science or study of morality. Etymologically, it is from the Greek word "ethike". It means that which concerns ethos. Its plural form "ta ethea" was found in the works of Homer, translated as "the abode or habitual places for animals, or a place of pasture… but in the works of Hesiod, ethos designates the dwelling place and habitation of men, (Ekennia, N. Justin, 2003:1). Today this concept "ethos" has undergone some transformations, from the basic sense of a dwelling place to designate the actual being at home in certain situations. We can now appreciate the sense in which Aristotle and the Igbo people appropriated the term "ethos". In other words, ethos points to the way and manner in which human beings can be at home in the world. It is the inner residing, bearing a man has towards himself, towards others and towards his world. Therefore, ethos or ethics or habit means the way we act and conduct ourselves. It is the science of that quality in human behavior by which an act is right or wrong. Thus, "if any detail of thought has a vital bearing on man's destiny or helps to shape his life, that detail of thought is suggested by ethics, and morality is that study" (Owen, A. Hill, 1928:1). Ethics is a branch of philosophy that studies the principles of right and wrong in human conduct. It systematically studies what we ought to do and how we ought to do them. One of the modern philosophers, Pope John Paul 11, as noted below, defined ethics as:

> *The science of human actions from point of their moral value, of the good or evil contained in them. Every human action involves a particular lived experience that goes by the name ethical experience...This whole lived experience has a thoroughly empirical character...(Wojtyla, A collection of Scholarly essays from Wojtyla's early Lublin Lectures, 1993:23).*

Ethics is fundamentally normative in John Paul's philosophy. It is rooted in experience. Within this context, the people of Ngor Okpala and Aristotle totally share John Paul's view. Ethics itself addresses people in their personal experiences for more fruitful and meaningful living and helps them to avoid obstacles that create chaos. To banish personal experiences from ethical life, for Aristotle, points to stripping it of its very essence. While Kant separated ethical experiences from the act or reduced ethics to rational agreement on norms, Plato presented ethics outside the realm of human management (Nwachukwu, 2010).

All the same, Socrates, Plato, Aristotle and Kant hold that ethics involves a system of mental activities that aids man access the degree of goodness or badness in any given situation. It is "essentially reflective, dealing with reason, giving solid justification for positions held" (Singer & Kuhse, 1999 in the edited work of Kuhse, H. 1997:63-89). Ethics provides the criteria of knowing whether an action or judgment is right or wrong, morally good or morally bad. However, there is no consensus in ethics regarding these criteria because a variety of opinions exist regarding what constitutes morally right or wrong actions. Yet, Ethics incorporates within its principles those religious and traditional values, which are of universal significance, defending the dignity of the human person, the sacredness of and right to human life.

According to Nwachukwu, "Ethics is particularly the science and study of morality" (Nwachukwu, 2010:152). The ethics of Aristotle handles and addresses the basic aspects of human person in the face of his daily responsibilities, his relationships with others, his personality as reflected in communications and interactions. When we describe somebody as being virtuous, it includes his integrity, moral well being, and relationships with people and not necessarily his religious preference or practices. Being virtuous entails the magnitude and manners a person is committed to the course of truth and justice. Actually, morality absolutely belongs to rational beings including their sense of their connectedness with their duties, functions and obligations towards the rest of humanity and preparedness to enjoy the greatest good and opportunity life can offer them.

As Nwachukwu would have it, "the need for emotional and spiritual intimacy in one's relationships is very important. And the moment human beings begin to integrate these social values and moral issues in their lives, the questions of divorce, family abuses, lack of respect or care for the elderly will be reduced"

(Nwachukwu, 2008). In other words, whatever causes divorce, family abuses; lack of respect for the elderly in society cannot encourage the growth of the Christian faith. In a way, when people no longer respect one another and behave in ways that contradict the Christian message, to advance the same Christian religion will be impossible. Paraphrasing Nwachukwu's thoughts on Aristotle's ethics, we shall come to the conclusion that man is so because he behaves ethically. It is my candid stand that Aristotle has demonstrated a skill or quality as a moral philosopher that marks him out and makes him unique from the rest of other moral philosophers who equally treated ethics in their field of specialization.

When we speak of ethics, it may appear, that ethics is an academic subject that applies to man indirectly. As observed already, ethics is basically and typically man himself. Besides, there is ethics in all aspects of man's endeavor. There is ethics, for example, in the, Government, Church, school system, in the market square, in the homes, kitchens, in the manner we dress, walk, eat, speak, and practically anything we do and that essentially makes ethics a social issue. That is to say, whatever involves man as such has ethics in it. It is because man is an ethical being that we talk of right or wrong behaviors and actions. In this light, when we reflect on the seeming blunder the westerners who brought us religion committed in Igboland, it was because they violated some ethical principles. Even in the teaching field, before any teacher or lecturer succeeds in bringing knowledge to his or her students, it is important that the teacher understands the psychology of those to be taught. A trained teacher cannot apply the same teaching methodology meant for the mentally retarded or people with mental disabilities to normal children. If he does, there will be no success or achievement of any educational objectives.

Therefore, the need for people to behave properly in our time cannot be overemphasized. In a sophisticated world like ours, the supernatural is being questioned because of the benefits from science and technology. But many people forget that science is a gift from God himself. We cannot because of the influence and realities of money, sex and power relegate the basics of life. That is why our discussions on social values and moral issues in this book are being broadened to include various moral values as they affect and impact on our families, love one another, sexuality, and aspirations in life. We must find the best ways to avoid getting involved with evils like telling lies against honest people and inflicting injustice to them too.

One may not be conscious of the need for being ethical minded. But it is always there potently activated or not. Ethics is a natural call to fall in line with the rest of humanity in actions that depict us as rational beings. That is why we maintain that there is ethics, essentially in all human beings do in life, whether they are aware of it or not, it is there. How can there be growth or advancement in any religion that lacks morality? Let us face it, can the dilemma in question be tackled without discipline or a sense of morality? What of cohabitation, and living together as social beings? It will be unheard of to talk of solid relationship that has no ethical principles guiding it. Or, can there be a religion that does not take the morality of the people into account or consideration? A belief in God or religious practice that does not consider how it impacts on one's attitudes and interaction with others is bound to fail. In a serious note, the Christian bible says:

> *He, Yaheweh, is merciful, tenderhearted, and slow to anger,*
> *very loving, and universally kind; Yahweh's tenderness embraces*
> *all his creatures.....Always true to his promises, Yahweh shows*

love in all he does. Only stumble and Yahweh at once supports
you, if others bow you down, he will raise you up (Psalm 145:
8-9; 14)

In another striking manner, one may ask: "Can human beings live and interact amicably without ethics - the sense of right and wrong?" That is why the study and practice of ethics and its principles are urgently needed in our time than in the past. In Igboland, for instance, people knew behaviors that went against the ethics of the land and avoided them. In such situations, scientific investigation to ethics was not necessary. Morality was part of the religion of the people, integrally bound together. Among the people of Ngor Okpala, to have religion is to have morality – they were inseparable. Ethics belongs to the same category or camp as moral philosophy and morality. As noted already, they belong principally to human beings and not to animals. Going back from the creation of mankind to this present time, there is no epoch in human history that has not faced the universal needs for liberty, security, happiness and the preservation of the human life.

Can life be preserved without ethics or morality? It is only a human being that can worship God or have a religion. To worship God entails the ability to understand the ordinances and commandments of such God. In other words, if life is important to each of us and we feel there is need to enjoy it to the fullest, then there is also the need to have some guidelines and principles that encourage what is good in our actions and condemn that which is bad. In his own words, Haring observed: "Morality is for persons," (Haring, Bernard, Wikipedia, Internet Dictionary) and not for any other beings in the universe like animals and angels. A clearer knowledge of this morality will help us understand to what extent religion can thrive in the practice of morality. Any behavior that involves another person, his feelings, reactions and adjustments might be ethically bound.

There are moral philosophies in various aspects of learning. Morality is differently viewed and interpreted by different scholars because of the nature of human actions and complexities. Yet, we know when an action is morally good or morally evil. Within this context, Koterski made these following observations:

> *There are many theories of ethics: the utilitarian theory of ethics…the ethics of Duty and Respect of Immanuel Kant….a third kind of ethics that attempts to go deeper by relying on insights of human character and …the tradition of natural law. This third one has its basis in the works of Greek philosophers, such as Socrates, Plato, and especially, Aristotle, (Koterski J. S.J., 2001:4).*

Further elaboration and elucidation of the remark Koterski made on this subject is necessary here. In the first place, the utilitarian theory of ethics generally lays emphasis on the equality of human actions. In this light, it considers the consequences of human actions to be done or already done. It examines the benefits for doing or performing certain actions. For instance, what is the implication of shouting in the midst of a gathering or in public? Shouting with no specific intension to alert others for a serious danger sounds neurotic. In this sense, shouting connotes the sense of distraction and peace of others. It is morally wrong to distract people in their businesses or create chaotic scenes. The situation just described is akin to what Aristotle would want us understand in his ethics because it does address a personal concern as this or that individual on the moment. For ethics to be meaningful, it has to address or focus on somebody. Unlike utilitarian theory of ethics that tells us what to do or avoid without any specific person or individual in mind.

In line with the primary objective of this book, we are concerned with individual reactions and behaviors that affect their perception of facts regarding to faith or religion. For example, when we speak of the dilemma of the growth of the Christian religion, we are concerned with factors that hinder individuals from practicing their faith authentically. Partners live and worship together. Any religious issue that affects one equally has some effect on the other. The question is what that issue might be. At times, people expect their ministers to teach them by examples. In cases where the other is observed, interest begins to dwindle and if nothing is done to resuscitate it, it creates a dilemma. There is dilemma of the growth of the Christian religion because something has fallen out of alignment or not properly understood. This is where psycho-pastoral perspective comes in human interactions. For instance, partners are meant to live in peace with each other. Assuming that one of them proves otherwise despite all the honest efforts his or her partner has done, what happens? In such cases, where an individual knows what it takes to maintain peace in the house and the other defiles it, the peaceful one must go ahead to seek peace and enjoy his or her life.

In the analysis presented by Koterski, Kant emphasized another aspect of ethics as pertaining to one's duty and the respect one owes to others. This is what Nwachukwu calls "deontology". According to him:

> This deals with, and studies the duties of individuals in their various states of life, gender, age, status and functions. It is from here that ethics, which is the study of right and wrong living, derives its intrinsic meanings. Thence, deontology, morality and conscience are so interwoven that we cannot speak of one without the other. The implication is that, faithfulness to one's

> *duties is important in any given relationship (Nwachukwu, 2010:224).*

In Nwachukwu's understanding, doing one's duties, acting morally right and obeying one's conscience is one and the same thing. I strong agree with him. In a shared responsibility, once each person does his duty, everyone else has some benefits from it. On the other hand, if one neglects to accomplish a common goal that is meant for the public good, it will affect all those who should be beneficiaries of the failed duty. Even in marriage life, every member of the family is meant to participate at the general up-keep of the house. While one person does one thing the other does another and the family enjoys the fruit of each other's labor. But when it is placed on the shoulder of one person, it may affect the family in a very adverse manner. We shall consult Kant's position again in this discussion.

Eventually, any ethical principle or responsibility that neglects the various situations people pass through in their every day-to-day life is not realistic. The need to behave and be responsibly and reasonably accountable for one's actions and their implications in the lives of others is at the heart of ethics and this is what he refers to as respect for the other. We owe and show respect to other people by the ways we carry out our responsibilities and duties. Failure to perform our duties is a sign of disrespect to others. At this point, it will be better we study what we mean by ethics and morality in this book.

Ethics and Morality

I am going to fall back to my previous work on this subject as directed by Nwachukwu in one of my DLMs – Distance Learning Model at GTF. It has to be noted that the word ethics is cultural, which means it has no one-way of expressing it. As we shall read from this book, others may reject certain behaviors that are considered and accepted by one culture. However, so many moral philosophers hold that ethics has all to do with how human beings behave and how their behaviors affect the rest of society. For example, to have money or wealth is awesome and encouraged but to acquire it through illicit manner is condemned by ethical standards. In this sense, one may begin to ask what these standards are. The standards here are such universal values that determine an act to be in compliance with order or out of order. Generally, we know when we are doing pleasant or unpleasant things. The nature of what we do is validated and assessed by the way it affects other people.

As earlier noted in this book, ethics is also known as moral philosophy, because it is the science of analysis between pleasurable and un-pleasurable behaviors. It is the science and study of morality. This is "a branch of philosophy which seeks to address questions about morality; that is, about concepts like good and bad, right and wrong, justice, virtue, etc" (Wikipedia, the free encyclopedia). Its etymological derivation as stated above, comes from a Greek word "ethike" which refers to "ethos" [an act] that which is possible or impossible. Ethos conveys the various ways each person feels safe morally. It simply means code of conduct, the study of the quality of a human act, different from other animals, by which we classify it good or bad. For example, it is unethical to lie against the innocent or cheat one's neighbor or friend. In the words of Owen, referring to ethics, he said: "If any detail of thought has a vital bearing on man's destiny or helps to shape his life, that detail of thought is suggested by ethics, and morality is that study" (Owen, A. Hill, 1928:1). As cited from Wikipedia Internet Dictionary, it is a branch of philosophy that studies the principles of right and wrong in human decisions, actions, deeds and conduct.

However, according to Nwachukwu: "Today, this concept 'ethos' has undergone some transformations, from the basic sense of a dwelling place to designate the actual involvement of a human being at home in certain situations" (Nwachukwu, 2010:152). From what Nwachukwu has said here, a lot of suppositions are imminent. For instance, to be at home has much to do with the way we perceive ourselves, others, things and practice our faith. We can now understand a bit of why the dilemma in the growth of the Christian religion in Igboland of Nigeria. The new religion was not comfortable with some of the people, hence the lack of interest in keeping to it. If the people had received the religion in the spirit of its founder and lived it in their lives, the dilemma in question could have been averted. Nothing in life can be more rewarding or enriching than being at home with oneself. It is only when we dance true to our nature and surroundings that life prospers to its fullness.

Practically, ethics examines how each person should carry out his duty and why it should be carried out properly. In this capacity, Pope John Paul 11 presented ethics as: The science of human actions from the point of their moral value, of the good or evil contained in them. Every human action involves a particular lived experience that goes by the name ethical experience *(Wojtyla, Op. Cit)*. From what Pope John Paul has said here, ethics involves experience, which may be compatible with societal expectation or against it. As noted earlier, ethics is the science of morality and morality concerns human actions from the point of view of their moral value. For instance, what makes a particular action morally good or bad? Have my actions affected us in a positive or negative way? Every lived experience is normative, a guide, a characteristic by which we continue or discontinue with it. Whatever makes the experience noble and exemplary points to its ethical and empirical character? Ethics is empirical because it deals with concrete human situations here and now.

Social Ethics in human life – a diverse reality

Ineluctably or not being capable of being avoided, ethics cuts across every human industry. Man cannot be one without ethics. Consequently, ethics has been a universal matter, without which, humanity will be equal to other animals. In this line of argument, Moore, a strong proponent of "Meta-ethics" in support of ethics insists that: "Meta-ethics is concerned primarily with the meaning of ethical judgments and/or prescriptions and with the notion of which properties, if any, are responsible for the truth or validity thereof" (Moore, G. E., 1903). For example, a person lost his wallet of money on transit. Now, there are some probabilities as what had happened to that wallet in question. It could be possible that the said wallet was not lost but stolen, in which case the matter becomes ethical. To lose an object is not ethical, unless somebody purposely threw it away; in which case, it becomes an act freely carried out.

As Murray would have it as cited in Nwachukwu: "A moral act is an act which is performed with knowledge and freedom" (Murray, 1960:328; Nwachukwu, 2010:258). According to "meta-ethics" principles, for any valid judgments to be passed on such property, the truth surrounding the lost or stolen wallet must be ascertained. This is the problem that has led to the dilemma of the growth of the Christian religion in Igboland of Nigeria. If the missionaries had examined the situation on the ground when they came to Igboland, and applied some sort of prudential judgment on what they encountered on arrival, the dilemma in question could not have been possible today. They were already biased and prejudiced about the culture of the uncivilized people of Africa. They failed to realize that the Igbo people were ethically minded people who viewed nature with the highest level of morality.

However, in line with what Pope John Paul II mentioned above, "normative ethics which is equally known as moral theory, concerns the study of that which makes actions right or wrong. In Rawls's analysis of this moral theory, there are complexities involved in determining what actually makes an act morally right or wrong in certain cases, as we noted earlier on. For example, there are certain actions considered immoral in one culture but celebrated as a normal way of life in another culture (Consult, Rawls, John, 1971). As it were, the missionaries would have considered moral implications of what the people were doing. Obviously, while the Igbo of Nigeria believed in certain practices that are unacceptable today, like the Osu caste system, there are so many practices they uphold as healing and therapeutic. Such positive practices should have been encouraged out rightly.

In another serious development, Socrates (469 BC – 399 BC), who was a well-known Greek philosopher encouraged society to turn from their external world to the inner selves, maximizing the beauty of creation to her own advantage. For Socrates: "Self-knowledge is considered necessary for success and inherently an essential good" (Wikipedia, Internet Dictionary). In his argument, he states:

> *A self-aware person will act completely within their capabilities to their pinnacle, while an ignorant person will flounder and encounter difficulty…. a person must become aware of every fact (and its context) relevant to his existence, if he wishes to attain self-knowledge. He posited that people will naturally do what is good, if they know what is right. Evil or bad actions, are the result of ignorance. If a criminal were truly aware of the mental and spiritual consequences of his actions, he would neither commit nor even consider committing those actions. A*

person who knows what is truly right will automatically do it (Ibid.).

While Socrates the wise philosopher has presented a beautiful account of what ethics stands for in his opinion, I do not accept all he has said here. It is true; being self-aware of what one does is being in touch with one-self. To say that "people will naturally do what is good, if they know what is right" is not always conceivable as can be observed from events today.

On the contrary, it does not work out that way. There are so many people who prefer evil to good. For instance, why do we have terrorists over the globe? A lot of people inflict injuries on others purposely without any regard or care. Again, for him to hold that "evil or bad actions are the result of ignorance" is not acceptable today considering what is going on in society. Many people purposely carry out ferocious actions on innocent souls. There are some who are nothing but bloodthirsty individuals. On the same argument, he held: "If a criminal were truly aware of the mental and spiritual consequences of his actions, he would neither commit nor even consider committing those actions" is another fallacious claim. It is not normally easy to say that "a person who knows what is truly right will automatically do it" has not been always the ways of the world. Many people know what is right and choose to act otherwise. Most criminals take joy in being so and brag as the most fearful people on earth. What do we say of those who belong to different secret societies and cults? They form evil gang to terrorize innocent citizens. Rather, it is more acceptable and feasible to hold that the rightness of an act challenges society to choose well. For instance, stealing is morally evil. Ignorance to such atrocious acts is not excusable.

Again, how do we validate the philosophy of Hedonism and its tenets that maintain: "Ethics is maximizing pleasure and minimizing pain". Unfortunately, 'hedonism' is: "The ethical theory that pleasure is the highest good and proper aim of human life" (Internet Resource). How can a life based on the pursuit of pleasure be ideal and a person getting devoted to the pursuit of pleasure and self-gratification and that everything is about pleasure lead to the growth of the Christian religion anywhere in the world? The greatest paradox being anticipated here is that a person can naturally be a hedonist without any official profession in hedonism. How are we sure that some of the missionaries or Igbo people of Nigeria have or had no such inclinations? A person who is driven with the sense of hedonism may not fancy any religion that emphasizes sacrifices. Human beings are mysterious and some of us are bundles of possibilities. No human imagination can discern most of the things that go up and down in our minds. At times, such uncertainties create problem in the growth of the Christian religion worldwide.

Judging from the heinous and damaging principle of hedonism, we need to take cognizance of few things. First and foremost, what does the content of pleasure mean in this philosophy and what it means to minimize or reduce pain, and from what injuries. In other words, to advocate for self-gratification regardless of the pain and at the expense to other people, is very wrong. Both the Cyrenaics Extremists and the Epicureans who tend to support and advocate for pleasure irrespective of how it is achieved is unethical. To advocate a philosophy, which encourages people to "eat, drink, and be merry, for tomorrow we shall die" (Wikipedia, free encyclopedia) is to attack the very basis of ethical principles. For 'tomorrow we shall die' has no qualification because, if one is sure of dying tomorrow, eating and drinking today makes no sense. This is in line with the philosophy of "consequentialism" whereby the ends of any act justify the means. In other words, if I can become rich by killing my neighbor, and I need to be rich, killing becomes morally acceptable. We said it earlier that the dilemma in the growth of the Christian religion in Igboland is traceable to human nature.

As it were, consequentialism is dangerous. Morality or ethics cannot be based on such values where the means justifies the ends. On the other hand, ethics and morality are based on behaviors that are most acceptable by society in every age and nationality. Actions have to be morally good or bad in themselves irrespective of what anybody may say of them. When an act is intrinsically good, it is good, but when it is intrinsically evil, no matter the best intention for doing it, it remains evil (Kant, Emmanuel, Wikipedia Internet Dictionary). The need for sound moral behaviors cannot be overemphasized in human nature. There is dilemma of the growth of Christian religion because some people have decided to make it that way. Morality does not depend on individual characterizations and definitions. As the popular adage goes, "One man's food is another man's poison". This adage reflects in most of the things we do in life.

Ethics provides the basic criteria for one to know whether an action or judgment is right or wrong, morally good or morally evil. These criteria are not relative in the sense of choice. They are universally accepted as such. Any action performed with freedom and knowledge has a corresponding ethics. It is possible that somebody can laugh to him or herself without meaning to hurt or affect another. In such a case, there may be no ethics attached or associated with it. It is always normal that there are certain actions or behaviors that are not ethically intended. For instance, to eat is an action but it is neither moral nor ethical. Still, in such a case, some questions may spring up: "Are you eating alone or with somebody? Where is the location of such an activity or the eating going on?" What does eating mean in the instance because someone in a restaurant may be there for personal reasons other than eating?

Invariably these questions determine to a great extent the ethics or morality of the action or eating. For instance, when we eat with people, we must observe certain table etiquettes or mannerisms. In the examples at hand, each situation is treated differently. In the first place, it is not necessary ascribing ethics to the action of somebody who is eating alone in his house. But when the same person eats alone in a restaurant, he is no longer alone as such. The presence of others should influence his behavior this time. More still, if that person is eating with others at the same table, his behavior there is important as it might affect them or morally be assessed. That is why each other's behavior has some imprint on others. Assuming the person in our story begins to distract others with loud talks and jokes, his action might be morally interpreted as offensive. To offend is wrong and to please is right. His action will either be positively assessed or negatively interpreted.

The same thing applies to a person who is eating and drinking with bad gangs or notorious armed robbers. If it were in Africa, the first face interpretation is that this very person is bad too. No wonder we have that popular aphorism that holds: "Tell me with whom you move and I will tell you who you are". These are hypotheses that have not been verified. For instance, that I visited a native doctor for scientific investigation in the art of native medicine does not make me one. Such things happen also. For somebody to eat with a well-known bad gang, does it automatically make him one? It is possible that one may use that strategy for other reasons that are not connected with evil or harming others. At times, one may be found in the company of other people, whether evil or good, accidentally. That was one of the reasons that led to the dilemma in question. The Igbo of Nigeria practiced certain belief systems based on their knowledge at the moment without thinking of the other side of the coin. For them, to change their mode of prayer and learn a new one was evil. That is why when flexibility lacks in any human interactions; any element of change will not progress.

Eventually, this is where we take Singer and Kuhse so seriously here. For us to hold a position we think is true, we must have examined such a position with reasons that support our claims. In this light, Singer and Kuhse observed: "Essentially reflective, dealing with reason, giving solid justification for positions held" (Singer & Kuhse, 1999 in the edited work of Kuhse, H. 1997:63-89), is the key to progress. Ethics and morality incorporate within their principles those religious and traditional values, which are of universal significance, defending the dignity of the human person, human freedom, the sacredness and dignity of human life and right. Such values as truth, honesty, justice, peace, joy, happiness, love etc, are intrinsically useful to every human being irrespective of culture, language, gender, ethnicity, and nations. We know when we obey or violate them. At this point, there is every need to discuss the ethics of Aristotle in the light of the foregoing discussions.

Aristotelian Perspective and Comparative Analysis: Implication for Ngor Okpala People

As an effective way of understanding Aristotle's moral philosophy or ethics better, it is important to situate it within the context of other moral philosophers. Aristotle belongs to the family of physicians, received his training and education that inclined him to study natural phenomena, (Biography of Aristotle, Internet Resources). Aristotle is an existentialistic philosopher who believed on the correct and concrete application of human actions as they impact on the person on the moment. He did not necessarily dwell much on the theoretical aspect of events that might not happen. For example, Aristotle was a student of Plato who was an idealist, and posited a world of perfection outside the physical reality. Instead, Aristotle disagreed with Plato that humanity and its existence are within human reach. That was the way the foreign religion first sounded to the Africans who had felt the presence of the God in whatever they did and believed.

Remarkably, both Aristotle and Plato disagreed on the essence of man as such. For example, because of the world of ideas of Plato, the human soul was presented as foreign to man. Rene Descartes also supported this view of Plato by positing that the human soul had existed before the body. In this sense, humanity should be perceived from its spiritual significations. According to him, the soul is totally and purely spiritual and it does not contain any "potentialities" of matter. This is a teaching that might not be accepted by the Africans. While the Igbo of Nigeria believe in the spiritual world, they equally believe such existence has absolute connection and resemblance to their every day lives and community. The people never accept any supernatural being that has no communication with the living. Unlike in the case of Plato and Descartes, the sojourn or indwelling of the soul in the body or in this sensible world becomes a form of punishment, "something antagonistic to the true being of man which ends in death" (Descartes, J. Rene, 1974:110).

In this light, one can easily surmise conflicts with the stand or position of Aristotle who believes in the importance of the body as the basis of man. He equally believes in the power of the spirit or the intellect. In fact, Aristotle accepted from Plato that the world or cosmos has some rationality because it is only through reasoning that one can come to the knowledge of absolute truths and universal forms. The people of Ngor Okpala wholly accept this belief or teaching. That is why till tomorrow, before an elderly man drinks local palm wine, he pours some on the ground, believed to be mother earth and stability of the living. At times, it is an invitation to the ancestors to join in the drinking. If the people were to separate the body from the spirit or vice versa as Descartes would want them, then the belief in the Almighty who is in control of the universe and the day-to-day affairs of the people could have become mere stories that have no foundations in history.

However, the major difference between Aristotle and Plato is centered on "universals" and "common sense". For Plato, the universe can exist without any reference to the particulars, which is dangerous for the people. But for Aristotle, there is emphasis on "common sense" knowledge (Koterski, Joseph, S.J., 2001:3). No wonder he holds that nothing comes to the intellect, which did not first pass through the senses. It is only through what we know that we can imagine what we do not know. For example, our belief in God can only be reasonable if there are traces of his handiworks on earth or believe that he created us in the first place. Moreover, for Aristotle, our physical reality is meaningful and essential to us and we know it to be a fact. We are not living in any world of ideas, as Plato would want us to believe. Particularly, the Igbo are community people. They live as one family, ontologically connected. To separate them is to create more dilemmas in their belief systems. From this stand point, we can now surmise or guess the nature of Aristotle's ethics is all about and the implications it has or holds for society in general and individuals or the people of Ngor Okpala in particular.

Paul Tillich's Paradoxical analysis of Aristotelian Ethics to Life

I have decided, not only to include but also apply the Aristotelian Ethics to the Tillichian idea of the paradoxical co-existence of good and the bad, especially with some implications for authentic Living. This approach is necessary here judging from the seemingly resilient nature of the people of Ngor Okpala in accepting the Christian religion from the missionaries. The flexibility applied in Paul Tillich's philosophy is essential for co-habitation and interpersonal relationships. For instance, an act is morally good or evil only when it has been performed. An action, which appears morally sound, paradoxically contains the potency or capacity of being evil too. The Igboland of Nigeria did not want to give any trial to the new religion partly because of the wrong approach the missionaries employed. Both the missionaries and the people should have known that nothing under this sun is permanent. The traditional religion, which the missionaries seemed to have condemned out rightly, has elements of salvation in it. Just as the Christian religion, which posed a threat to the traditionalists initially could have been allowed to manifest its elements of salvation too. In other words, Paul Tillich's principles are apt for enculturation and adaptation.

There are always elements of 'despite of' this or that in every human industry. Rigidity is always instrumental to the dilemma of the growth of the Christian religion in Igboland or Ngor Okpala. In the light of the idea of Paul Tillich, 'happiness' in Aristotle is not far from 'sadness', friendship has elements of enmity in it. We have already studied extensively Aristotle's ethics in this book. However, for the sake of emphasis and to prove the importance of Paul Tillich's philosophy, I deemed it necessary to do so. With regard to the paradoxical co-existence of good and evil, as it applies to the ethics of Aristotle, this section studies and examines the ethics of Aristotle and that of the Ngor Okpala people of Igboland of Nigeria for the purpose of using them to improve their understanding of the flexibilities that take place in life.

This 'comparative analysis' essentially focuses on how Aristotle and the Igbo of Nigeria conceive human conducts in terms of their moral implications, which could affect their perceptibility of other people's religion or culture. There are so many aspects of moral philosophy. Yet, it has to be borne in mind that "morality is primarily for persons" (Bernard Haring, Internet guide selection, I.G.S, 1971) and not for brutes or spirits. In another striking note, Koterski remarked:

> *There are many theories of ethics: the utilitarian theory of ethics ...the ethics of Duty and Respect of Immanuel Kant....a third kind of ethics that attempts to go deeper by relying on insights of human character and ...the tradition of natural law. This third one has its basis in the works of Greek philosophers, such as Socrates, Plato, and especially, Aristotle, (Koterski J. S.J., 2001:4).*

The utilitarian theory of ethics as we saw earlier focused more on egalitarianism - the political, economic and social equality for all thereby neglecting the intrinsic value of the individuals. This aspect of ethics is in one hand unacceptable in Ngor Okpala community, but in another not welcomed. It is accepted in one hand that anything that neglects the welfare of the individual person equally affects the community as a whole. But on the other hand, the community is the foundation of the individual. An individual cannot take a decision that binds on the community whereas the case is the other way round. On Kant's ethics of duty and respect, the Igbo, especially the Ngor Okpala people may appreciate them only if they include the communal notions of justice. Regarding the third category that relies on human character and the law of nature, the people will gladly appreciate it.

These ethical theories assist us to understand the Characters involved in the discussion. For instance, Aristotle came from a long line of physicians, received training and education that inclined him to study natural phenomena, (Biography of Aristotle, I.G.S, 2007). It was his point of departure from the idealistic position of Plato that relegated the practical coherence of the universe. Plato, in line with Descartes as noted previously, held that human soul had existed before the body. And as such, the soul is purely spiritual and it does not contain any "potentialities" of matter. In other words, the sojourn of the soul in this sensible world is a punishment, something antagonistic to the true being of man, which ends in death (Descartes, J. Rene, 1974:110).

However, Aristotle agreed with Plato that the world or cosmos is rationally designed. And that through reasoning we can come to know absolute truths by studying universal forms. While Plato would hold that the universal exists apart from particulars, Aristotle advocates for a philosophy of "common sense" (Koterski, Joseph, S.J., 2001:3), which is the basis for all scientific and technological enquiries. Aristotle, a promising student of Plato, maintained that "nihil est in tellectu quod non purius fuerit in sensu", that is, 'there is nothing in the intellect which was not first found in the senses' -- knowledge is both inductive and deductive. We reason from and observe the activities of the world or particulars around us to other realities or knowledge of universal laws or essences. That was one of the major mistakes of the missionaries. They simply presented heavenly issues on hungry people who struggled daily for their bread.

For Aristotle, man has the potentialities to better his existence on earth once he is guided by the right reasoning. Therefore, human existence would have simply become a matter of chance if the only thing that mattered in our lives were the realm of ideas and perfect forms of Plato.

On the other hand, the Igbo people of South Eastern Nigeria are homogenous, (one language, one color, one belief system) with slight dialectical differences, hence, a bit heterogeneous. As far as this book is concerned, I essentially focused on Ngor Opkpala of Igbo land because of their peculiarity in terms of hospitality and benevolence. The dialectical nature of their religion is such that, the ways they live their lives on earth is determinant of what happens in the world to come. Again, for the interest of this book as noted earlier, the word "Igbo" can stand for a noun, an adjective, singular or plural. The need for this limited range of focus is necessitated by the simple fact that Ngor Okpala people of Igboland are more homogeneous in nature. They share the same moral or ethical principles like those of Aristotle. The homogeneity of their moral conducts may make this project interesting. The Ethics of Aristotle have some values to share with those of the people of Ngor Okpala. The entire cosmology, spirituality, epistemology and anthropology of the Igbo people are geared towards the best ways to make their lives meaningful. Their communal structure marks them out from the rest of the western culture that tend to emphasize individualism. However, we need to properly understand the implication of the word "Ethics".

The Ethics of Aristotle vis-à-vis that of Ngor Okpala People

Descriptively, Aristotle discussed the goal of moral philosophy or Ethics in his Nicomachean Ethics. He is credited for his two

Treatises: the Nicomachean Ethics and the Eudemian Ethics. But some scholars argued that probably the words "Eudemian" and "Nicomachean" were added later, perhaps because the former was edited by his friend, Eudemus and the latter by his son, Nicomachus. In another assumption, the Nicomachean Ethics is noted as a later and improved version of the Eudemian Ethics. (Preliminaries on Aristotle's Ethics in Stanford Encyclopedia of Philosophy, revised 2005). All the same, the above Sources summarized the Ten Books of the Nicomachean Ethics of Aristotle and their Divisions into chapters. In a nutshell, the Ethics of Aristotle is centered on responsibility, personality and character formation, moral evaluation and the best options to achieve the end of human life. When life is at its best, the practice of religion will be encouraged rapidly. In other words, Aristotle is asking: "what are the conditions and situations under which a moral agent can be responsible for his actions?" For him, we are our actions. These actions define our personality and form our 'character'.

The word "character" (Ithos) as noted already is important for Aristotle. We need certain character traits; continence (enkrateia) and incontinence (akrasia) that help us live life at its best. Enkratic person acts with reason or mastery. An akratic acts against reason or mastery due to some pathos. To understand what it takes for a human being to be a good person, he examined the nature of arête, "virtue, excellence" and vices involved in moral evaluations, (Nic. Ethics 11-X). In a sense, "the Nicomachean Ethics is a study based on experience that aims to find clear principles that will help us to distinguish good from bad and right from wrong" (Koterski, J., S.J., 2001:5). For Aristotle, human activities have goals and there must be a highest good which we ultimately aim at (Nic. Ethics 1-2) and this highest good or the end of life he calls "happiness" "(eudaimonia = having a good spirit)" in (Koterski, 2001:6) or "living well". In achieving this "happiness or living well", Aristotle treated the notions of pleasure, wealth, friendship and honor. These are subordinate goals that promote the well being of people because these values even philosophical forms cannot provide adequate account of the ultimate goal or happiness in question.

By historical antecedents, the acquisition of wealth, material goods or the achievement of intellectual knowledge does not guarantee happiness. This is because happiness "involves a life of activity ... an end in itself, not a means to an end" (Koterski, 2001:6). In other words, "the good for human beings, then, must essentially involve the entire proper function of human life as a whole, and this must be an activity (ergon-function, task or work) of the soul that expresses genuine virtue or excellence" (Nic. Ethics 1-7). As such, human beings should aim at a life that is in full conformity and compatible with their rational natures. In effect, acquisition of wealth, knowledge or satisfaction or desires is less important than the achievement of Moral Virtue (hexis). Accordingly, a happy person should manifest a personality well balanced between reasons and desires, with certain degree of moderation. In this sense, "virtue is its own reward" and "true happiness can therefore be attained only through the cultivation of the virtues that make human life complete (Aristotle: Ethics and Virtues in Britannica, I.G.S). The nature of Virtue in Aristotle is not all that clear at first instance. Normally, temperance, justice and courage count as virtues. But for him, Ethics is an intensely practical discipline and not theoretical.

That was why he disagreed with his grandfather, Socrates who equated knowledge with virtue. It is virtue if one knows the right thing and does it, (Koterski, 2001:29). Virtue is skill or state of being, which naturally seeks its mean (mesos) relative to us. Virtue manifests itself in action, (The Internet Encyclopedia of Philosophy).

It is a condition of life-long activities that actualize and play a role in any well-lived life. Virtuous activities do not come by chance because happiness consists in using our reasons well over the course of a full life. And "doing anything well requires virtue or excellence", (Stanford Encyclopedia of Philosophy). The virtues of character for example are our dispositions to act in certain ways in response to a similar situation. It is a habit of behaving in a certain manner over a period of time. A virtuous habit of action is always an intermediate state between the opposed vices of excess and deficiency; too much and too little are always wrong. The right kind of action lies in the mean. Hence, he concludes that virtue lies in the middle, "virtus in media stat", (Nic. Ethics 11-6). For instance, with respect of spending money, generosity, which is virtue, is a mean between the excess of wastefulness and the deficiency of being stingy. We must avoid extremes of all sorts and seek moderation in all we do. Moderation is an edge to the growth of Christianity. Much emphasis on wealth today has created more dilemmas in this direction.

Eventually, he insists that responsible actions must be voluntary, unless involuntarily done under duress or ignorance because moral actions are within our power to perform or avoid (Nic. Ethics 111-1). On this note he advocates for other goods like long-life friendships without which, in the midst of other goods, man cannot choose to live, (Nic. Ethics V111-3, 4). In the above Book, he noted three kinds of friendships, the friendship of common interests, mutual utility and for overall goodness of the other. According to him, genuine happiness lies in actions that lead to virtue. He strongly recommends contemplation as the highest form of moral activity that is vividly continuous and leads to divine blessedness while realizing the various aspects of human virtues as well, (Nic. Ethics X-8), because virtue alone provides the true value one needs to live well. As whether virtue means anything for the Igbo, needs to be investigated too.

The Ethics of the people of Ngor Okpala of Igboland, Nigeria

It is not a sweeping generalization to note that the Ethics, morality, religion and culture of the Ngor Okpala people of Igbo land are one and the same thing. Their entire cosmology and belief systems are deep rooted "within the ambience of ancestral or community life or in solidarity with the Umunna or community" (Nwachukwu, O. Anthony, 2002:341). For the people, morality is synonymous with their normal living. It is a pattern of life bequeathed to them by their ancestors. A violation of the moral order affects not only the humans but also vegetation and livestock. Their virtuous activities are their normal ways of living. Such qualities like truth, justice, honesty, unity and peace are virtues and inevitably parts of their life styles. Living out these virtues in practical life situations joins one to the ancestors who own Igbo land. They are the models of morality.

In order to maintain the moral standards (horos) of the land, the oldest man, being the custodian of morality of each community holds the "Ofo na Ogu", that is, symbols of authority and justice. It "is a visible sign of the legitimating influence of lineage ancestors in the affairs of man", (Ejizu, C. I. 2000:58). Compliance with the natural norms of the land defines the Ethics of the Igbo people of Nigeria. Of course, in Igbo land, women do not own properties. Everything belongs to the men. Thus, violation of moral standards holds its emphasis more on the male adults. This view sounds different from that of Aristotle and the missionaries, which may create a dilemma.

The Comparative Analysis

Both Aristotle and the Igbo people of Nigeria fundamentally recognize the ontological value of life. They equally address the same question: "What is the goal of life?" Each of them accepts happiness as an end in itself. The moral philosophy of Aristotle finds a place in Igbo land, especially on the areas of identifying a person by his actions, habit or character. Ones 'actions speak louder than words" is an aphorism among the Igbo and that the way a tree bends is the same way it falls. This confirms the constancy of the repeated human good actions or conducts of Aristotle that leads one to ones happiness.

However, the Igbo people may differ from Aristotle on the various notions of virtue. A virtuous activity is part of the normal life of the people. While Aristotle disagrees with Plato on his assigning the reality of this physical existence to a world of perfect nature, the Igbo people agree with Plato to an extent.

The Igbo believe that their present lives are lived in the light of the hereafter. Even in the case of death, they believe that "the way a person dies here on earth determines where he goes in the spirit world", (Ikenga-Metuh, Emefie, 1998:16). For instance, a person who led morally bad life would not join the abode of the ancestors from whom the Igbo derive their morality. For Aristotle, friendship is a value that helps one to achieve ones happiness. The Igbo hardly talk of friendship, but relational companion in terms of brother or sister. They say: "Enyi madu bu nwanne ya" meaning that a person's friend is his or her relation, brother or sister. That is why an offence committed against one person has communal effects and it is treated as such. In Aristotle, an individual may aim at cultivating virtuous life and aspire to happiness. It is not so in Igbo land. Happiness is communal and morality is communal. If a good person dies, the entire community grieves or mourns him. But in the case of a bad person, the bereaved family makes propitiations or is punished. Strict measures are taken as a warning to others to avoid falling victim to the bad man's offence and the consequent punishment on the community. All the same, the Ethics of Aristotle challenges that of the Igbo people of Nigeria in the sense that an individual has every right to aspire for his or her own happiness or life goal irrespective of society in which he or she lives. Moral standards cannot make a person a prisoner in his or her own land because of traditions.

Apparently, the ethics of Aristotle has got to do with responsibility, personality and character formation, moral evaluation and the best options and ways to achieve the end of human life. This depends on what we regard as the end of human existence. For the Igbo of Nigeria, the end of human life is an application of values of right decisions and choices in conjunction with societal acceptable values. Aristotle is poised to discovering the conditions and situations under which a person or moral agent can be responsible for his actions and what he believes as the ideals. In his opinion, the way each person behaves says much of his responsibility, personality and character formation. For Aristotle, we cannot separate actions from who we are as rational beings and this is why his philosophy is an antidote to the dilemma of the growth of the Christian religion in Igboland. The peoples' cosmology, religion and life are one and the same thing.

In this regard, Aristotle's ethics is an important tool for the reconstruction of the human mind to accepting values that will assist him or her live and enjoy life. His ethics is important, especially today that a lot of people no longer care about the effects of their actions on other people due to the influence of science and technology. That was the same attitude that created a dilemma in the cherished religion of the Igbo people. The modern person or westerners must be made to understand that happiness does not consist of cheating other people or amassing wealth regardless of the situations of others. Rather, happiness and good life consist in living virtuous lives whereby each person respects the views and boundaries of others and his or her own views too. On this note, we shall include among all others, in our review or study of the ethics of Aristotle under the following two headings:

a. *Virtue:*

The issue of virtue is very essential in our time than any other time in history because of the present day atrocities. There is no way life can be possible without being virtuous in our actions and deeds. According to Internet resources:

> *Virtue is goodness: the quality of being morally good or righteous, a paragon of virtue, good quality: patience is a virtue, admirable quality: a quality that is good or admirable, but not necessarily in terms of morality; a cardinal or theological morality: a cardinal virtue, e.g. justice or moderation, or theological virtue, e.g. hope or charity; chastity: the moral quality of being chaste, especially in a woman; worth: the worth, advantage, or beneficial quality. (Encarta [R] World English Dictionary, 1998-2005).*

In this light also: "If you mean a person's virtue, it is the morality of the person. In literature, a woman's virtue generally means her virginity. If you mean something like the phrase "Patience is a virtue", then it means that patience is a good quality to have" (Ibid). The possession of virtue in human life is not limited to religion or any faith tradition. It is part and parcel of human life. To live without one virtue or the other is to be brutal in nature. We need virtue in our lives to claim our identity as rational human beings.

Consequentially, every human being should aim at a life that is in full conformity and compatible with his rational nature (Nic. Ethics 11-X). Moral Virtue is the foundation for all happy and healthy living. There could be no dilemma in the growth of the Christian religion in Igbloland if people were to be happy, enjoying one another. Any joy that is selfish is false. In this sense, the Christian bible asks this question: "A virtuous wife who can find her? She is far beyond the price of pearls. Her husband's heart has confidence in her; from her he will derive no little profit. Advantage and not hurt she brings him all the days of her life" (Proverbs 31:10-12). From biblical perspective, to be virtuous is to be alive. What does it mean to live than to bring joy and progress to other people? When our lives are shining examples to others, the dilemma in question will lessen drastically. Experience is the best teacher and people learn faster from others' actions than words that may not bear any fruits.

Moral virtue is life. It is accommodating and embracing. It is quite different from the acquisition of wealth, knowledge or satisfaction of personal desires. To have virtue is to have everything. Good living is consistent with being self-rewarding. Hence, Aristotle noted: "Virtue is its own reward" and "true happiness can therefore be attained only through the cultivation of the virtues that make human life complete (Aristotle: Ethics and Virtues in Britannica, Internet Resources). In this way, he concludes that virtue lies in the middle (Nic. Ethics 11-6). It is the application of moderation and avoidance of excessiveness or pomposity. Virtue is the usefulness of us. It is our skill, or the state of our being, which naturally seeks its mean, relative to us, in achieving its end. Virtue is not theoretical but it manifests itself in what we do, in our actions, (Internet Encyclopedia of Philosophy). Once any religion puts on a virtuous face, it grows and enlivens peoples' hopes and aspirations.

b. *Happiness:*

This is where Aristotle proves his practical philosophy. All human activities have goals and there must be a highest good, which we ultimately aim at (Nic. Ethics 1-2) and this highest good or the end of life he calls "happiness. A 'goal' is wider and more beneficial than an objective. While objectives look at the particulars, goals consider the universals that equally apply at particular cases. The goal of virtue is holistic and embracing. According to Aristotle: "Virtuous activities do not come by chance because happiness consists in using our reasons well over the course of a full life. And doing anything well requires virtue or excellence, (Stanford Encyclopedia of Philosophy; Nic. Ethics V111-3, 4). It was within this context he treated three kinds of friendships, the friendship of common interests, mutual utility and for overall goodness of the other. One acquires virtue when one associates with others for the achievement of common interest and not being selfish or avaricious. In mutual utility, he advocates for an egalitarian society where everybody will be happy with each other and achieve the goal of life - happiness. While it may not be possible to achieve such goals because of the complexities of human nature, Aristotle has fired the first shot that can lead us to true happiness.

According to him, genuine happiness lies in actions that lead to virtue. If you become rich by stealing, it is no virtue or happiness. If you are unfaithful to your partner, consider it selfishness and not happiness or virtuous. Virtue leads to happiness that is the result of genuine and sound moral living. It was in this context that he condemned pleasure, especially when derived from wealth as the basis for happiness. In Koterski's own words, an action is a virtue if one knows the right thing and does it, (Koterski, 2001:29). Thus, knowing the right thing and doing it gives happiness and that is virtuous too.

Any other thing short of these guidelines will ultimately bring one to a regrettable situation. Even the missionaries who brought the Christian religion to the people of Igboland, their attitudes could have assisted the people appreciate their new religion better than they did at first. Virtue is the key to sound human relationships.

Effective Evaluation of the point at hand

Generally, social values and moral issues touch every aspect of human behaviors and the best way they can lead to fulfilled lives is by acquiring virtue in them. Our extensive research here has supported Aristotle and other social and moral philosophers squarely as ways of guiding individuals appreciate and practise their religions and live happily. That is why Aristotle conceives virtue as the highest good that brings happiness to a person and should manifest his personality always by striking balance between reasons and desires, with certain degree of moderation. Excessive life patterns are not welcomed in Aristotelian moral philosophy. Too much of everything is bad. Today, a lot of people do not want to be told what to do, at times; they purposely dodge their responsibilities. Therefore, virtuous life has to be consistent, universal, and particular also, but must aim at the individual and general good of society. Ethics is lived in compliance with moral order and unity. As it were, the book has provided individuals with the tools to live virtuous lives allowing moral laws and principles to govern their relationships and relations with themselves.

Effects of 'Paganism' and Heathenism in Africa

The practice of "paganism, heathenism, fetishism or idolatry," has long been associated with the Africans and their religious consciousness. But the question that challenges us here is: "Is it true that Africans are the pagans invoked here?" This is why prejudice is spurious, a vice and crime. It is unnatural to judge somebody you have not interacted with or come in contact with. Being impetuous about concluding a matter one has not studied well may ultimately lead one to an affected blunder. Rumormongers and querulous individuals will always be found in every part of the globe. Society will never lack true and false prophecies, even those who wish that the world might end earlier than God has fixed it for himself. Permit me to examine the definition of the word "pagan". According to Webster's Dictionary Thesaurus, the term 'pagan' means: "A person who does not acknowledge God in any religion, a heathen". On the same par, 'paganism' means: "The belief in and the worship of a false god; heathenism".

There is no smoke without fire, especially within our common sense knowledge. This matter will thoroughly be dealt with in this book. From human experiences, research and findings, Africans have a religion that puts God first in their lives. Reiterating the points already noted in this book, if Africans have lacked anything in their lives, it was far from being religion. The missionaries testified to this as evidenced in this book. Then, the question is: "What is paganism or heathen in the religion of the people? African Traditional Religion is practiced world round today because of its objectivity and beliefs in such values as honesty, truth, justice and peace. The peoples' religion has singled them out as people who are closely connected to their faith, belief and adherence to the true one Almighty God. There had never been any time in the history of Africans that they did not profess a belief in "Chukwu" the great God. In this sense, Africans or the Igbo of Nigeria are not pagans as such.

The discussion has become so interesting in that one should not be condemned before ones accusation. The word 'paganism' is not African and has no relevance there. Therefore, most of those missionaries who came to Africa with hidden agenda other than to evangelize the people have some questions to answer in this regard. The people have always and firmly stood on their faith in their religion. Then, how did the idea of fetishism come about? Idolatry is a universal problem, and not peculiar with Africans. Among the westerners, many people present themselves as idols to be worshipped as gods. With this mentality infiltrating in Igboland of Nigeria these days, the dilemma of the growth of the Christian religion becomes feasible. The issue of 'juju or 'voodoo' in the consideration of the western world is not associated with African's alone. Human jealousy and envy have exacerbated the human situation and escalated into a situation of destroying and putting innocent souls to death. These are equally forms of juju or voodoo. It does not matter what it means in the assassination of an innocent soul, it is all within the group of juju and voodoo.

In a research work of this magnitude, exaggerations have to be avoided. That the people had beliefs in certain powers or forces should not be taken literally to mean that they were heathen. There are certain behavioral patterns that are empowering, generating spiritual energies that keep the people in balance. In this perspective, can we correctly hold that beliefs in objects, dreams, witchcraft and things like that equally affect the growth of the Christian faith as such? This again calls for further investigations into what beliefs in objects, dreams, and witchcraft mean in our context. In Igboland of Nigeria and throughout the African nations, certain objects are highly valued as medicinal and therapeutic and the people cannot discard them on religious reasons. As we shall see in the course of this discussion, for instance, "Odo" signifies peace and the people apply it in different ways to wish others peace. The Africans have not replaced their God with any object. But, with the advent of

Christianity some of the Christians who no longer believe in such objects criticize the traditional religion thereby creating loopholes for the dilemma in question.

On the part of dreams, this is a human factor. Individuals differ on the interpretation of dreams. The issue of dreams is not African, but a universal phenomenon. Dreams are biblically proved. When Joseph dreamt (Genesis 37: 5-11) and narrated to his brothers of his kingship, he did not have the Igbo of Nigeria in mind. That his dreams came true did not mean all dreams share equality and credibility. There are instances of dreams in the bible and in everyday life. It is possible that some people are endowed with special gifts for dreams and interpretations. There are no general consensuses with regard to any belief in dreams or not. Everybody is entitled to his or her dreams and should not constitute obstacles in the practice of the peoples' religion. Once a person is remarkable as a true dreamer, he is always and respectfully looked upon to deliver his message within the context of his claims or position. In African traditional religion, a dreamer has never been worshipped or looked upon to decide the mode of worship or religious celebrations.

Many have argued that witchcraft; sorcery and magic are all associated with the African traditional religion in which certain individuals are dreaded as possessing magical powers. Just like the case of dreamers, those who practice witchcraft or sorcery can foresee the future through their supernatural powers. Assuming that some Africans or people from Igboland of Nigeria practice sorcery and witchcraft, what has this belief got to do with the religion of the people as such? Even in the western world, we have more magicians than in Africa. There is need to understand properly what witchcraft means in our context. According to The Random House Dictionary of the English Language (RHDEL): The Unabridged Edition -

RHDEL: "A witch is a person, now especially a woman, who professes or is supposed to practice magic, especially black magic or the black art; sorceress, one who uses a divining rod; to bring by or as by witchcraft; bewitch; charm…witchcraft – the art of or practices of a witch; sorcery; magic, magical influence, witchery" (RHDEL: The Unabridged Edition). In the first place, why should witchcraft be associated with women and black magic or art and not men, white magic or art? What can be more witchery than a mother suffocating her own baby to death for any reasons at all? The dilemma of the growth of the Christian religion in Igboland of Nigeria is a human factor, involving the individual on the spot and not necessarily the art of worshipping God or belief system.

The human environment and dynamics are important factors in this discussion. That was why we extensively examined the various perspectives of the culture of the people of Igboland in this book. Hence, one indigenous writer, Chinua Achebe, rightly observed in his book titled "The trouble with Nigeria" that: "Indiscipline pervades our life so completely today that one may be justified in calling it condition par-excellence of contemporary Nigerian society" (Chinua Achebe, 1983). Indiscipline is a threat to the growth of the Christian faith generally. As an African addressing his own people, Achebe frowns at the rate of indiscipline in Igboland. Definitely, if he were to address the general public on the same topic, no country could have been exempted from his accusation. Indiscipline seems to have entered into the fabric and marrow of many people in society today. Achebe has made a serious point. When the human intellect is falsely fed by the senses, the net result has always been regretted.

Thus, the indiscipline experienced in Igboland is responsible for a lot of crimes that go on there on daily basis. In this light therefore, the problem or dilemma of the growth of the Christian religion is not that of the missionaries but the people. We see and hear and read about indiscipline in the homes, in the private sectors, in government and in legislative assemblies, on the roads and in the air. The malaise takes so many different forms and shapes - sometimes brutally crude, at other times more subtle - that a comprehensive definition of it would be very difficult. In a general sense like this one, it is possible that indiscipline has created more problems or dilemma for the growth of the Christian religion in most cultures of the world. Indiscipline is a universal issue that needs to be curbed. If people could take life more seriously and respect bounds and boundaries, indiscipline will lessen and many will be energized to trace their spiritual source energy.

With regard to our present target in this book, it is obvious that indiscipline is a failure or refusal to submit one's desires and actions to the restraints of orderly social conduct in recognition of the rights and desires of others. As a malaise, it demands a general compliance to fight it as much as possible. Indiscipline makes one primitive, un-churched, irresponsible and animalistic. Discipline differentiates us from brute animals. This value is universal and it is not limited to Igboland. In fact, in real traditional Igbo set up, the issue of indiscipline was never raised. For instance, any Christian who is not disciplined cannot advance the kingdom of God on earth, be the person a minister or not. The importance of discipline has led some people to maintain that it is the first law of heaven. In the context of the Igbo people of Nigeria, before Christianity came to their land, everybody complied with the laws and customs of the land without exception because the ancestors were perceived to be in charge of the governance of the land. The ancestors were revered, as God's own representative and the custodian of peace and order. Unlike today, Christianity appears to have lost its force and spiritual significations. More people shout the name of "Jesus" than in the past. But only few comply with the injunctions and legacies Jesus left for society to follow. This is what we refer to as dilemma. Indiscipline is a chronic disease that demands immediate and special attention.

In his own words, Achebe insists: "The goal of indiscipline is self-interest, its action, the abandonment of self- restraint in pursuit of the goal" (Achebe 1983). It would be inconceivable to talk of the growth of Christianity in Igboland without addressing the problem of corruption in our society, in the state, Church and in the nation. This is so because, as long as corruption remains the bane of our Nigerian society, no meaningful attempt at any religious order will be effective. Without adequate care and safeguards against the evils of corruption in Nigeria, especially among the Igbo, which has passed the alarming and entered the fatal stage, there will be no growth of the Christian religion in that part of the world. Definitely, Christianity in Igboland and in so many parts of the globe will naturally die if we keep on pretending that things are all right, the grace of God is plentiful.

The growth of religion is incompatible with corruption. In other words, religion cannot thrive within the atmosphere of corruption. Corruption is fatal and lethal to the practice of religion and harmonious co-habitation. Unfortunately, corruption is the child of western civilization. In real African or Igbo cosmology, corruption was never acceptable in any form. To be involved in corruption is to choose death not life. According to Dr. Lambert Nwigwe in his book "A patriotic invitation for a moral Renaissance of fresh" the Igbo of Nigeria are corrupt because the system under which they live today makes corruption easy and profitable. They will cease to be corrupt when corruption is made difficult and inconvenient" (Nwigwe 1983:12). Corruption, Nwigwe went further to say, "goes with power, and whatever the average man or woman may have, it is not power. Therefore, to hold any useful discussion of corruption we must first locate it where it properly belongs - in the ranks of the powerful" (Ibid). The emphasis on the points Nwigwe has noted here are on the "today" which, in a way, exonerates the Igbo of old. Unless the Igbos work hard to stamp corruption out of their lives, reorganize society, have family life improved, and build industries to give employment to the idle youths to keep them out off mischief and the streets; the Christian faith will continue to be jeopardized.

Disunity and lack of trust in government

Moreover, other factors that the book would address that impede the growth of Christian faith in Igboland include disunity and lack of faith in the government. It is necessary to have in mind that our discussion is a preposition of a people who authentically have and practice religion. The simple implication is that not all cultures and people who claim to have religion practice it. It is one thing to have a religion and another to profess and abide by the values of that religion. The Igbo of Nigeria belong to the latter option. Not only do the people have strong belief system in their religion but also they do whatever it takes to protect and defend it at least violation. Therefore, our allusions here pertain to those government or leadership positions where the constituents have and practice a religion as ways of their lives. Casting doubt on a government or leaders because of their incompetence, ineffectiveness and unacceptable decisions directly or indirectly affects society in a great manner including religious matters. For instance, the uproars and un-restful atmosphere in the Northern part of Nigeria has affected religious practices there. Cases have manifested where worshipers were burnt alive during religious services. In a way, this is the dilemma that corrodes the growth of the Christian religion in Igboland.

Unity can only be as good as the end purpose for which it is desired and achieved. There is no unity in cheating, embezzlement of public fund, refusal to pay workers their salaries and in deceit. Obviously, it is glorious when groups of people come together, unite themselves and build a school, church, a hospital, a good road, pipe borne water, electricity and basic infrastructures that will keep the people going green. By so doing they build an egalitarian society where everybody will have a fair chance, play and justice. What happens when a group of other people supposedly gets together in order to rob a bank? Is their unity not undesirably doomed? Therefore, we cannot extol the virtues of unity without first satisfying ourselves that the end to which the unity is directed is impeachable or not having any flaws. Neither can we have justice without truth. For religious people, faith in God is a desirable way of life, for humanists, it is acceptable to believe in the intrinsic worth of man. But, what do we say of having faith in money, talismanic objects and fetishism that are seen among so many people around the globe today, particularly in Igboland of Nigeria? Besides, tattoo industries are growing worldwide, including Nigeria. These are extra-mundane measures aimed at ridiculing religion and its mission. For instance, cases have featured where armed robbers who were killed at gun fires have been seen wearing the crucifix and Rosaries. These nuances portray a total denial of the supernatural in the course of human history, thereby reducing religion to a choice of chance, hence the dilemma.

Nothing can be more powerful than having faith in what one believes in. It does not often mean believing in God. But a belief in God that is not backed up by strong faith is just like asking a person totally born blind to read and interpret a document. It is sheer neurotic if not psychotic to have religion without the corresponding faith that energizes its practice. Or do we accept to have faith that is not accompanied by good work? So many utterances were made in the bible to buttress this point. Due mainly to this mentality, Paul in his letter to Titus made the following remarks:

> *To all who are pure themselves, everything is pure; but to those who have been corrupted and lack faith, nothing can be pure – the corruption is both in their minds and in their consciences. They claim to have knowledge of God but the things they do are nothing but a denial of him; they are outrageously rebellious and quite incapable of doing good (Titus: 1:15-16).*

The above quotation specifically boils down to the individual who claims to be religious or have faith. This tendency is the cankerworm that eats the taproot of religion in Igboland and elsewhere in the world. Holier-than-thou attitude has destroyed the growth of the Christian religion in Igboland, especially in Ngor Okpala Local Government Area. The people are open-minded in their interactions and dealing with others. They hate camouflage-related type of Christianity or surface Christianity that emphasizes superficiality that lacks any reasonable substance.

James succinctly made this point clearer when he noted that there was no faith that was not accompanied by good work. For instance, how can we tell people to be well, feed fine, keep warm, and feel happy, et cetera when we have no intention of assisting them achieve those comfortable situations? In concluding his observation on the matter he added:

> *Faith is like that; if good works do not go with it, it is quite dead. You say you have faith and I have good deeds; I will prove to you that I have faith by showing you my good deeds – now prove to me that you have faith without any good deeds to show. You believe in the one God – that is creditable enough, but*

the demons have the same belief, and they tremble with fear. Do realize, you senseless man, that faith without good deeds is useless (James 2:17-20).

Faith is more of life especially when it is placed and built on something acceptable. Before our faith grows like living things, it must have a focus, a bearing, a foundation from where it leads to maturity and fulfillment. Ordinarily, many people often and first ascertain the nature and worth of building up faith on something that is promising and enlivening. We ask crucial questions such as, faith in what or whom? Just as in the matter of unity, we normally try and x-ray the composite factors involved as to ascertain to what extent such unity can be achieved. For instance, there can be no unity among individuals who cheat and deceive each other in the name of friendships, associations and unions.

Therefore, a likelihood conclusion is derivable that virtues like unity and faith in material things are not absolute, but conditionally based on the satisfaction of other mundane purposes. That was our main reason for predicating or establishing that faith is life particularly when it is backed up by meaningful actions. The socio - cultural vitality of the Igbo depends on their willingness and ability to ask searching questions that concern and involve them as a community. This tendency calls for vigilance on what might surprisingly spring up among the people. By this way, anything or habit that brings mental rigor, stiffness of temper or harshness is avoided. Unfortunately, Nigerians, especially the Igbos being smooth and easy-going people are not famous for fermenting troubles. They have never doubted that their God is always protecting and guiding them. Yet, things have rapidly changed today that a lot of questions are being asked as regards what has brought about the state of uncertainties and anxieties.

Elements of cultural disparagement/disparity

Each person has right to exist and be respected as such. Disparaging a people whose identity is not in doubt brings about huge disorientations and disparities. The Igbo are happy people who take pride in their being and achievements in the face of poverty or sickness. Any factor that seems to bring about inequality in their cherished values creates divisions instead of progress. Both in richness and poverty, they are one, undivided unity and body. As Chinua Achebe would ask, "Why did we not think, for example, of honesty which cannot be so easily directed to undesirable ends? Justice never prompts the question: justice for what. Neither does honesty or truth" (Achebe 1983). Such values as honesty, justice and truth are embodied in the lives of the people. There was no disparagement in matters related to marriage, leadership, governance of the people and the laws that guide the people. The elders have their divine roles as far as the smooth running of the affairs of the people is concerned. But with the advent of the western civilization, a big cut was inflicted on the morality of the people. Today, lack of discipline in society is affecting every aspect of the human condition – social, political, cultural, religious, economic et cetera.

Thus, as the "New Igbo" of Nigeria continue to struggle in their gloomy situations of misery and poverty, the Nigerian Bishops, during the Synod of African Bishop's Conference in Rome, added their voices to some of the major effects and dilemma of the growth of Christian faith in Igboland of Nigeria. Such voices included: "The battering of wives, the disinheritance of daughters, the oppression of widows in the name of tradition, forced marriages, female genital mutilation, trafficking in women and several other abuses such as sex slavery and sex tourism" (Synod of African Bishops, October 3,2009 through October 25, 2009). This is more of inhumanity to man. I tend to describe and differentiate the Igbo of old from those of today – new Igbo, who love money more than life and appear very mendacious, prone to evil, lying and deceitful.

Eventually, this book is trying to elucidate more on these points mentioned by the 'Synod' fathers, and proffers some solutions to this nagging problem that militates against the growth of Christian faith in Igboland. We shall preview why, despite advances, the standard of living of the population, the condition of widows and divorced women remain deplorable in society. The situation, though, may be worst in many developing nations with their unique social, cultural and economic milieu, which at times ignores the basic human rights of this vulnerable section of society. Women and children must be protected at all cost because of their vulnerability and delicacy. I am much aware that widowed /divorced women suffer varying psychological stressors in society generally and Igboland in particular because they are often ignored. It has been concluded in various studies that such stress could bring about harbingers or professionals who initiate or pioneer this unique movement that takes care of psychiatric and psychotic illnesses, like depression, anxiety, and substance dependence. In a situation like this, pastoral psychologists, the treating physicians, environmental theologians, social workers and others who come in contact with these women are required to integrate them to their rightful place in society. As it were, this is the main objective of this undertaking.

At this point, it is necessary to reflect on the theology of Pastoral Care, and the Psychological and a case approach to an AIDS Patient in Igboland of Nigeria. Obviously, Pastoral Psychology is in the area of psychological practice in that it addresses the concrete problems individuals go through in their efforts to lead normal lives. In this instance, we shall study how pastoral psychology is interwoven with environmental theology that considers the individual in his situation, circumstances and conditions in relation to his aspirations in life (Rev. Dr. Jude Osunkwo, GTF/Oxford, 2012). This is an aspect of theology that meets and addresses the individual at the moment. By 'theology' in this context, we are not speaking of received theologies that may not address peoples' physical and spiritual problems at the same time. Any theology that excludes the body and emphasizes only the spirit is defective. God can only be perceived as an embodiment. Therefore, any discussion that involves pastoral care is equally psychological in that the latter embraces every aspect of human endeavors and interactions, his feelings and actions. There can be psychology without pastoral care, theology or religion, but we cannot have either of them without psychology. Considerably, we shall examine the dilemma of the growth of the Christian religion within the context of the theology of pastoral care as inseparable part of psychology.

Approaching Pastoral Psychology/Care in the face of AIDS Victim

As a professional in my field of study, I have poised to deeply reflect on a particular scenario in which a person with AIDS in Africa or Ngor Okpala of Nigeria should be approached or treated. Call this a theology of pastoral care or an aspect of pastoral psychology; it is the same and one thing. The emphasis is on human beings who need some help from their situation, which ordinarily might appear hurtful or depressing. The question is: "What can I do now to assist this very individual in this particular case?" The question of religion or belief in God or theology is not always the way out in matters like this one but skills gained from research and experience. That is why pastoral psychology is a child of concern in which experts attempt to apply professional tools and skills in addressing 'concrete' human problems. Human problems are hydra-headed and versed.

By 'concrete', we mean stressful situations or emotional traumas that can throw individuals out of balance.

We need to know that, it does not matter what an individual goes through in life or may call a problem, as long as it affects his body chemistry and spiritual equilibrium, he needs a psycho-pastoral attention. In this section, we are discussing the healing presence, the relevance, place and role of God in human suffering, pains and his realization in a concrete dimension. One basic question that stares us on the face is: "Is there any need for religion when there is no absolute trust in a supernatural being who has the power to influence human actions?" If there is no such belief, then the discussion on the dilemma of the growth of the Christian religion becomes futile and pointless. Again, if we adopt the dictionary definition that "pastoral' refers to the duties of a pastor" (Webster's Dictionary Thesaurus), must we always connect or invoke God before we can carry out every pastoral care? The matter becomes more complicated when a pastor specifically refers to "a Christian clergyman in charge of a Church or congregation" (Ibid). By implication, the dictionary definition has limited pastoral care to the duties of Christian pastors. Can that also be conceived of a pastoral psychologist?

Ultimately, one can be tempted to ask who a pastoral caregiver is in terms of ministering to or addressing the need of people who have no religion or do not believe in God like the atheists. For an instance, does an Atheist who is instantaneously and emotionally distressed have need for any pastoral care? This is to say: "Is theology absolutely necessary in pastoral care?" This is what makes this book interesting. For instance, does the hood of a pastor define pastoral care or the compassion that characterizes the lives of good-spirited people? In this capacity, can an Atheist who does not believe in God exercise or offer pastoral care in any form? In what capacity can a person be called a pastoral caregiver? As far as I am concerned, pastoral care presupposes a call, a mission, a compassionate and supportive presence, and the preparedness to listen and be moved to extend oneself to another person. Pastoral care cannot be subjected within the confines of pastor-church relationship.

Generally speaking, among created order and in most aspects of our human co-existence, there are various forms of care. For instance, most mothers, both human and animals have the natural tendency to protect their younger ones. They do this not because of any religious obligation or mandate. Every good government tends to place much premium on the economy and security of her citizens. Examples of these sorts of governance abound in many countries. Therefore, we are constrained to discuss what theology of pastoral care means in terms of the difficulties, sufferings and pains many people are experiencing today irrespective of the vast religious affiliations that surround them. The discussion may sound as "fictio mentis" - an object of the mind, when we do not situate it on a particular case that might involve God and man in the healing process. From these perspectives that involve God, man and woman, we can discuss a particular and practical case of need that I will present what I may refer to as theology of pastoral care.

As a way of acquainting our readers with a psycho-pastoral dimension of the book, a woman just lost her husband in a motor accident and called her pastor to inform him of what happened. The pastor picked the phone and responded, thus: "Who is on the line?" With tears in her eyes, she shouted: "Pastor, please it is me, Mrs. NP, my husband has been knocked down by a car and he has been pronounced dead, I am finished, I am finished pastor!" The pastor responded: "When did this happen? It is a pity, I am preparing a homily to preach at a crusade this evening, I hope you take care of yourself and I will pray for him" and hangs the phone. Here is one of those cases in pastoral psychology, where certain skills are consequential. Ordinarily, every clergyman is a 'pastor' or minister of the word of God, but not all pastors are professional caregivers. A little elucidation of the point at hand is essential in this project.

In the first value interpretation or evaluation, it is possible to say that the pastor did all he could have done in the given situation just described. There are certain pertinent questions one should ask regarding the situation as presented here:

What was Mrs. NP looking from the pastor?

1. Was she actually in need of prayer at this moment?
2. From the pastor's response or answer, is it not possible to guess that the pastor lives very close to Mrs. NP?
3. It could be possible that Mrs. NP has no other relation or child except her spiritual leader. Or, is it not possible to conclude that the woman has great faith in God?
4. The pastor simply gave an answer to her concern and not a response.
5. Did Mrs. NP need to know what the pastor was doing or where he was preparing to go?
6. Was there any element of compassion in the manner the pastor answered Mrs. NP's phone?
7. What was the implication of asking Mrs. NP when the accident occurred?
8. Had time any major role to play in that instance?
9. Could the pastor have made out time to visit with Mrs. NP or did he play his role as such?

10. If Jesus were to be invited physically in Mrs. NP's matter, how do you think he could have approached or responded to the whole issue?

There are thousand and one questions one could raise here with regard to the above situational event. Without over flogging the issue, when life is at stake or involved, every attention or effort is intensified and shifted to save it. Mrs. NP was devastated and needed somebody to be there for her. It was natural that by calling her pastor could have meant she had found God or some sort of consolation. All the same, from the manner the pastor addressed her concern; she was left with more physical and spiritual pains than she had bargained for. This is why supportive presence is very important in human interactions, communications and interpersonal relationships. The Igbo of Nigeria have a saying that states: "Anaghi amu akaikpe na nka" meaning that one does not learn to use the left hand at old age. The implication of this proverb is that once an individual has formed a particular habit from childhood, it would be very hard for him to change it at old age. In our context, it means that being a pastor does not necessarily change anybody's personality traits, generically speaking. It is only with the grace of God and practice that some people supervise themselves and sensitively apply values of other-regarding in what they do.

There were other manners of approach the pastor could have employed to recognize the predicament of Mrs. NP as an important human document. That is why my studies in psychology have revealed that only those who are spiritually connected to themselves can feel emotional connections with other people. In the first place, the pastor did not seem to hear the pains in the poor woman's plight. Apparently, such poor understanding of religion or practicing religion on its instrumental level will definitely lead to the dilemma in question. First and foremost, the pastor would have acknowledged the magnitude of the loss in one of these ways: "Oh my God, your husband passed or died? This is very hard to imagine. I am so sorry to hear it. Please, calm down, I shall try to come and see you and hear you correctly. I am a bit confused! This sounds unbelievable to accept, etc". One does not need to have a religion or belong to any Christian fellowship or become a pastor to feel with those who have some emotional pains or in similar situation like Mrs. NP. No wonder, some people maintain that life is larger than logic. This point will become clearer as we read through this book. Before examining the theological implication of psycho-pastoral counseling and care, let us try and apply psychological tools in dealing with other concrete human situations.

Psychology and its Therapeutic effects in the Peoples' lives

The Catholic Bishops of Nigeria were once reported to have said that: "Every disaster, suffering, death and unpleasant event is regarded as a punishment for some evil done by the victim" (Catholic Bishops of Nigeria, pp.75-78). Based on what is happening among some of Ngor Okpala people and many parts of the world today, is it possible to justify the above statement? It was a serious over statement to hold such obnoxious belief. That was the belief among the people that suffering was a punishment from the ancestors or God. However, events occur within varying circumstances. Such views can only be accepted in the context of the Igbo of Nigeria who believe that everything or misfortune has a cause, either by the victim or punishment from the ancestors as noted already. The situation becomes different or is proved wrong when we consider so many areas where natural disasters have stricken like the case of Haiti, Japan and so many other places. Such natural disasters indicate that poverty can cause severe panic attack but not an earthquake for instance.

Unfortunately, most people have presented "Haiti as the poorest country in the Western Hemisphere" (2010 Haiti earthquake, Wikipedia, the free encyclopedia, page 3). While I do not doubt that survey or piece of history, there are some people in Nigeria who are suffering terribly because of high level of corruption and bad government even worse than some people in Haiti. That some people are suffering more than others, do their situations suggest that they are the worst sinners on the planet? This is what I cannot accept as a platitude. Suffering is part of life and it exists in degrees. There are certain categories of sufferings, some are natural and some others are man-made. For instance, can a lazy person make major progress in life without being assisted? Research has proved that laziness is a disease that can lead to un-foretold sufferings and hardships even when a victim is assisted.

After I finished studying and reflecting on the nature of suffering that many people go through in their lives especially in Nigeria, I was saddened by the recent catastrophic events created in many places by natural disasters. Our main sources in this book will immensely reflect some of the extensive readings and findings on related and various works in psychology and how they apply to the people of Ngor Okpala. Moreover, after I asked myself certain unanswered questions with regard to the All-Powerful nature of God and his unmatchable control of the Universe, the quotation from Matthew's Gospel came to mind (Cf. page 149). Thus, in this section of the book, I delved extensively into the relevance of psychology and its therapeutic effects in the life of the needy especially as it concerns the people of my town, Ngor Okpala. However, before we can justify this unavoidable approach, there is the need to view psychology from its theoretical perspective and then its practical application to concrete human situations as it affects Ngor Okpala people of Igboland of Nigeria.

From a theoretical viewpoint, it is easy to cite instances where psychology could be most effective in people's lives without any application to the problems thereabout. For example, the synoptic episode of Matthew has relevance for both theory and practice. While I extensively examined that quotation in the light of what is happening in Ngor Okpala and many other places of the globe, I equally brought out its theoretical aspect as a guide to anticipate the need for psychology in human life. In the words of Nwachukwu: "The borderline remains that; psychology remains therapeutic in theory and practice, depending on how it impacts on each individual person, consciously or unconsciously" (DLM, GTF. 2007).

According to Prof. Robinson: "The most important aspects of human psychology are precisely those unique factors which make us human" (Robinson, Daniel, N. Part 1, p.5). By this claim, the humans are differentiated from animals due to certain characteristic features. The basic question we should ask now is: "What are those important aspects of human psychology that make us human?" They include:

- ❖ The sensory programs such as the sense of smell, taste, touch, see, and to hear especially what is happening in the world around us like the devastating event of poverty in Ngor Okpala.
- ❖ Motor programs, by which we walk, climb and run, especially to assist those in dire need of our support as those under investigation.
- ❖ Cognitive programs, by which we are able to interpret the hardship of most people around the world, express our

sympathy to them, intensify ours efforts to come to their rescue and feel for them.

Both human beings and animals share these characteristics in certain degrees. As far as sensory organs are concerned, animals have them too. Animals know when there is danger and run for their safety. They eat, hear, see and taste just as human beings and enjoy more powerful sensory programs. Even their motor programs are more effective than most human beings. Many human beings cannot climb or run but most of them do in pronounced levels. On the level of cognitive programs, animals are so intelligent. They lack rationality and analytic ability to count numbers and engage in science as humans do. This is precisely the only difference between them and us.

Eventually, the therapeutic nature of psychology depends largely on the various functions we perform as human beings. Juxtaposing this situation with the dilemma in the growth of the Christian religion in Igboland of Nigeria, it appears that these faculties have been frustrated or underused. The issue of syncretistic activities hits at the animalistic nature of man instead of his rational nature. When somebody calls a spade a spade, he has little or nothing to hide about himself or the position he stands for. Some people play on their intelligence at times without telling themselves the truth and carry same attitude to others as well. Once people are not straightforward in themselves and interactions with others, expecting the growth of the Christian faith with them is to say the impossible.

Our activities, cognitive, affective, intellectual, sensory knowledge, mental, emotional, and the various manners in which we are defined, as rational human beings should guide even our belief systems. It is only when we employ these faculties properly in assisting others, and ourselves that psychology becomes therapeutic both in theory and practice. This is the role the Christian religion is meant to play in the lives of her adherents. Any belief in God or something one does not trust and approach with the same level of conviction cannot yield any fruit for that one. Just as the case was before the advent of the western civilization and Christianity, the Igbo of Nigeria lived long lives because of their truthfulness and integrity of purpose both in words and actions. The Christian religion came as a form of camouflage or disguise for perpetuating evil in society. The people resorted to swearing and oath taking to decide the truth of any matter. But Christianity came and condemned it. The net result today is that hardly do people tell the truth any more.

With the common trend of events today, one can simply fantasize the need to assist others or the poor ones in many parts of the globe. That kind of attitude refers to psychology in its theoretical level. For instance, according to James: "Nobody must imagine that he is religious while he still goes on deceiving himself and not keeping control of over his tongue; anyone who does this has the wrong idea of religion" (James1:26). This is the cause of the dilemma in question. When people present a falsehood of their persons, the practice of religion suffers. It is easier to wish somebody well without any execution of any sort. In the biblical perspective, psychology becomes therapeutic when it is translated into action.

For instance, this long passage from James summarizes our point here:

Take the case, my brothers, of someone who has never done a single good act but claims that he has faith. Will that faith save him? If one of the brothers or one of the sisters is in need of clothes and has not enough food to live on, and one of you says

> *to them, 'I wish you well; keep yourself warm and eat plenty',*
> *without giving them these bare necessities of life, then what good*
> *is that? Faith is like that: if good works do not go with it, it is*
> *quite dead (James 2:14-16).*

That is why James goes on to describe the nature of religion that can lead to the growth of the Christian religion in Igboland of Nigeria and elsewhere. For instance: "Pure, un-spoilt religion, in the eyes of God our Father is this: coming to the help of orphans and widows when they need it, keeping oneself uncontaminated by the world" (James 1:27).

Religion produces much fruit once the adherents put their feelings of sympathy for the poor into actions or deed. In this way it becomes practical and therapeutic and in this sense the aspect of psychology we talk about here equally becomes a reality (Red cross, CBS News, 13 January 2010). In the light of what makes us human in the face of human problems, as we have them in many parts of the world, there is need to listen to what Spencer has to say in these words:

> *Physiologists and psychologists say that the mind is a manifestation*
> *of the brain. According to them, "without the brain, there is no*
> *mind. Within the brain lies the potential for self-awareness and*
> *purposeful activity. Somehow the brain gives rise to the mind.*
> *Whether thought is then self-initiated, merely responsive to*
> *external stimulation, or reflects an ongoing interaction between*
> *people and the environment is a hotly debated issue in psychology*
> *(Spencer Rathus, 1989, page 61).*

In the light of the above observation, every phenomenological event that involves a 'thought' or a 'feeling', there should be accompanying, underlying neurological events too. Spencer Rathus has furnished us with some guidelines as regards why there can be dilemma in the growth of the Christian religion in some parts of the world. The mind being the manifestation of the brain extends to all the activities carried out by the brain itself. In practice, each person behaves true to type and this very psychological trait in human nature could lead to a lot of things. No decision is taken in a vacuum because of the role the brain plays in choice making. That is why Spencer is arguing that it has been a controversial issue in psychology as whether thought is self-initiated or caused by some other factors – mere responsive to external stimulation or a personal interaction and reaction to the environment. These possibilities equally affect the manner in which individuals behave. For instance, a belief in God can only be possible when it is backed up by the will to freely exercise faith in the supernatural. Some sort of persuasion does not lead to practicing religion. In other words, when people are not convinced to practice or continue with a particular religion due to the working and reasoning of their brains, obviously faith in such religion declines and dilemma becomes the result.

In terms of our actions, our decisions and the choices we make on daily basis, including to worship or not, belong to any religious group or not, et cetera, psychology has its important role to play. However, as long as individuals get assistance from each other, due to their various mental and bodily capacities, the therapeutic effects of psychology can easily be measured. This raises the question: "Is there anything man does in life that has no psychology in it?" We said it already. The answer is no. This is where the matter becomes necessary in its therapeutic role in human life as dramatized in most earthquake hazard areas like in Haiti (Earthquake Hazards program, US Geological Survey). In such situations and places, human brain stimulates people with the feelings of sympathy among good spirited people, and assistance begins to arrive from different zones.

On the point at hand, due to the nature of poverty plaguing the human society especially the people of Ngor Okpala, we are challenged to dwell more on the practical aspect of psychology and its therapy which the people of these areas need right now. Yet, on the issue of theoretical aspect of psychology, it is hard to define at times. For instance, a common greeting may not go with any practical demonstration, yet it carries some therapy in it. There is no problem or contradiction to maintain that psychology, by its divine design is aimed to alleviate the human situation as the case at hand. Psychology is only relevant in human history when it is applied in the particular cases individuals find themselves. Days are gone when emphasis is centered on its theoretical aspects like what James told us earlier. In the words of Goot: "The science of psychology faces a crisis because for some time many of the most formative leaders . . . have not done justice to the distinctive character of psychology as a human science" (Goot, 1987, p.1). The situation at some poor stricken countries of the world calls for action and not theory.

In this light, what Goot is saying here at the science of psychology is facing a crisis because for some time many of the most formative leaders who should give the guidelines on how to utilize this important subject have not done what they should have done or the justice to the distinctive character of psychology as a human science as noted above. I am aware of the efforts most psychologists are making to establish the scientific status of their discipline, especially to alleviating human problems. It has to be noted that the human person and his activities are so diversified to the point that no psychologist can handle all aspects of human interactions and activities. There are so many things we do not know about ourselves, let alone others and these complexities create problem for us even in the practice of religion.

The need for the distinctive role of psychology in everyday life is vital. Some see it "as an institution - those activities and professions which shape human habits, social consciousness, and common knowledge" (Goot, p.1). It is hard to believe that psychology seems to remain "largely silent and reluctant to address our complex problems to the existential dilemmas in human experience and interpersonal relationships" (Frick, 1989, p.6). Such existential dilemmas include the growth of the Christian religion in Nigeria today. This is a concern that may not be completely solved in this book. We may go on to posit the questions: "How can psychologists address the complex human problems, the existential and religious dilemmas of the Ngor Okpala people? I strongly believe that "with man at the center, however . . . humanistic psychology ... can take man's full range of inner experience into serious account" (Frick, p.6 in Nwachukwu's GTF DLM, 2007).

This book is a serious call on Human Psychologists, especially those of our time, to bend down and find solutions to the increasing poverty rate in society. This is the psychology that should look beyond the physical down to the excruciating stressors and emotional pains people are going through in their struggle to make ends meet. For instance, a person with tattered clothes who also appears hungry may not be more worried or conscious of his external looks than the emotional problems that keep him restless. Therefore, emphasis should be placed more on why people go through such stressful situations in their lives. Whenever we speak of poverty, the first things that come to mind are the basic necessities of life. At times, a person who is surrounded by plenty may still experience spiritual poverty because of lack of good relationships and friends. These are burning issues in human psychology that should be given attention in this book.

Thus, human psychology should not turn "out to be a matter of degree rather than kind" (Robinson, Part 111, p.33). Actually, this is one of the causes of the dilemma in the growth of the Christian religion in Igboland of Nigeria. Religion should not be presented as an academic subject, theoretically oriented as it is conceived in many parts of the world today. Rather, if religion has any meaning in peoples' life, it must be geared to solving some human needs. Even with the therapeutic nature of psychology, what can be more therapeutic in human life than religion? Religion is meant to bring peace in peoples' lives and offer people the hope that despite the difficulties of this life, there is a being involved in their problems. As adherents of this being, they put their words in actions. But, when on the other hand, the so-called adherents begin to rub people of the little hope they have, either by trick or insinuation, then, such religion must begin to fail.

Just like the case of religion, society needs a psychology that is functional and operative, which can address her problems. This is what "distinguishes psychology from the other social sciences because of the scientific methods it employs to understand the mind and behavior" (Romero & Kemp, 2007, p.1).

This is the time for the distinctive role of psychology in the life of a people who are desperate in need of economic redemption to show itself up. That is why it has been presented in many quarters "as an institution - those activities and professions which shape human habits, social consciousness, and common knowledge" (Goot, p.1). Psychology cannot be "largely silent and reluctant to address our complex problems to the existential dilemmas in human experience and interpersonal relationships" (Frick, 1989, p.6). Our psychologists must address the complex human problems and the existential dilemmas of the Ngor Okpala people now that they are almost rendered helpless because of bad government and evil people in society. This, I repeat, is when "with man at the center, however . . . humanistic psychology ... can take man's full range of inner experience [that of Ngor Okpala people] into serious account" (Frick, p.6).

That is why Prof. Robinson insists in this DLM at Graduate Theological Foundation that human psychology should not turn "out to be a matter of degree rather than kind" (Robinson, Part 111, p.33). For human psychology not to turn out to be a matter of degree rather than kind, much work has to be done in making extra efforts to understand the problems individuals go through on daily basis. This is where the law of quantum physics comes in. The observer cannot be separated from the experiences he is making. In other words, the human psychologists have to condescend to the level of people, carry out fieldworks in order to find out what human problems are. Distribution of questionnaires is very important in any research work and collection of data for the analysis. At times, it is advisable that researchers go in person for oral interviews with the population they are studying. Most often questionnaires do not reflect adequately the real problems that plague the people.

As a matter of urgency, what the people of Igboland and so many others on the globe need right now is not those who have high degrees or PhDs in psychology or who have not. They need a Daniel, a deliverance and immediate assistance. Days of high grammar are over. Society needs those high grammars translated into their daily activities. They need a psychology that is functional, relevant, empathic and operative which addresses their problems here and now and this is what really, according to Romero & Kemp, "distinguishes psychology from the other social sciences". This is essentially because of "the scientific methods it employs to understand the mind and behavior" (Romero & Kemp, 2007, p.1). Therefore, any psychology that excludes the possibility of coming to the assistance of the people in need, especially most of Ngor Okpala people, is not needed now. Psychology has to be therapeutic and in touch with people by providing them with some remedies in the form of "hand-to-mouth" method that addresses the people in their fate, pain and great losses.

In this sense, a lot of psychologists have tried to make this subject relevant in every human situation as the ones in war-torn areas or natural disasters. On this note, I consider it more expedient to examine the thoughts of these two psychologists, Romero and Kemp (Romero & Kemp, 2007:xxv - xxvi) further in their detailed account of the meaning of various aspects of psychology and how we can apply them to the situation of the people in question. Their presentation of what psychology is – theory and how it can be employed to solve human problems here and now – practice, will be of immense assistance in this book. In this sense or understanding, first of all, let us examine their analysis on the various meanings of the word "Psychology" as implicated in its different types, because, according to Prof. Robinson "what makes an event psychological is that it is the result of human goals, desires, aspirations, etc" (Robinson, p.5).

As I have embarked upon finding a solution to the dilemma of the growth of the Christian religion in Igboland of Nigeria, for instance, if by the end of this survey I succeed in my aspiration, then my efforts become psychological and therapeutic. Psychology is the human mind at work. This business of the mind includes finding reasons and disposing the mind to accepting the Christian religion for what it is without abandoning the traditional values inherent in the indigenous religion. If by making a right decision in life one succeeds, that achievement or success is as the result of the psychology applied. The various steps and deliberations we take in executing a particular objective have much to say about the psychology employed. For instance, if I love to eat a particular costly dish, I cannot just have it unless I work hard in order to afford it. Wishful thinking does not achieve much because it is not backed up by certain psychology of motivation that reinforces each step taken to achieve the goal. Consequently, we are going to study these various shapes and kinds of psychology one after the other. We shall do so in this sequence or order and how each could be relevant to the problem facing the world today, especially Ngor Okpala people, because a hungry person does not sing alleluia, hence the dilemma.

1. *Social Psychology:*

It may be necessary to have an idea of what social psychology means in general. As an aspect of psychology it means: "The branch of psychology that studies persons and their relationships with others and with groups and with society as a whole...studies the dynamics of interaction in social groups" (AudioEnglish.net). This appears theoretical at first evaluation. This is an aspect of psychology that studies the effects of how individuals interact with each other and how such interactions affect their behaviors even in the practice of religion. This is a basic psychology because the manners in which my behaviors affect others are important tools in establishing rapport or disharmony among them. For instance, in natural disaster areas, like Haiti and Japan, with these earthquake experiences that have challenged the consciousness of the people, to what extent, can each of them be of assistance to each other when, in actual fact, almost everybody is in needy? Had this branch of psychology been applied in the relationships between the missionaries and the Igbo people, the dilemma we are studying here would have been reduced in a great extent?

In the light of the Gospel of Matthew that concluded this section, is it possible to determine how many people that have fallen sick, when many have died already (Death toll hits 200, 000, USGS). Who is expected to visit whom at this point? Without the assistance of the International Communities, is it possible for these people to survive? This is where the humanistic aspect of psychology comes in. How do we define or describe what those in prison go through when almost everybody in such natural disaster areas has no more freedom in any sensible aspect, no housing, privacy, or food etc. Again, who are to be blamed for not feeding the hungry when practically, everybody is scrambling and in serious search for food? Can Matthew's Gospel ever be validated based on what is going on in many part of the globe? There can be a way out especially when humanity like the US renders helping hands to those in need.

2. *Developmental Psychology:*

Actually, Romero and Kemp have furnished us with a powerful working tool. This aspect studies the changes in people's behaviors due primarily to their ages. It is just as the name applies. Developmental psychology studies the various stages people pass through from infancy to adulthood. This raises the question: How will a teenager (boy or girl of 16 years), for instance, in Haiti who has been rescued from death and adopted by some good Samaritans feel when he or she comes back to Haiti at a later age of 40 in his or her life? Definitely, without over flogging the obvious, the situation will be different. This is a serious problem facing psychology in its therapeutic function and mission. The teenage boy or girl in question can never have any peace of mind, no matter to what part of the world he or she has been taken, or how properly cared for, when he or she has lost his or her original family circle. Then, we can imagine how the elders who were the custodians of Igboland felt when the missionaries came and introduced many changes in their culture without any reference to their gray hairs or respect for them. Lack of respect for seniors or elders is a major factor in the dilemma of the growth of the Christian religion worldwide.

In such situations, as years go by, such children in the case of Haiti who are rescued now and transported to other countries for shelter and care will always feel depressed in the midst of plenty because their developmental processes did not resolve properly. That lack in their personality development will always affect their behaviors and interactions with others because a fixation has occurred. This is the time for psychologists to do their work, by reminding these affected children and their surviving parents or siblings to understand the magnitude of what has happened, its lasting effects in their lives, and how they can begin to appreciate their being alive today to tell the story and maintain their family histories. Taking a child away from his natural in-habitat to a different or another country without these basic pieces of information, or talking about the tragedy, is not going to assist anybody in future. This is where psychology becomes counseling in nature. There is need for a rehabilitation of these children to their original or loss memories. In the same way, introducing a new religion to people who have practiced their own for ages is like taking them away from their roots to a foreign one. This attitude consciously creates a dilemma.

3. *Personality Psychology:*

This is the branch of psychology that studies individual differences in behavior. This is very essential. Relationship is only possible when individual differences in behavior are understood. These could be cultural, ethnic, socio-religious or political differences. Personality differences are important factors in interacting effectively with other people. We can now surmise what led to the dilemma in the growth of the Christian faith in Igboland of Nigeria. There was no study of the different personalities involved in the evangelical mission. The mission came as an imposition. The Igbo people were not approached as important human documents. Rather, they were seen as barbarians who had no soul. In a situation like that, how can any growth of the Christian religion take place? Even with the situation at Haiti or Japan, people are going to perceive it differently and act accordingly. For example, there are some individuals who cannot understand why they lost family members and everything they lived for or depended on. In such horrifying situations, if no assistance is rendered, they can easily give up. While some will accept it as one of those natural happenings that nobody has control over and try to deal with them, others will not. Hence, we say that whatever affects the body equally affects the mind.

4. *Psychology of Consciousness:*

This is a timely psychology for the Ngor Okpala people, which studies their experiences in life, the imposition of a religion they did not ask of, the sufferings they go through today. What could be more difficult and painful in their experiences than the sufferings they are going through today because of bad economy and government? We need to understand how our present economy and situations affect us generally. As a way to healing and restoration, we need self-supervision in other to adjust to what we cannot change and that is precisely what psychology of consciousness is all about. It studies us and our experiences and how those experiences shape our lives. There is nobody in society who is not aware that things are hard. Experience is the best teacher, many say, the Ngor Okpala people have been taught this in a very excruciating manner. Matthew's Gospel spoke of being in prison, but from what is happening in society, especially with the Igbo of Nigeria, some would have preferred to remain in physical prison than going through the spiritual torture they are forced into by the level of sufferings being experienced.

5. *Psychology of Emotion:*

This is an important aspect of psychology in that it looks into us as human beings. In line with the psychology of consciousness, that of emotion studies the feelings that color human experience. Even in the area of religion, the people were not treated as having the consciousness to decide for themselves, as to accept what they wanted or refuse what they did not like. There is an adage in Igboland of Nigeria, which says: "An animal that is hard to catch normally forces the hunter to apply a means that defeats running". In other words, since the animal runs so fast, for the hunter to catch it, he has to be very diligent in approaching it. The psychology of emotion is best applied to the situation at Ngor Okpala right now; in order to assist people cope with the level of sufferings they are going through. Often it sounds theoretical and impossible for any psychologist, let alone an ordinary person to describe the feelings of others based on physical appearances. Feelings are the engines that keep life afloat.

There are various ways our feelings color our experiences or rather, the other way round. For instance, if your friend borrowed money from you and promised to pay back on a certain day, you will not feel good if he or she disappoints or does not keep to his or her words or promises. Worse still, if your friend returns your kind gesture with ingratitude, you may not take it likely any more. Whatever we say of you is simply a guess because only you, and nobody else knows the level of hurt your friend has caused you for behaving the way he or she did. Again, in the case of those affected by natural disasters, assuming you are a victim, how will you, as the reader of this book, feel to live without your friends, family, home, food or water? Does life mean anything again for anybody in this situation? The situation created by this natural disaster has colored your feelings about yourself and the world as a whole. Psychology of emotion is one of the theoretical ones that is hard to understand especially when applied to the individual's sad situations as the one we are talking about here. In this instance again, the need for a professional pastoral counselor is important.

6. *Psychology of Motivation:*

This is the psychology that is needed in every aspect of human life, in the classroom, hospital setting, in family circles etc. The people of Ngor Okpala needed some sort of motivation in their belief systems before the new one took place and in their sufferings too. Suffering is not relative to Ngor Okpala alone. The naked reality is that there is suffering in the world today due to economic recessions. Psychology of motivation is what is needed to deal with the present situations. People have to be motivated to accept what they cannot change in the face of poverty or natural disasters. From infancy to adult development, this is a psychology that can encourage people move forward in their lives. As the case at hand, if the missionaries who brought religion to the people had motivated the people in what they had already and introduced their new message in that light, the dilemma in question today would have been avoided to a great degree.

Human beings usually are their own problems. We have maintained a systematic assertion on this note. The ways some people choose to go, or companies they keep, at times, determine whether they become progressive or retrogressive. The study of why we do what we do is necessary to give meaning to our actions, decisions, choices and life. The poor people of Ngor Okpala and others across the globe should come to terms with their present reality or situation and accept it as their own cup of tea, and fight to get out of it. This is where the International Community has major role to play. Thanks to America that has provided the most astonishing relief strategies to assist the poor countries of the world. For instance, in the case of Haiti, providing immediate mobile hospital with a ship that has brought many back to life is worthy of mention in this aspect of psychology.

This, as it were, validates the therapeutic nature of psychology, both theoretically and practically. What of the various therapies in the form of food, clothing, medical assistance and rehabilitation efforts being made to alleviate the deplorable situation in Haiti and Japan for instance? Once there is reinforcement in the little efforts one is making, motivation becomes the result. The big question is: Why did the early missionaries fail to implement such therapeutic skills in their evangelical mission? Actually, they presented the Igbo people with some gifts as ways of enticing or attracting them to their mission. That was not necessarily done from humanitarian point of view. They did so in the spirit of "give them this and we shall control them". That was not the focal point of the Gospel message, as we know it today. Most of the people did not feel comfortable because of their antagonistic tendencies towards the people.

7. *Psychology of Learning:*

Knowledge builds on knowledge, we say. As observed by Watson, "Behaviorism was the school of thought in psychology that sought to measure only observable behaviors" (Watson, John B., Internet resource). In this light, psychology of learning pertains to acquiring of knowledge as a process. The behavioral psychologists are well known for this branch of psychology. In their own terms:

> *Learning is a relatively permanent change in behavior that is the result of experience. During the first half of the twentieth century, the school of thought known as behaviorism rose to dominate psychology and sought to explain the learning process. The three major types of learning described by the behavioral psychology are classical conditioning, operant conditioning and observable learning (Internet Resources).*

A little elucidation is necessary here because these different types of learning processes have some implications for the growth of the Christian religion. In this light, anything that creates progress in the practice of the faith eliminates the dilemma. There is a 'classical conditioning,' which is a situation in which learning occurs by association of a particular stimulus with a particular response. For instance, if I give you money whenever I call your name, the tendency is to conclude that each time I call you; I am going to give you money. The case of Pavlov's experiment comes to mind where a dog constantly responds to an invitation to eat by the ringing of the bell. That was mainly the approach the missionaries employed as if the people were simple robots. History still holds it that the missionaries used gifts to bring the people together instead of the word of God. That was the beginning of the dilemma we experience in the growth of the Christian religion today.

In the case of 'operant conditioning', it is a learning process whereby the probability or willingness to learn is determined by the amount of treatment given, either by reinforcement or punishment. For instance, if I know that by attending Mr. B's lectures, I will feel happy, I will not like to miss any of his classes. But if on the hand, I get hurt whenever I attend his lectures, I will try to give excuses for not attending his lectures. Such operant conditioning learning process could have served the Igbo people better. From the manners in which their teachers or evangelists presented themselves, could have been enough incentive either to join or avoid them. Regarding 'observational learning', this is also a learning process in which learning occurs through observing others or imitating them. In other words, my learning process depends on how far they motivate me or discourage me in what they do or teach. Again, this is a method that would have served the Igbo people, especially Ngor Okpala better. As they say it: "Seeing is believing". The good or bad lives the missionaries showed them could have as well assisted them in making their decision on the new religion. There are several social learning theories that we did not treat in this book. We chose the few to demonstrate to people how the things we learn can affect our behaviors including our approach to religious matters.

The psychology of learning is very important in human developments. It applies more on those suffering from one natural disaster or form of poverty like the people of Ngor Okpala. Generally, we say that experience is the best teacher. This is where it fits best. Experiences teach people some behaviors. For instance, if you have very low income and you have nobody to assist you financially; you will definitely minimize or be careful with your resources. In this light, this is the psychology that studies how experience changes people to be more capable in their world. The episode at hand [suffering and bad governance] has brought enough changes in Ngor Okpala. Practically, this ugly situation or the peoples' experiences are going to change, not only how they will perceive the physical world, but also how to guide themselves in future. In case of some of those in natural disaster torn areas like the Haitians and Japanese who have never liked to leave their countries for other places in the world, may begin now to think or plan traveling overseas for safety. They have to do whatever it takes to live and be happy once again. Obviously, religion flourishes more in a peaceful atmosphere. When people are happy, they avoid arguments as whether the Christian religion has done some good or bad. Of course, any religion that abhors peace heads to ruin.

8. *Psycholinguistics:*

Psychologies evolve as human problems emerge. As noted earlier, there are as many psychologies as there are human inclinations, behaviors and problems. Psycholinguistics studies human language. For most of us who have hospital related jobs and ministries, the importance of this psychology cannot be overemphasized. This branch of psychology is so relevant today especially considering the fact that if people can't communicate due to language problems, even to give some medical attention to them will be impossible. That was the last stroke that broke the Carmel's back in the evangelization of the Igbo people. Language was a major problem. Relationship appears impossible when people cannot speak or communicate to each other. The Igbo of Nigeria, particularly the Ngor Okpala people must be understood first in their cultural milieu before any meaningful or effective ministry is possible. However, in terms of feeding and clothing, communication is easier because the only language the people need is not only sympathy but also body language, the scrambling with their hands indicating what they need. Individuals should be allowed to decide which religion means something for them.

9. *Educational Psychology:*

The International body has been commissioned to render assisting hands to natural devastated areas like those mentioned in this book. While educational psychology is aimed at the dynamics of teaching in general, any teaching that neglects the comfort of the human person as the type faced in Ngor Okpala is not objective at all. This is a type of psychology that should be made compulsory in school systems in all levels. Actually, the need for this psychology and its therapeutic effects are necessary in human situations, especially when the peaceful equilibrium of the individual is disturbed. Education is both formal and informal. Based on the matter at ground zero in natural devastated areas, the two are important. While the general public needs to know how to get about their daily business in the face of suffering and death, the young must be sent to school for formal educational opportunities. In other words, any efforts made at this time to assist those suffering from one economic operation or the other will be both psychological and therapeutic. Ignorance of the Christian religion demands some educational process where the general public especially those who never went to formal school would be educated on the implications of the new religion in their lives. Initially, that was not the case.

10. *Psychotherapy:*

This book is an urgent invitation to psychotherapists to exercise their professionalism on those who are experiencing emotional problems without any delay. There is no gainsaying that the Ngor Okpala people and those of natural disaster torn areas have been traumatized, mentally disorientated and distressed. They need our attention. This is the psychology that can adequately handle their problems. As a pastoral counselor, and psychologist, this is my major area of specialization, attending to people with various emotional and stressful problems. Therefore, any assistance rendered to the people of Ngor Okpala is the work of psychotherapists and this validates this book in a very special manner. Even those who seem to be physically sound, once the atmosphere of suffering is prevalent, some still suffer mental disorders, including some of the rescuers in Haiti and Japan who are dumbfounded by the number of deaths recorded over there. As noted, when people are mentally balanced, they are disposed to worship properly.

11. *Health Psychology:*

Psychology deals with human problems and needs. Again, various psychologists, psychoanalysts and psychotherapists are challenged to understand and monitor peoples' interactions and behaviors as to determine who is mentally disoriented or actually healthy. For example, it is very simple to determine the health of a person by his utterances and behaviors and give such person the medical attention or therapy he needs before his situation worsen in the face of grief and loss. Missionaries should take note that change brings about fear and resistance.

12. *Counseling Psychology:*

There is no other time on the planet when those suffering in Africa or other parts of the globe need counseling psychologists than now. The importance of pastoral psychologists cannot be overemphasized in our time. Sufferings and sickness have multiplied in our time due to greed and selfishness in many quarters. The situations of those suffering, especially in war, natural disaster torn areas are unimaginable. They need to be reassured that they still belong to this world. The very basis of their lives has been shaken and uprooted. Their families, marriages, relationships, occupations, careers, in short, their future, have been scattered and most of them have lost hold of anything meaningful in life. In the face of all these stark realities, help and therapy are the keys. Again, the Gospel of Matthew becomes more relevant here than ever. Ngor Okpala people definitely need some sort of counseling in their evangelizing process.

Eventually, this is the time for counseling psychologist to demonstrate their expertise and credibility as such. The role of psychology and its therapeutic functions in the light of what is going on in most parts of the globe are open-ended enquiries that challenge psychologists of all nations and Universities to become more aware of the emotional problems that confront these people today. Call this an appeal or a state of emergency, community psychologists and psychotherapists have to apply techniques that can assist people come to terms and deal with their lots on the ground and "understand their conflicts and how to resolve them" (Sonderegger, p.146).

At this point, it becomes necessary to cite the famous biblical quotation from Matthew as a guiding instrument of our data information here. Based on what has happened in many natural-disaster-torn areas and to some Ngor Okpala people, how can psychologists and every rational being be evaluated today? According to that lengthy but important Gospel of Matthew, we read:

> *When the son of Man comes in his glory … He will place the sheep on his right hand and the goats on his left. The King will say to those on his right hand, "Come, you whom my Father has blessed, take for your heritage the kingdom prepared for you since the foundation of the world. For I was hungry and you gave me*

food; I was thirsty and you gave me drink; I was stranger and you made me welcome; naked and you clothed me, sick and you visited me, in prison and you came to see me. Then the virtuous will say to him in reply, "Lord, when did we see you hungry and feed you; or thirsty and give you drink? When did we see you a stranger and make you welcome; naked and clothe you; sick or in prison and go to see you? .... Next he will say to those on his left hand, "Go away from me, with your curse upon you, to the eternal fire prepared for the devil and his angels. For I was hungry and you never gave me food; I was thirsty and you never gave me anything to drink; I was a stranger and you never visited me". Then it will be their turn to ask, "Lord, when did we see you hungry or thirsty, a stranger or naked, sick or in prison, and did not come to your help? (Matthew 25: 31 – 46).

The big question that stares everybody on the face is: "Who are the virtuous mentioned above and who are the unrighteous in the face of the basic and essential needs of the poor or needy as highlighted in the above quotation? Having examined the therapeutic perspective of psychology in general, we shall discuss briefly the factors that affect our thoughts and behaviors – The Rational Emotive Therapy and how our thinking can change our behaviors.

Center for Rational Emotive Therapy - Albert Ellis Perspective

In the words of Nwachukwu: "This clarion call compels us to examine the principles of cognitive-behavioral therapy" (Nwachukwu, 2010:xxxiv). According to Capuzzi & Gross as cited in Nwachukwu: "The manner in which people think and feel affect their lives" or behaviors (Capuzzi & Gross, 2003:214; in Dr. Odikanoro Vincent – 2008:4-20, cited in Nwachukwu, Ibid).

What Capuzzi & Gross have noted here has great implication for the dilemma of the growth of the Christian religion in Igboland of Nigeria? More so, it is in line with what Albert Ellis has outlined in his REBT – Rational Emotive Behavioral Therapy. Therefore, with the suspicion with which the Igbo of Nigeria welcomed the Christian message, it was not possible for the religion to grow. It was not even given a chance. The people of Igboland having seen the white man's religion as opposing that of their own, they felt cold about the new religion. While some accepted it with open arms, some refused entirely. Because some people did not want to lose the religion of their ancestors, remained on the middle and that gave way to syncretistic practices.

However, Albert Ellis presented his REBT in a more convincing way that if people could think positive about the events of life, they will be more relaxed than nursing irrational and negative thoughts that lead them to stressful and emotional problems. Thus, we are going to discuss Albert Ellis and his Center for Rational Emotive Therapy essentially for the benefit of the Igbo people of Ngor Okpala to start thinking positively about their religion as to give a mortal blow to the dilemma that is dragging their religious consciousness to the mud. In the final analysis we find out that psychologists are aiming at the same goal. Positive thinking is important in the progress of an individual and society. Before we delve into Albert Ellis theory, let us examine bit of his background history.

His Life story and Educational growth:

History held that Albert Ellis was born in Pittsburgh, PA in 1913. He was among the first American psychologists who developed rational emotive behavior therapy (REBT). As noted by Capuzzi & Gross, it was first and popularly known as Cognitive Behavior

Therapies (CBT). Rational Emotive Behavior Therapy is one and the same as Cognitive Behavior Therapy. The only difference lies in the manner of emphasis. It was Albert who founded the Institute of Rational Emotive Behavior Therapy, abbreviated REBT. Fortunately, his Institution was non-profit organization whose major objective, mission and aims were to promote Rational Emotive Behavior Therapy (REBT) as a systematic and comprehensive educative and preventive theory.

No wonder, being the founder, Albert Ellis's Institute promotes REBT theory and practice. It achieved this objective through the training of professional, paraprofessionals and the public at large. This theory was a big launch in the history of psychotherapy in general. Hence, posterity considers him as the principal originator of this revolutionary movement. This claim was confirmed through the 1982 professional survey of U.S. and the Canadian psychologists in which he, Albert was considered the second of the most influential psychotherapists in history. Others who were considered along with Albert were Carl Rogers who was ranked first in the survey and Sigmund Freud with the third place. At this point, we need to study the meaning of rational emotive behavior therapy in this context.

Meaning of REBT - rational emotive behavior therapy

REBT is a systematic and comprehensive undertaking applied to study all psychological treatments that go with emotional and behavioral characteristics of individuals. Rational emotive behavior therapy is specifically designed to dig deep into the human emotional problems for possible solutions. Generally, a lot of emotional problems are misunderstood as psychotic cases, at times as mental that demand psychiatric treatment. With this development, Albert Ellis has proved to society that most of the times, the accusations we apportion to problems or sicknesses are mere fantasies created by human mode of thinking and feeling. For instance, if someone has complained that traveling to a certain town or under few weather conditions will create problems for him, there is no point encouraging him to do so. Such irrational thinking at times makes one to accuse someone else when no offence has been committed. The manner we think about our friends determines many a time the way we approach them. In this sense, the therapy is holistic in that it tends to examine the whole body chemistry of an individual as to offer a lasting solution to him and his problem.

In a practical note, rational emotive behavior therapy also deals with all aspects of human distractions and disturbances. However, as already pointed out, it places much premium on the thinking component and program of the person. We have continually pointed out that human beings are bundles of possibilities and exceptionally complex and mysterious. In a situation such as this, there is no form of expressing one's feelings. In other words, there is no simple way human beings show when they are emotionally disturbed or is there a single way in which their emotional limitations are ever foreseen as to ascertain the best treatment to be given them. Individuals differ and may share in the same emotional frustration, but the ways they get about them or feel them, will always differ.

Essentially, this is the major problem encountered in this process of REBT because, many a time, their psychological problems in this process arise from their misperceptions, distortions and thinking about reality. Thus, pastoral psychology calls individuals and society to excogitate from the minds some of those negative principles and ideologies that weigh them down. For instance, when the Christian religion first came to Igboland and in Ngor Okpala, the people did not imagine that anything good would come out of it. That was the initial resistance the people mounted in accepting the religion. The people never thought there could be any other religion on the planet to challenge their traditional way of life that has formed part of their socio-cultural identity. Misperceptions demand that we study a thing properly before making any decision on it.

The rational emotive behavior therapy is aimed at guiding individuals to the right actions. When cognitions are mistaken due to misperceptions, they create some sort of emotional under-reactions or over-reactions to normal and unusual stimuli. When, what is perceived to be evil is actually good, the judgment passed on it is being under-reacted. On the other hand, when what we accept as a treasure turns out to be destructive to life, the judgment we passed on it is being over-reacted. Hence, in pastoral psychology just like the case of Albert's REBT, we talk of "under-reactions or over-reactions". This theory is a unique guide to human decisions, choices and behaviors. This is where we appreciate the magnitude of work the missionaries did when they came to Igboland of Nigeria. They were simple people who came to bring a new religion and civilization to a third world country. They were not professional psychologists as to assess the way the people felt about them or behaved.

Therefore, those people who are habitually dysfunctional in behavioral patterns like the cases of "Attention Deficit Hyper Sensitive Disorders" (ADHSD) need to be assisted to repeat positive actions that fight against their negative responses to stimuli. In this sense, such dysfunctional individuals may be enabled to keep repeating instructing responses even when they think that they are behaving wrongly. In a very strict sense, rational emotive behavior therapy is a psychotherapeutic approach to irrationality of behaviors. In this process, it proposes that unrealistic and irrational beliefs cause many emotional problems. This is a platitude because the manner in which people think and feel leads to the way they behave and act. Primarily, the focus of 'rational emotive behavior treatment' is to illicit changes in thinking habits, which will lead to changes in behavior; thereby, alleviating and improving the symptoms that create such irrational thinking. For instance, if the missionaries had in any form praised some of the cultural observances and customs of Ngor Okpala people that could have gingered them to believing the new religion without any difficulties. Then, the issue of dilemma could not have arisen as we have it today. As a principle in this process or therapy, Albert believes that those who think irrationally have to be assisted to see things from positive perspectives and think rationally.

In a sense, the treatment of rational emotive behavior emphasizes the importance of changing irrational thinking patterns that cause emotional distress into thoughts that are more reasonable and rational. This is the primary focus of this process of therapy. It leads to total transformation of the problem behaving person. When people are out of control because of poor perception of reality or other life threatening factors, hyper phobias, Albert's REBT is an effective option. For instance, when a parent has a child with problem behavior as a result of irrational thinking, three things are involved:

1. The parent cares for his or her child;
2. The parent cares for his or her future and tries to assist, though with failures;
3. The parent, though the child is problematic in behavior, wants some peace too.

Histories where parents have abandoned their children because of their recalcitrant behaviors are rare. This sings the importance of pastoral psychology. It is a guide to individuals in various life situations who may be faced with one emotional or pastoral problem or the other. In most cases, it is very difficult to differentiate emotional problems from pastoral ones. For instance, to lose one's job is both emotional and pastoral. Also, to have ones baby in an Intensive Care Unit in a hospital equally creates both emotional and pastoral problems for one. This is where the role of a pastoral counselor comes in.

This is why pastoral psychology is an interesting subject. Some people emphasize on the need to feel better when nothing positively and practically has been done. That is not where the emphasis should be led. According to one of the principles of pastoral psychology, "For you to feel better, you have got to behave well first". As a pastoral psychologist, this is my philosophy borne out of research. Studies have proved that most people, who make noise about enjoying life, have not fought for it. Once you have worked hard in life, done everything humanly speaking well, you do not make noise when you are surrounded with so many luxuries. You tend to see them as parts of your growing processes in life. When you see people squander and spend wealth or money extravagantly, invariably, some of them never raised any finger in acquiring them.

Rational emotive behavior therapy is a healing process that is based on the assumption that human "emotional reaction" is largely caused by our conscious and unconscious evaluations. This is in line with what Capuzzi and Gross termed cognitive behavioral therapy in which feelings color thoughts and actions. For instance, if an individual feels anxious, agitated or depressed because he, in one time or the other, is convinced that life is unbearable because he failed in his efforts to achieve something, the process of REBT maintains that it is his belief that makes him feel psychologically disturbed. REBT encourages positive attitude to life because disappointments will always occur in human interactions. In other words, there is no perfect world anywhere. Again, if we feel hostile and disappointed simply because those we trusted surprised us by their unfair attitudes, then we are admitting that people cannot change. People will always disappoint us in certain ways. At times, expecting too much of everything from others may not work out exactly the ways we had anticipated.

Feeling frustrated because of other peoples' actions, when, most often they are being reasonable and fair with society, our thinking this way is our own cup of tea and irrational. When we nurse the idea that others are pursuing us or preventing our progress, we may not achieve much again. Applying the principle of rational emotive behavior therapy in our everyday life will go a long way to bring peace in our lives even in our practice of religion. Irrational thinking is a disease. We cannot be living in the world of irrationality, in which, if we become sick, instead of looking for a medical attention, we accuse others for it. This is exactly what most Ngor Okpala people have done with Christianity. When such people are not ready to put the hard teachings of Christianity, they begin to point accusing fingers to the religious leaders or missionaries who brought the religion. To be effective in this process, we must always think positive even when things are not moving the ways we want them because our rational emotional behaviors go together with our belief systems and convictions.

Eventually, we have come to the theories of Albert Ellis and the three basic ways this process of REBT works in human life. According to him, rational emotive behavior therapy is based on three theories, which begin with the letters "ABC". In his own words Ellis (2003) wrote: "In rational emotive behavior therapy, clients usually learn and begin to apply this premise by learning the ABC model of psychological disturbance and change" (Journal of rational emotive & cognitive behavior, p.21). The question is: what does he refer to as 'psychological disturbances?" For Albert Ellis, psychological disturbances of human beings are based on emotional thinking and belief. It is a confirmation of our earlier assertions. There are lots of events that can create psychological disturbances in our lives, especially when we feel disappointed by a person we have trusted as reliable. In order to bring the therapy anticipated in this process, Ellis places much emphasis on his three theories of ABC as the primary tools of treating people with emotional behavior problems.

This is where Albert Ellis has achieved his scholarship the management strategies he has recommended for tackling and treating people with these irrational thinking disorders. Let us briefly review his three theory methods in this order:

The letter "A": This stands for activating experiences, such as family troubles, unsatisfying work, early childhood traumas and all other things, we can point out as the sources of our unhappiness. In every counseling process, there is always the need to talk about problems of clients. It is only through their stories that the pastoral counselor can be of great assistance in the healing process. In this elementary level, to activate the client's experiences, the counselor will try to elicit information from the person with the problems. He might ask the client questions such as: "How many are you in the family? Does your wife always agree with you in whatever you do or say? Each question is determined according to the hints the counselor gathers from his or her client. In case, the client hesitates to answer a particular question, the counselor may not force him or her to answer it. Discretion has to be taken here.

The letter "B": Here, the letter stands for beliefs, especially the irrational, self-defeating beliefs that are the actual sources and causes of our happy moods. This is very important for any healing to occur. At times, disappointments lead people to start doubting the existence of God. Even, in such irrational thinking, many have lost their faith. We can now see how indisposition can equally lead to the dilemma of the growth of the Christian religion in Igboland of Nigeria. Therefore, in a situation like this, the counselor may ask the counselee if he has a religion and to what extent he is involved in it. Irrational thinking on religious basis could have sprung up through the attitude of a close friend who acted in a manner unheard off, of a man of God. Early child sexual abuse could create such an unbearable and sad atmosphere or experience in the life of the person that nothing can be done to make him happy. There are many inferences we can draw from this healing process as regards what must have created dilemma in question for the people of Igboland of Nigeria, particularly Ngor Okpala people.

The letter "C": This is the third theory through which the counseling process progresses in Ellis' therapy. It stands for consequences, the neurotic symptoms and negative emotions such as depression, panic attack, anxiety and rage that come from our beliefs and thinking. As it were, Ellis (2003) observed the following: "Although the activating experience may be quite real and have caused real pain, it is our irrational beliefs and consequences that create long-term and disabling psychological problems" (Journal of rational- emotive & cognitive-behavior, p.21). Albert is optimistic that there could be real problems in our lives that create stressful and hurtful situations. Yet, while he believes that such problems could be handled squarely and objectively, the irrational and negative manner in which we think about them is responsible for the psychological disturbances we experience. In this manner, rational emotive behavior therapy should be a welcoming process for the client that should bring an ultimate joyful treatment and lead to positive effects and rational beliefs.

Therapy of rational emotive behavior

This is the skill or tool employed for effective treatment of individuals with depressing problems. REBT is an active treatment to those who suffer or go through some emotional distress. The aim of rational emotive behavior therapists is to change irrational beliefs to rational ones. Often, he challenges the client to think positively or rationally. He equally promotes rational self-talk, supervision and various strategies used to achieve these goals, especially by making the client understand and think of how important he or she is in society. It is a practical strategy because once individuals with irrational thinking problems begin to realize that society looks at them as being important, they begin to feel that way and by so doing, they think rationally. That was a serious quality the missionaries lacked in their efforts to bring the Christian religion to the people of Ngor Okpala.

Besides the three theories of Ellis we have reviewed in this book, this process – REBT employs other strategies or stages through which the goal of the therapy is achieved. In his own assessment, the achievements of the goals of rational emotive behavior therapy are based on the following: Preparation assessment, Aftercare, Risks, Unconditional self-acceptance, Normal and Abnormal results. As in the case of those three theories, we shall treat these ones in this other:

Preparation Assessment:

This is more of activating experiences stage. The major differences are points of emphasis, which are centered on specific needs the therapist would like to know of his client. In other words, as the name suggests, before a client begins the rational emotive behavior therapy, there are certain assessments he has to undergo with the therapist. These assessments feature in the form of closed door interviews. The assessment therapy in professional levels is called 'bio-psychosocial'. This is a formal and highly structured interview designed to elicit certain pieces of information for the healing or counseling to succeed. Such assessments will include the client's medical history, both in the past and present, his psychological history, personality type, temperaments and development.

Further investigations include the family history, associations, third party syndromes, and if he is involved in drugs, alcohol, medical process, drugs already taken and possible effects on the client etc. In most cases, the educational background of the client is put into consideration. What level? Is he a drop out? Was he doing well at school etc? Also the client's criminal records are sought, marriage life, friendships, nature of jobs held in the past. Questions like these will be expected: Had or has he any job satisfaction in the type of job done? As regards employment history, how did he relate with his co-workers? In family assessments, the therapist will find out if the client still has living parents, how many siblings and the family tree too. The interview is so helpful as it aims at providing information for possible diagnosis or tentative one, which may be required for medical or psychotherapist's attentions.

Aftercare Follow-up:

Just like in any pastoral care giving, pastoral psychology employs the same procedure. Aftercare follow-up becomes necessary when and only when there is doubt as the success of the rational emotive behavior therapy. In such a case or situation, a follow-up appointment becomes expedient. But, in a situation where after the process, counseling session, the client feels or indicates that he or she is in positive condition, and able to take care of him or herself, there will be no more rational emotive behavior treatment or therapy. That is why this aftercare follow-up has always been a decision between the client and the psychologist or therapist. To avoid the risk of relapsing to irrational thinking or abnormal behavior, the aftercare follow-up is highly recommended, especially when the client has shown signs of returning to his previous behaviors that brought about the therapy in the first place.

Risks:

These are danger signals in almost every counseling process. That is why the counselors must be very careful in the manner they approach their clients. In a situation where the client does not open up to the pastoral psychologist or therapist due to his unfriendly or unprofessional manner of approach, it does not matter what the counselor might do, there will always be risks of therapy failure. For a professional who knows his skills and the best ways to apply them, there is little or no risks associated with his approach and the treatment. But in the case of clients who defile all efforts made by the counselor due to his irrational thinking and behaviors, risks can easily occur.

From research, we have discovered that rational emotive behavior therapy may likely fail because of the psychological disturbances of the clients. The success and failure of the therapy depend primarily on the client's dispositon to abide by the guidelines and instructions the counselor is giving him or her. However, there is every likelihood that the therapy may fail especially when the client or patient has multiple psychological disorders such as – Attention Deficit Hyper Activity disorders (ADHD), paranoid personality, aggression, anxiety, panic attack, depression, and post-traumatic perceptions and experiences.

Unconditional Self-acceptance:

In Nwachukwu's observation: "The engines of healthy relationships are within each individual. Healings do not come by accidents or without reasons. This 'power of the individual to care for and cure him or herself' primarily comes from his or her positive memories, energized by sound moral life and good works and not from remorsefulness" (Nwachukwu, 2010:214). This is the same thing Ellis is talking about here as regards irrational thinking. Once positive ones replace such negative thoughts, the clients begin to heal. According to Benson cited in Nwachukwu: "This visceral truth is, something we can count on, something that remains the same despite the dramatic changes we often experience in our public and private lives" (Benson, 1997:24; Nwachukwu, 215).

In a more elaborate form, Nwachukwu, analyzing Benson's invaluable contributions in the field of therapy, noted:

> *That "something" we can count on, that "something", which remains the same irrespective of the emotional pains, difficulties and changes in our lives and relationships, differs from one individual to another. That something, which does not easily affect our relationships despite poverty, individual sicknesses, mistakes and weakness must be terrific and explendid. Some may call it love, personal convictions, others hope, but Benson*

*calls it "remembered wellness" as already noted. For me, it is
"sound moral life" guided by Truth, Justice and Peace – TJP
(Nwachukwu, Ibid).*

In effect Nwachukwu is supporting the rational emotive behavior therapy of Albert Ellis. In the first place, our negative memories create emotional pains for us. Therefore, to think positive or rationally according to Ellis, one has got to cash in one's positive experiences and associations. The borderline is, once a person begins to have recourse to issues that caused him depression in the past, he is likely to wind up getting depressed again. That is precisely what the rational emotive behavior therapy of Ellis is talking about here.

Basically, rational emotive behavior therapy depends more on individual unconditional self-acceptance than what others have said of him or her. One's self esteem is important in this discussion. Of course, once one does not feel good about oneself, one will definitely begin to lose interests in the things around one including the practice of religion. That was why we included poverty as one of the major causes of the dilemma of the growth of the Christian religion among Ngor Okpala people. The effects of poverty cannot be underestimated in the growth of religious faith. People have got to trust in themselves first before they can ever think of trusting others even God and that is what Ellis regards in this book as unconditional self-acceptance. Our value or worth should not depend on others. We are bound to recognize who we are in the face of uncertainties of life, without minding so much on the values others have set for themselves.

In this capacity, Ellis emphatically stresses the importance of self-awareness, unconditional self-acceptance and importance in his rational emotive behavior therapy. According to him (1957):

"In rational emotive behavior, no one is damned, no matter how awful their actions are and we should accept ourselves for what we are rather than for what we have achieved" (Journal of individual psychology, p.13). Ellis, by that singular sentence has raised an important fact for human development and advancement. In other words, self-condemnation is damaging and destructive. No wonder Nwachukwu maintains that: "There is no one, no culture, race or religion that is beyond or above the favor of God" (Nwachuwku, 2010:109). Every person on the planet is unique and different from others. These differences assist in utilizing the benefit of plurality in life. No one is completely insignificant.

Each person has something to contribute to make the world a better place. Failure to realize this fundamental fact of life, led the missionaries to create dilemma in some aspects of the Igbo people. Religious bigotry has never encouraged the growth of faith in Christianity. Therefore, the success and failure of rational emotive behavior therapy depend to a great extent on the individuals and how far they accept their worthiness and self-esteems unconditionally. In this light, once persons with some emotional problems begin to realize that there are no other persons like themselves in the entire universe, the more realistic they will be in assessing the beauty of their world. That was the main point we made regarding the need to view oneself as an important human document who has some unique contributions to make to better self and the world.

Normal Results:

By this, Ellis presents the naked reality to clients or people going through REBT. It is a fellow-up from the foregoing factor of conditional self-acceptance. Once an individual has established himself in the recovering process, that person must hold more on those behaviors that could encourage progress in the process. Normal result levels are those stages in which the patients or clients will begin to appreciate and understand the repetitive patterns of irrational thoughts and disruptions in their lives. These disruptions are created be certain symptoms of rational emotive behavior problems. For instance, when a client is healing from alcoholic problems that once created irrational thinking and behavior in his life, at the sight of drinks, he will begin to recollect the danger of alcohol without being guided by anybody.

In such a situation, he is building up resistance strategy and tool to fight alcoholism in his life. That is why Ellis holds that in this process of normal results individuals in rational emotive behavior therapy may begin to develop certain skills that could help them improve their specific problems. The capacity or ability to say no to what one is addicted to may be strength. In this sense, the therapy has yielded normal results, acceptable to self and those around one. Such results may include remarkable improvements in one's self-esteem, awareness, confidence and the paradoxical sense that life is cyclical, what is seen as good today may turn otherwise tomorrow, hence the need for flexibility. At this stage when a client begins to reason analytically, that life events can change unexpectedly, he has thereby started to produce normal results in the healing process.

Abnormal Results:

We have noted this fact before that people behave true to their nature and type. There are certain individuals who appear resilient in accepting order and corrections in their lives. In such cases, when a client has gone through rational emotive behavior therapy and refuses to abide by the skills recommended for healing, there is nothing more the therapist can do. Actually, according to Ellis there are no abnormal results as such. The abnormal results talked about here are as the failure of clients or patients to accept the healing process they have been introduced into. Unwillingness to accept change and adhere to therapeutic guidelines may not produce any fruitful results on the part of the clients or patients. The same thing applies to the Igbo people of Nigeria, especially people of Ngor Okpala. Their unwillingness to accept the new religion will always lead to dilemma of the growth of the Christian religion there.

Rational emotive behavior therapy for co-occurring problems

This is a more severe situation for the counselees. In the first place, what does "co-occurring problems" mean in our context? These are problems that coexist with previous ones, problems that fall together. Co-occurring means: "Occurring or operating at the same time, 'a series of coincident events" (Internet Web. Def.). In other words, rational emotive behavior therapy problems re-occur, as the healing process appears positive or to be going fine. Rational emotive behavior therapies usually over-relapse among people with co-occurring psychological problems. We say that the mind is a playground; only the individuals know best what they are going through in their lives.

In this light, those people who have complex psychological problems are victims and vulnerable to encounter rational emotive behavior disorders due to traces of their irrational beliefs and thinking. One of the most powerful psychologists in this area, Emmett Velten & Patricia Penn (2010) remarked: "Some of the most disturbed people can be significantly and often quickly helped to understand how they perceive, think, feel and behave to upset themselves and also to secondarily upset themselves about their upset-ness" (Professional resources exchange, p. 453). This is so because most of the people who suffer from rational emotive behavior problems; often do not even know why they are upset. In cases like this, the therapist makes efforts to assist them realize the cause of their upset-ness. Some of the psychological problems are traceable to the diagnoses and assessments of individual situations.

The ability to understand and comprehend the rational emotive behavior problems and their consequences are assets and great insights to psychologists to have more effective clinical work in order to help those who are suffering from rational emotive behavior disorders. Based on this important observation, Daniel David & Steven Jay Lynn (2009) wrote: "REBT/CBT theory and therapy have a strong evidence base and probably qualify as empirically validated, with more evidence for some aspects and disorders and less evidence for other aspects and disorders" (Research, theory and clinical practice, p. 360). Some of those who have shown positive signs after the rational emotive behavior therapy have equally proved that psychotherapy to irrational thinking can change. It is important for people with rational emotive behavior therapy disorders to prove themselves by their rational thinking and positive attitudes.

Similarly, Jack Trimpy in his scientific work entitled "The Small book" has equally proved that his approach to the rational emotive behavior therapy is the same with that of Albert Ellis. Their treatment of the disorder is the same thing. Considering Ellis's stand on this issue, we see that the irrational thinking under discussion is associated with those who have behavioral problem especially those who are intoxicated with alcohol or drugs. In the same vein, Trimpey (1974) once wrote: "Some social differences may show up between people who use different intoxicants but these are significant. Recovery is the same" (The small book, p.7). For instance, alcoholism is varied as the different items people take in this capacity. Comparatively, intoxicants affect people differently depending on the nature and level of alcohol taken. Jack Trimpy maintains that what is more important is not so much the intoxicants as such but the process of recovery. Messrs. A. & B. may have the same quantity of alcohol; it does not mean that they are going to be affected at the same level.

Alcohol may bring somebody to a different level of life assumption. At times, an alcoholic does not see any danger in alcoholism, even in his actions. Some of them think that everything about them is normal, when those around them know that they are out of alignment in their behavior. In actuality, they do not have much rational behavior. Yet, some of them in their irrational assumptions and claims end up believing that they are on top of the world. Reacting to this natural and at times, ugly fact of life, Trimpey (1974) remarked: "It is because we feel the way we think that rational recovery is such an effective way for chemically dependent people to gain control of the emotions that perpetuate the drinking cycle" (The small book, p. 17). This is only achieved when the irrational thinking and behaved persons avail themselves with the skills inherent in rational emotive behavior therapy. For instance, when an alcoholic begins to feel and think that most people out there or in society do not support alcoholism generally, rational recovery begins to occur in the alcoholic. There are so many other reasons or factors like substance abuse; sex maniac and indecency are some of the consequences of irrational emotive behavior problems. In this sense, those who have been addicted to alcohol or drugs do not reason or think properly.

However, rational emotive behavior therapy works best for those who are willing to change their irrational thinking and behaviors. Research has proved that there are no specific precautions or therapies that can bring patients to normal life level except their willingness to accept change. In other words, all those who wish to avail themselves with the treatment of rational emotive behavior problems must be ready and willing to change their irrational behaviors, which are the constant causes and symptoms of irrational thinking. There are so many areas of need the rational emotive behavior therapy can apply to bring irrationality to rationality of thinking and behaviors especially those suffering from such disorders like depressions, post-traumatic disorders, anxiety and stress.

This was a problem in the implanting of the Christian faith in Igboland because the people believed that what they had was the best and did not feel like having something more. The Igbo adage summarizes it better: "Nku no na mba na-eghere ha nri" meaning that the firewood of a community cooks their food better than that of other people. Therefore when an alcoholic or drug addict begins to think or feel that he or she is recovering from alcoholism or addiction, he or she will invariably begin to show signs of recovery too. That is why I earlier said that belief works best in actions. With regard to an individual belief system, let us examine how this faith is contended with or disputed in the face of contingencies and unpredictability of life.

Theologies vis-à-vis pastoral counseling/care

When we speak of the theology of pastoral care or pastoral psychology, there is need to specify the theology we are talking about. There are so many theologies as there are theologians under the sun and various aspects of pastoral care. We have ancient, biblical, catholic, protestant, modern and contemporary theologies. While we do not intend to dwell on any of them, theology places the supernatural on the center. For instance, when we speak of the theology of pastoral care, does it mean the same thing in all religions? Where do we place the different theories of God as Omniscient, Omnipotent, Creator of the whole human race, and the First Person of the Blessed Trinity, theologies of third world countries and ecumenical theology etc? All the same, how do all these theories fit into the whole process of pastoral care or psychology? Citing the case of one with life threatening disease, like cancer or AIDS, does this one who is in a lot of pains here and now need the definition of theology? This is to ask, do we need to study theology as an academic course to effectively do pastoral care or professionally assist people in their pitiable conditions? This is where we take our bearing and discuss the topic at hand.

The theology of pastoral care or psychology calls for the best concrete means to bring some spiritual support or a healing presence to a particular situation of human need and pain. Thus, by the theology of pastoral care and psychology, we are talking of an operational and functional theology that offers compassionate assistance to the sufferer, irrespective of religious preferences. A little distinction between pastoral care and pastoral psychology which is pastoral counseling properly understood has to be made at this stage. When a pastor like the one we mentioned in our case study claims to be a pastoral caregiver, few questions are inevitable. Are such claims on the same footing or status as a pastoral psychologist or counselor claiming to be one? Therefore, we have to differentiate pastoral care and pastoral counseling or psychology in our context.

Understanding Pastoral Care and Counseling

In the words of the American association of Pastoral Counselors, "Pastoral counseling is a unique form of counseling which uses spiritual resources as well as psychological understanding for healing and growth..." (Pastoral Counseling. Wikipedia, the free

Encyclopedia. En.wikipedia.org/wiki/pastoral counseling. Accessed Oct. 11, 2010). By "spiritual resources" we do not imply religion or going to heaven because to be spiritual is not the same thing as being religious. As cited by Prof. Nwachukwu A.O. "Spirituality" is better understood in the words of Svoboda:

> *Our spirituality is expressed in the little daily decisions and choices we make, what kind of food we eat, how we talk to the clerk in the store, how much time (if any) we devote in prayer, Our spirituality also includes the big choices we make: whom we decide to marry or befriend, the kind of home we live in, the type of work we choose to do. When life presents us with few options, our spirituality influences the way we accept and work within the confines of such restrictions (Svoboda, Melannie. 1996:5).*

By spiritual resources, therefore, we include all the perceptions before us: the environment, character manifestations, attitude of the counselee, response mode, uttered words, and facial impressions. According to Au in Nwachukwu: "Spirituality is holistic when it acknowledges that all aspects of a person's life must be subjected to the transforming influence of the Incarnation" (Au, Wilkie. 1989:219). Even, in Smith's own words: "Spirituality is an elusive term and has as many definitions as people who write about it" (Smith Jane W. in Vision Vol. 17 No. 9, NACC, October 2007:5). In other words, spiritual resources might be more inclusive and extensive as applied in this book. In this light, a pastoral counselor employs factors gathered from the environment to determine the situation of the process. In a way, pastoral care resembles counseling in this capacity because, in each case, the environment, one-on-one interaction plays a major role. This is what it means to place the convenience of the client first in any pastoral process, whether it is counseling or in caring.

Another major difference between pastoral counseling and pastoral care lies in methodology and how one employs a skilled approach. Unprofessionally, pastoral care can assume the form of preaching, where a pastor counsels his parishioner or a group of individuals concerning certain behavioral issues. On professional level, listening is more important than talking in both pastoral care and counseling. In pastoral care, we do not preach to those who need our care, either in the hospital setting or elsewhere. However, attentive listening is very crucial and an important management strategy for attending to our patients and clients. Pastoral care can be given to the dead in the form of prayer and extended to the living through exhortation and consoling the bereaved. In support of the difference between these therapies, Benner remarkably said: "Also, while pastoral care can be offered to the mentally retarded and the unconscious, pastoral counseling can only be offered to the conscious and to people who are aware of their problem and are capable of making a decision and changing after providing the necessary insight (Benner, 2003:20-21).

This is an important point that our readers need to note. As a pastoral counselor, versed in pastoral and psychological (counseling) care, I am professionally trained to treat individual cases differently depending on its nature and magnitude. By this we mean that the emotional problems people go through in life are so many that a counselor uses his or her expertise and professional acumen to determine the most suitable manner to approach them. There are stressful situations ranging from loss of jobs, friendships, divorce, loss of relations, parents, children, pets, and property. Worse still, when gratitude is repaid by ingratitude, it triggers off spiritual and emotional pains that can only be handled by a pastoral counselor or at times, with medication too. What of people with various forms of addictions – drug addicts and alcoholics for instance, the approach to their cases is different. Besides, personality traits and temperaments are different and they equally affect behaviors in a substantial level. On a more serious note, to what extent can drug addicts and alcoholics practice religion or encourage the same in others?

In terms of psychological context: "Pastoral counseling can take place in hospitals, nursing homes, rehabilitation facilities, independent living centers, psychiatric facilities, correctional institutions, and residential care facilities (Pastoral Counseling. Wikipedia, the free Encyclopedia, En.wikipedia.org/wiki/pastoral counseling. Accessed Oct. 11, 2010). While pastoral counseling can occur in such places as mentioned above, the counseling is almost done one-on-one basis. With regard to these distinctions as observed here, pastoral care can equally take place in those areas as enumerated therein. Yet, the approach to issues in each case slightly differs as noted above. In case of pastoral care, chaplains carry out their ministries within the four walls of the facility in question without specifying location or moment of meeting. Even in the case of the pastor cited earlier, pastoral care can be carried out over the phone, but not pastoral counseling or psychology. Though, pastoral care takes place in the hospitals and various parishes, it can also hold in a car, park, on the road depending on the nature of problem that surfaces or springs unexpectedly.

Unlike pastoral care, pastoral or psychological counseling can hold in a hospital setting, but it must be within a particular location, office or place of meeting. For instance, you cannot engage an alcoholic who has just approached you for help in public without stating the time two of you can meet and look into the matter. This does not mean that in pastoral care, the issues of patients, staff of family members can be discussed in public. Patients' Confidentiality is part of the policies that guide pastoral care and counseling. While we do know that in pastoral care, patients decide whether to have it or not, a chaplain can walk into a patient's room without previous notice or information. This cannot happen in pastoral counseling. However, in counseling, pastoral care and psychology, the patient or counselee provides the clues and tools through which the care will be executed. Counseling is not by force or persuasion. Counselors try as much they can to build faith and confidence in their clients so that they will be disposed to open up and tell their stories. Besides, pastoral care is not as important as the heart expressed in compassion and love.

That was precisely the point Benner made with regard to setting, as previously noted in Benner (2003). Pastoral counseling, like any other form of counseling is structured. It has an official beginning and ending. In pastoral care, formalities differ. For instance, in pastoral care, a chaplain may walk into a room of a patient when the doctor is attending to the same patient. In some moments while the doctor may welcome the chaplain and ask him to wait, he may tell the chaplain to give them some privacy. In some other times, a chaplain may not visit with a patient whose curtain is drawn while another chaplain may go in without minding the curtain. There are certain manners chaplains go about their duties in the hospital setting that do not follow any laid down formality. Unlike in the case of pastoral counseling, it is a practice that is highly marked by formality and not a practice that should be done anyhow and anywhere like a chaplain praying for a patient on the hallway. This way of approach is unacceptable in pastoral counseling.

Pastoral counseling follows a system that allows the clients some freedom and trust to tell their stories. Nothing is achieved in any pastoral counseling where the clients or counselees are not given maximum privacy. Under this background, like in other forms of counseling, Benner (2003) identified three stages and their corresponding tasks in pastoral counseling. He described them as encounter, engagement, and disengagement stages (Consult Rev. Dr. Oliver Offor, PhD Dissertation, 2012). The stages describe the process that has to be observed in counseling for effective results. Just like in the case of pastoral care, the pastor or chaplain must avoid being judgmental or apprehensive of what the patient wants at the moment. The clients or patients take the initiative in expressing what they want from a pastoral caregiver.

These very stages are so vital in any counseling process and stage and they basically differentiate pastoral counseling from pastoral care. This is the modality for pastoral counseling and psychology. We are going to examine and discuss the 3 stages in this order:

(a). Encounter Stage

Generally, this is the first step, the preliminary stage in pastoral counseling. Just as the name implies, it describes the initial meeting of the pastoral counselor and the one to be counseled or seeking help. The counselor's goal at this point, according to Benner is "to establish a personal contact as we noted earlier with the client, set the boundaries for the counseling relationship, become acquainted with the client and his or her central concerns, conduct a pastoral diagnosis, and develop a mutually acceptable focus for the work they will do together" (Benner 2003:72). The establishment of this working relationship is sine qua non for achieving success in that counseling session. In other words, it is at this time, in Goldboom's estimation, "that the pastor gets to know the client as a person, that is, getting to know his or her age, social and economic background, racial or cultural background, marital status, and the problem that brought him or her to counseling" (Goldboom 2006. Pp.2-3). As it were, this is the core and beginning of success in any counseling profession.

The same thing happens during the Sacrament of Reconciliation or Confession in the Catholic denomination. The impression the pastors create for those who are having their first Sacrament of reconciliation determines how they will approach it in future. For instance, it does not matter what an individual may confess at the Confessional, the pastor should not yell or scold him or allow his voice be heard by others. Every discussion or confession the individual holds with or confesses to the pastor must remain absolutely and confidentially secret. According to Corey and Corey: "This is fundamental for successful counseling because it is at this stage that the counselor allays the fears and concerns of the client" (Corey & Corey, 2006. P.36), and also, "it is from this stage, that the pastor, in addition to his or her personal dispositions, begins to put into practice the counseling skills (Benner 2003:75) especially the listening skill. In this context, 'pastor' refers to a professional who has the knowledge and skills in psychology or counseling and not just a clergyman in charge of a parish or congregation like the case we saw earlier on. It is also important that presumption is avoided in counseling. The counselor must make sure he understands the point the client has put forward as a springboard to fruitful interaction and results. That was why Miller et all observed: "This process of relationship building through listening is the clarification stage (Miller et al, 1995:16). In a friendly and objective manner, the counselor repeats his question for more updating in the process. After the clarification and establishment of rapport stage, the counselor naturally enters into 'liminal' stage, the counseling session proper. According to Benner, it is called the engagement stage.

(b). Engagement Stage

As noted already, this is the 'liminality' of the counseling session. It is the actual counseling where the counselor employs his skills in addressing the stories, problems and values of the counselee. This is the working stage and the heart of the counseling relationship. In subsequent sessions, this engagement stage features as the reason for meeting. The stage may last for few other sessions. For instance, it is the stage at which both the counselor and the client get down to business or to the issue that brought them together or the client into counseling – seeking help from a counselor. In Benner's evaluation, this session occupies one to three sessions. The role of the counselor at this stage is irreplaceable. According to Benner: "The tasks of the pastoral counselor in this stage is to explore the client's feelings, thoughts, and behavioral patterns associated with the problem area, as well as the development of new perspectives and strategies for coping or change" (Benner, 2003:74). The success of counseling not only anchors on the ability of the counselor to understand the counselee properly but also being able to create the environment in which the client happily anticipates the meaning of the meeting generally.

(c). _Disengagement Stage_

In any professional pastoral care or counseling, the manner in which the session ends matters a lot. It is this ending session that helps the counselor to assess the success or failure of the meeting or the result of it. In Corey & Corey's views: "This is also known as termination or final stage in other forms of counseling" (Corey & Corey, 2006; Rutan et ali, 2007). As noted already, this stage brings the counseling relationship to an end. This is a reinforcement stage. Once the counselor feels that his meeting with his client is successful, he might at this moment, decide not to fix another meeting for any other reasons. But where there are some misgivings that his efforts did not achieve the desired goal or things did not go well, he might consider it expedient to have another meeting with his client.

According to Benner: "It involves an evaluation of progress and an assessment of remaining concerns, a referral for further helps if need be, and the termination of the counseling relationship" (Benner, 2003:74). As in the case of the stages a counseling session revolves, the end, termination or disengagement has its own pattern too. According to Hill:

Termination involves three things – looking back, that is, counselors reviewing with clients what they have learned and how they have changed; looking forward, that is, counselors and clients set an ending date, discuss future plans, and consider the need for additional counseling or referral; and saying goodbye, that is, clients express their thanks to counselor and both share their feelings about ending and say their farewell (Hill, 2004:.410).

As a way of elucidation, the counselor and counselee have to weigh the degree of agreements and disagreements as to determine where progress is made or not. This will involve a total review of the initial stage of their meetings as to know whether they actually made some achievements or not. Once the counselor recognizes tremendous improvements and huge success on the matter or issue being addressed, he encourages his client with praises. This reinforcement energizes the counselee and builds strong sense of belonging and success. For instance, counseling an alcoholic is a gradual process where the counselor guides the victim to understand the need for drinking and the harm of getting drunk. Their meeting may lead to a situation where the alcoholic freely takes decision to quit drinking or smoking.

Generally, as a guideline, the counselor should always be cognizant and aware that bad habit is not formed in a day. Once formed, it takes longer time to heal. Every counselor always bears that in mind, especially that people regret leaving or quitting the habits and situations that have appeared satisfying or rewarding to them. It was on this note that Dayringger made the following observations:

> *So pastoral counselors need to take great care that the intensity of the positive transference is sufficiently diminished in the later stages of therapy, in other to permit a leave-taking, which is not too traumatic. It should be noted that pastoral counselors have a unique problem regarding termination. As a part of their pastoral ministry, they normally have a more post-counseling contacts and conversations with clients than 'secular' therapists (Dayringer, 1998:125).*

It is true that termination has to occur. But it is not always easy. Therefore, counselors should have ways of contacting their clients from time to time assuring them of their continued support and assistance. In other words, the termination process is gradual and free. Based on the foregoing perspective, we shall present a particular case where pastoral care, psychology and theology are interwoven and play vital role in the wholeness of the distressed individual.

Encountering God with an Ngor Okpala person with AIDS

Infections: A challenge to pastoral care and counseling.

There are few more things we need to know about the Igbo of Nigeria or the nation generally. Nigeria is both homogenous and heterogeneous. She belongs to diversified cultures with different languages, life styles, mannerisms, looks, wears and peculiar sicknesses like malaria or chicken box for an example. As it were, the people's understanding and manner of dealing with sickness differ from one another. This makes it imperative to examine few peculiarities with an Ngor Okpala person.

Characteristics of an Ngor Okpala Family

The characteristics of Nigerian families in general refer to the various environmental situations and life situation in which people find one another. By family here, we include the biological, blood, personal, communal, economic, and political, socio-religious relationships and states of life and those who form part of that life. In many places, family only refers to the husband and wife with their children. The Ngor Okpal people practice extended family system and each of these family members is included as belonging to the same family. The family system in Nigeria is so interesting that any emphasis or study that tends to separate the people from one another might be counterproductive in the practice of the faith too.

Family is not different from the people's belief system. As a way of emphasis, personal family means that in Ngor Okpala, everybody has a family, even a bastard who does not know his family tree. In terms of communal, families make up the various compounds, and every compound belongs to a clan, village or community. The community determines the sanity and spirituality of the family and that is why nobody sins alone. Any crime committed in the family is always treated as a community affair. Religion is integrally linked to the family as such. That was the point Augsburger was alluding to, when he said that as regards the case with less developed nations, like Nigeria, religion and religious beliefs play a major part in the daily lives of family members (cf. Augsburger, 1986:200). The issue of religion playing major role in the daily lives of the people has much implication for this book. Any infringement on this their life wire must surely lead to a dilemma.

The economy of the family has great impact on the lives of the members of the community especially when there are certain contributions to be made for the progress of the community. In such cases, it is a thing of shame to be laughed at, as a result of family's failure to meet up with any community levies or contributions. Therefore, emphasis is placed on being hard working and industrious. In Igboland, laziness is considered a disease and a lazy person is never seen as a person of worth. Thanks to God, science and technology have eased out most of the strenuous and manual labors of the people, in the past, emphasis was centered on farming alone. Hence, there were so many crops, palm wine, mat makers, hole diggers for various purposes.

On the part of the political life of the family in Ngor Okpala, there is a system of governance that respects seniority and the elders of the land. We spent time in this book explaining the implication of customary laws and 'Omenala' of the people. Socially, every family is compelled to conform to a general morality and ethical observances. Any failure on the part of a particular family to comply attracts heavy punishment from the community as a whole. Family characteristic in Ngor Okpala, even in the whole of Igboland, includes the people's culture, manner of dressing, dialects, the type of food people eat, their markets, farming season and harvesting period. Each of these events are linked to the family system in Igboland. The family is the life of the people, multi-cultural, interdependent and related to each other.

Character formation is largely built on religion. Up to this present age, character has not been determined by wealth or affluence. People are assessed based on the moral probity and creative contributions to the community. To be respected as a person for Igbo people, one has to be morally sound in character. Anything that is short of this expectation is regarded as useless. Mbiti, one of the African erudite writers believes that "religion embodies many beliefs; beliefs which Africans find hard to destroy even after the conversion to Christianity" (1991:29). These are some of the causes of the dilemma we encounter today with regard to the growth of the Christian religion in Nigeria. The mistake was initially made when the missionaries did not seem to appreciate anything in the traditional religion of the people. Most of these beliefs, we treated them in this book. Some of them include the beliefs in the ancestors, the Supreme "Chi" or God of the Igbo people, the creator and sustainer of the universe, Spirits that inhabit the earth and so many other gods, who are the intermediaries of the major God, "Chukwu". Some of the people practiced magic and witchcraft, sorcery etc. The people strongly believe in reincarnation, if not physically realized then spiritually so. Good life is one thing that never dies in Igboland. Once a person of sound moral quality dies, his or her death is celebrated and people pray to have such people in their families. The people equally believe in the law of Karma in which whatever a person sows in this present life, he must reap in this life and the next to come. These are the values that shape the character of the Igbo people. In his continuing assessment of the religious lives of the people, Mbiti observed:

Religion has been largely responsible for shaping the character and culture of African (Nigerian) peoples throughout the centuries. Even if it has no sacred books, it is written everywhere in the life of the people. To be an African (Nigerian) in the traditional setting is to be religious.....Africans (Nigerians) are notoriously religious (1991:30).

Beliefs are linked to faith. Once one's faith anchors on one's belief, it sticks and forms part of one's life. In such situations, nobody can separate belief from faith and life because people firmly and accordingly act on them (Mbiti, 1991:29). On this basis, Dr. Oliver Offor noted: "Thus it is very important for every pastoral counselor to understand the beliefs that dominate the life of the people in other to assure proper and effective counseling" (Offor Oliver, GTF/Oxfrod, 2011).

According to Nwachukwu: "In the light of the African belief and eschatology, a famous Nigerian writer, Onwubiko, observes that: "Religion and religious belief and their effects on the African community are the key to understanding the African world and ideology" (Onwubiko O. Oliver. 1999:23). Undoubtedly, religion is synonymous with family life in Africa and that constituted a great problem for the early missionaries in that part of the world" (Nwachukwu: 2010:208). Bishop Chikwe citing Mbiti in his paternal address to Igbo Catholic Community and their friends in Baltimore, USA, remarked:

Mbiti rightly puts it that the Igbo are scrupulously religious in whatever they do. They eat, work, play, dance, and even sleep religiously" (Chikwe, Victor. A., June 28, 2009).

In this context, religion is not only a belief in the absolute but also life carried out in practical terms and deeds. In this sense, religion can totally be embraced as an aspect of spiritual psychology. This is religion in the true sense of the word - a movement that changes, challenges and encourages the individual to quit hypocrisy and holistically and intrinsically embrace oneself and others as fellow pilgrims on the same eternal journey of life (Culled from Nwachukwu, 2010).

Repeatedly, the point has been hammered in this book that the people's entire religious beliefs, their culture and cosmological worldviews are inseparably one and the same thing. In Odoemene's own words:

> Religion does not only serve the interest of the society but also of the individual, in that religion provides answers to the questions and the search for meaning, leads him into loving confrontation with the source of his being and integrates him into the society to enable him participate in the religious rituals of the community and values (Odoemene, N. Anacletus. 1993:54).

Inevitably, writing about the role of human conscience in religious practices, interpersonal relationships and society, Davis K. noted: "Religion serves to compensate people for the frustration they invariably experience in striving to reach socially valuable ends" (Davis K. 1948:526). How can there be any growth of the Christian religion when it creates some frustration in certain quarters?

The issue is "what brought about the frustration in question and what are those socially valuable ends?" Again, this is where spiritual psychology challenges each person to respond to his or her internal energy in the pursuit of sound moral lives. That means, while religion seems to provide hope or compensate society for the injustices, frustrations, lack of Truth, Justice and Peace - TJP she suffers because of bad government, politicians, citizens, spiritual psychology assists her and individuals to realize the need to faithfully avoid behaviors that lead to such frustrations. In this sense, religion can meaningfully guide and resuscitate relationships particularly in moments of hopelessness and confusion just as spiritual psychology itself. That was why Odikanoro, citing Capuzzi & Gross in his Ph.D. work, noted:

> *Indeed, spirituality and religion have been a source of stability and hope for minority groups for many generations and are part of their socialization (Capuzzi & Gross, 2003:436-437 in Odikanoro, Vincent I., 2008:19).*

The big question that comes to mind is: "Why is religion not for majority groups of society?" This is basically because it serves as a source of stability for minorities and the few that understand and accept its moral implications in their lives. Therefore, any religious belief that has no practical application to individual concerns and problems of the moment is misleading. Then, if religion and spiritual psychology have such unique and enormous roles in the life of the individual, how can the situation be described when some of the ministers who are meant to facilitate these healing opportunities to society turn around to perpetuate the frustration by false Gospel?

According to Idowu: "Religion is very much and always with us. It is with us at the very moment of life" (Idowu, Bolaji. E. 1976:1). People are free to accept or refuse it in their lives. In Bouquet's own words: "Religion cannot wisely or safely be ignored or neglected" (Bouquet, A. C. 1941:23) because a "person's real religion lies in that something that has taken possession of his life" (Ezeonyia, V. Vincent. 1998:30). The "something" meant here has nothing to do with acquisition of material wealth, education or social status but God. Personally, I am not against material possessions that people honestly achieve through hard work and accountability. To be rich implies poverty or an escape from it. As such, any little help rendered to the poor as a way of solidarity, matters a lot. However, for someone to use his or her wealth to punish or terrorize the vulnerable of society is sickness and death. Thus, "religion is popular only when it ceases to be truly religious. Religion by its very nature is unpopular - certainly unpopular with the ego" (Fulton, Sheen in Marlin, George & Co. eds. 1989:263). Therefore, for a minister to strive for popularity in the world contradicts the essence of the Christian mission and leads to greater frustrations and dilemma of its growth (Consult Nwachukwu, 2010).

With regard to the socio-economic conditions, Nigeria is indeed a blessed nation with so many natural resources, with crude oil in the lead. Yet, "despite this oil wealth, poverty is widespread and basic indicators place Nigeria among the twenty poorest nations in the world" (Walter, L. ed. 2003:312). According to Dr. Oliver Offor:

> *Wealth and power are distributed very unevenly. The great majority of Nigerians, preoccupied with daily struggles to earn a living, have few material possessions and little chance of improving their lot. One-third has no access to health care simply because they live too far from clinics or other treatment centers, and many others cannot afford the fees charged by clinics. Secure and well-paying jobs are scarce, even for those with considerable education. Food is typically expensive. Housing too, is costly despite its rudimentary qualities prompting the poor to build basic homes in shanty towns. Sewage disposal systems in most cities are also basic or primitive, and polluted streams, well, roadside drains, and other bodies of water increase the risk of infectious diseases (cf. "Nigeria" in Online Encarta Encyclopedia Standard. (Accessed October 18, 2010, Offor Oliver, GTF/Oxford, 2011).*

With the infiltration of western civilization and culture, different kinds of sicknesses have emerged. Some of these sicknesses go with their nature of shame and humiliations, especially sexually transmitted diseases (STDs). For instance, Nigeria being blessed with extended family systems and people living as brothers and sisters, such diseases like "gonorrhea" – caused by bacteria that can grow and multiply easily in the warm, moist areas of the reproductive tract are unavoidable. But sex is held sacred especially by the Igbo of Nigeria. The people of Ngor Okpala consider a violation of fidelity and conjugal union as a serious offence against God, their ancestors and the land.

Due mainly to the differences in the peoples' culture and the unique way of looking at sicknesses, people are very cautious to contact any shameful sickness for their families. Yet, as long as people interact and communicate with one another, certain infectious diseases are easily spread around. The shame that is associated with certain sicknesses will help us to understand and appreciate the nature of sickness one is suffering from and the way the sufferer is being looked upon. Besides the sickness that may land somebody to the hospital, bad manners and offences are considered the worst form of sickness too. There are certain notions of sickness in Nigeria, particularly in Ngor Okpala that are commonly perceived and dreaded among the entire ethnic groups. Such notions include: 419, inconsistency of governmental policies and mismanagement of economic resources, increase of armed robbery, invasion of deadly sicknesses (like Aids, chicken boxes, malaria), falling standard of education, bad drinking water and roads in most parts, poor health care facilities and power supply, multiplicity and proliferation of churches with increasing number of false prophecies et cetera. As noted, these equally count as diseases that need to be cured. However, in this book, our attention is focused on a particular AIDS case in Igbo tradition of Nigeria with particular reference to an Ngor Okpala person.

In the past, before the advent of Christianity or western civilization, the people were never associated with the thousand and one diseases we have today. People lived and died at a very ripe old age. Death was never a problem for the people as of those days because they knew that good life would always bring someone to the company of the ancestors - their role models. Worst still, with the advance in technology and science the people have intermingled so much with other people across the globe. These mingling and interactions have brought their positive and negative effects in the lives of the people. The most recent of these deadliest diseases in Nigeria is 'acquired immune deficiency syndrome [AIDS]' - "a disease in which there is a severe loss of the body's cellular immunity, greatly lowering the resistance to infection and malignancy" or "HIV" – human immunodeficiency viruses" (Internet Source, 2011). To say the least, the people are really frightened by the mere mention, let alone the presence of this disease in their land.

In Igbo Tradition, particularly among Ngor Okpala people, AIDS is seen as an abomination, a curse from our ancestors. The cause of AIDS is out of the question. A lot of questions have been raised about how this monster disease came into Igboland in the first place. A mention of 'AIDS' in Igboland portrays a thing of shame and humiliation. No family will like to be linked with this disease, not necessarily because it is life threatening, but the shame it brings to affected families and compounds. The intensity with which the people of Ngor Okpala dread AIDS has reflected in a high sense of suspicion as who could be a victim. This has equally affected marriage relationships and friendships in some degrees, leading to the dilemma in question.

Because the Igbos are homogenous, speak the same language, have the same looks and wear the same dresses, etc, whatever is regarded as an abomination, taboo, atrocity or evil in one part of Igbo land is given the same amount of consideration in other parts too. Yet, there is need to note that among these Igbo people themselves, there are slight differences in their dialects, ways of doing certain things in terms of cultural observances, rite of initiations and symbols etc. Despite these differences, it is easy for somebody from the Igbo tradition to recognize a fellow Igbo person, the differences notwithstanding. For instance, among the Ngor Okpala people, sickness is principally divided into two categories: natural and unnatural or man-made. Each of these could be personally or communally experienced. All the same, personal sicknesses are viewed and felt by the community in the same way as the individual does except the sufferer knows more where the pain pinches.

Natural sicknesses or sufferings in Ngor Okpala include infant mortality (Ume), impotency, lack of male issues or children (end of family lineage), poor harvest, history of misfortunes (enweghi aka aku or oku), mourning or grieving of a lost partner (igba mkpe), outcast and free born controversy (osu/diala), bachelorhood, incest, oath-taking between two families before reconciliatory rite is done (Isu ogwu oriko), protracted sickness such as convulsion, mental case, madness, being notorious in bad life (thieves, prostitution, giving birth at one's father's house, trouble makers) and AIDS etc. Man-made sufferings include: drunkenness, poverty (lack of land, unable to take care of the sick, no good housing facilities), laziness, debtors, complete illiteracy, bad gang etc.

It is most painful to observe that among these categories of sicknesses, AIDS has become an evil-infected disease that does not attract the sympathy of the community. There is practically no attention given to most AIDS patients in Igboland. Once one is infected with this virus, one must try to hide it from the community. An AIDS patient in Ngor Okpala is allowed to die in his or her family of origin. Though efforts are made by western medicine to treat them but so far, it is hard to mention a particular hospital in Ngor Okpala where such people are treated. Burial in Igboland, especially in Ngor Okpala is one of the highest honors given to a person that led good life. In such burials, the communities as a whole will gather to bid the person farewell.

Among the people, sexuality is highly held sacred. Unlike in the case of an AIDS victim, nobody cares when the victim dies and there is no befitting or communal burial for him or her. As far as my investigation is concerned, this has mainly been done privately. Of course, it is a thing of shame for any family to have such a patient in their group. As of few years ago when this outbreak became known, once a person has been associated with these infections, he or she was hidden. In such cases, only few close and family friends were allowed to peep into or have a glance at the dying member. It is traumatic indeed to watch a person created in God's image treated in this manner. Such mentalities, whether brought about by culture or technology, create dilemma for the growth of the Christian religion among the people. Even in the western world as well as Christianity, AIDS has posed a serious threat and a big challenge to life. In many quarters, especially in the western world, emphasis is placed more on prevention than in curing the disease.

The family members of an AIDS patient suffer greatly and pray that the victim dies and to save them from further shame and melancholy. Once it is discovered that there is an AIDS patient in Mr. BB's family, the news always flies and spreads to every hook and cranny of that town like a hurricane fire or "a tropical cyclone with winds exceeding

74 miles per hour" that leaves no object standing (Dic. Def.). This is where the Christian religion is tested and subjected to criticisms. If the Christian message is meant to bring solace to the downtrodden and the poor, where does a HIV patient fall within? There appears to be a lot of contradictions in what the Christian Bible and doctrines teach and what the adherents do. Is HIV a disease or a curse? Or, does one suffer from this disease because of one's sins or is it just a natural occurrence that happens in one's lifetime? There could be more questions than these. One fact is clear; in as much as life is not respected or treated fairly because of one's poor situation, the growth of the Christian religion will be hard.

Consequently, based on the situation at hand about this particular case of an AIDS patient in Ngor Okpala, we can still raise some questions from other angles. For instance, where does the theology of pastoral care come in now? What are the limits of pastoral care and counseling? If God, Jesus, the First Chaplain pastoral counselor were to visit Ngor Okpala community or town and meet a particular AIDS patient, what would his attitude to it be? Could he have done anything different from our pastors, if he had ministered to people with HIV? Is it possible our Bishops, Monsignors, Priests, Pastors, Ministers and the majority of our strong faithful people are aware of the excruciating pains HIV victims go through, and yet nothing substantial is done for them? The fact that these vital organs of the Gospel are silent over an issue that affects their ministry, the growth of the Christian religion will suffer. This is where our emphasis may not be placed on God this time. I feel that pastoral care and counseling go beyond religious affiliations and seek the face of God in others and in love, extend to whoever is suffering from any type of sickness including HIV. That is the only way to enliven the growth of the Church.

AIDS should not be an obstacle to the mission of pastoral care and counseling. They should go beyond all boundaries of color, race, nationality or language and reach the suffering Jesus in the person of the AIDS patient. The theology of pastoral care and counseling is a theology that unifies, vivifies, creates, recreates and eschews all forms of discrimination. It is a theology of love, caring, compassion and supportive presence. The theology of pastoral care and counseling is an action theology that posses a big challenge to any religion that does not accept each other as brother or sister. Though, most pastoral counselors or psychologists do not have religion, once life is at stake, every emphasis should be centered on it. This is where, we repeat, pastoral care and counseling go beyond the confines of religion and Church.

Emphatically, from my CPE training and studies in pastoral psychology, I have learned a theology that can help me see beyond the disease in a person and approach him or her as a human being in need of assistance like every other person. Ambush theology is out of place here in which people fear to approach God as a loving father. To minister and counsel those suffering from AIDS is part of professional and pastoral objectives. That was why I saliently did Residency Training in a hospital where AIDS patients are taken care of. The burning zeal led me to be certified as an effective Pastoral Caregiver and Counselor. Hence, this is my denominational aim to base this study on the benefits of those suffering from AIDs in Igboland. This study will not only save AIDS patients from the ugly predicament which society has placed them, but also bring about the growth of the Christian religion among the people. Christian religion has to be practiced in the spirit of the Founder. The theology of pastoral care and counseling sees the face of Jesus in those with AIDS and spends time to listen to their stories without allowing them to die miserably. This is the mission of pastoral psychology.

In these heart-breaking studies of AIDS patients being left to die miserably, time has come to call a spade a spade and accept them as human beings with equal rights and freedom. In a way, there is no way one can exhaust the theology of pastoral care and counseling with reference to AIDS patients in my country, particularly among the Ngor Okpala of Igbo tribe. The call to alleviate their anguish, shame and misery is urgent. This is the only way the Christian religion will be meaningful and grow. The Pastors of soul, both Sacramental and "solar scriptura" need to understand the language of the theology of pastoral care and counseling and take the same risk Christ took with leprosy and minister to AIDS patients in Nigeria. This is a theology that does not require a definition but dynamics and practice. It is a theology that does not differentiate or ask questions as to what denomination one belongs.

Pastoral psychology is one of those courses that could be recommended in schools because it's practical application to the various cases, which individuals suffer from or are unable to manage. The theology of pastoral care or counseling is that of healing and life. It is the theology of the healing presence of Christ or the other, of heartfelt concern and of the 'golden rule' of our salvation: "Do unto others what you would have others do unto you" (Matt. &: 12). This is a theology of silence, a theology of attentive listening, a theology of supportive presence and a theology of participation in the suffering and pains of other people. By so doing, the dilemma of the growth of the Christian religion will become a thing of the past. The individual person has more to contribute to the growth of the Christian religion in question and not the ideologies and debates associated with the dilemma.

Therefore, the moment pastors of souls and pastoral counselors begin to listen and hear the hidden sound of the pains of Jesus in the suffering of other people, the more practical pastoral ministry will be and the more fruitful and blessed the functions and not positions as pastors or pastoral caregivers in the Lord's vine yard will be. The Lord's vineyards include such homes, offices, governments where the presence of truth, justice, honesty, love and peace is felt and lived. The theology of pastoral care and counseling is based on our preparedness and willingness to render and minister to the spiritual needs of other people, including AIDS patients, irrespective of their religion or creed. This is a theology that has gone beyond the words of the bible to seek for the homebound, the homeless, accident victims, the hospitalized and what have you. The inclusion of pastoral psychology in our everyday living will go a long way to increase the growth of the Christian religion, not only in Igboland of Nigeria but also in other countries of the world.

Elements of dehumanization

This book vigorously deals in details on the Osu caste system, an indigenous religious belief system, practiced by people of Igboland. It raises concerns why this caste system has not improved since the advent of Christianity. It is my fervent desire to bring this discriminatory, dehumanizing and obnoxious caste system to the attention of the international community. The fact that this practice or belief that hits at the very fabric of the Christian faith has remained untouched, how can anybody or sensible person or Christian expect any growth in the faith. The major reason is that issues of discriminatory practices and cultural mishaps around the world are not tabled for discussion in the international community. If not, why cannot such repugnant and discriminatory Osu caste systems be dealt with or addressed?

This system as predominately found among the Igbo of Nigeria has given a strong blow to the dilemma of the growth of Christian faith in Igboland. These sacred persons of South – Eastern Nigeria, a region inhabited by the Igbo race are persons purported to have been dedicated to the powerful deities of the land. This was the point, for which Achebe lamented in the Arrow of God, saying:

> *A disease that has never been seen before cannot be cured with everyday herbs. When we want to make a charm we look for an animal whose blood can match its power; if a chicken cannot do it we look for a goat or a ram; if that is not sufficient we send for a bull. But sometimes even a bull does not suffice, then we must look for a human (Achebe, 1978:133).*

The choice of human beings in sacrifices was necessitated as the only way "to avoid future calamities in the community" (Uchendu, 1965:89). That the people of Igboland of Nigeria have perpetuated this uncharitable practice is not the fault of the missionaries as such. The big question that should surprise everybody is: "Why could not the Christian message wipe it out?"

We are aware that the Christian religion condemned it out rightly. For instance, the Christian Bible specifically stated that: "When the Scripture says…it makes no distinction between Jew and Greek: all belong to the same Lord" (Romans 10: 11-12). The question again is: "Who should implement this biblical injunction?" Why could not the Christian message prove the Igbo wrong in the practice of such heinous customs or life system? The situation is better elaborated in another version of St. Paul's letter, thus:

> *There is one Body, one Spirit, just as you were all called into one and the same hope when you were called. There is one Lord, one faith, one baptism, and one God who is Father of all, over all, through all and within all, Ephesians 4: 4-6 (Confer Malachi 2: 10; Colossians 3: 11-12).*

Therefore, disobedience to accepting unity, oneness, and others as belonging to the same family creates dilemma or is responsible for the lack of the growth of the Christian faith in Nigeria. Questions continue to mount in thousands, if the Christian message was meant to unite the people of Nigeria or not? Why have the people remained divided in accepting the message? Do we still call this disobedience?

Elements of domestic violence

Another important aspect of the work would be on the problem of domestic violence and women rights in Nigeria, as it affects the growth of Christian faith in Igboland of Nigeria. According to Hadiza Iza in his book titled: "Sources without Borders", studies have shown that globally, domestic violence accounts for nearly one quarter of all recorded crimes, and that women have been subjected to various forms of violence ranging from rape, battering, trafficking and even murder" (Hadiza Iza Bazza, 2009). Although the degree and magnitude of violence differ from society to society, the occurrence has profound and destructive consequences on the psychological, physical, emotional and social lives of the people and at times leads to disbelief in God to guide humanity.

The fact that domestic violence prevails across all strata of the Nigerian society is no longer debatable and its effects on the growth of the Christian faith cannot be over emphasized or denied. We shall in this book continue to examine the various ways and means through which domestic violence has continued to constitute a stumbling block to the growth of the Christian faith in Igboland of Nigeria. Efforts would be made to analyze the impact of Western education, colonialism, the Nigerian civil war and other problems of contemporary Nigeria on women. Violence is equally committed on children. Many children in Igboland of Nigeria are forced to leave schooling and become baby-sitters. Most often, these children are given to cruel families who do not care whether the children survive or not. Again, some of the female children are sexually abused and assaulted too.

Actually, the impact of Colonialism and advent of Christianity in Igboland of Nigeria would be among other issues to be discussed and emphasized in this book as being contributors to the dilemma of the growth of the Christian faith among the people. Today, despite the numerous messages of salvation which Christianity holds for the people, many of the Igboland of Nigeria still see it as a foreign or white man's religion because of it's hypocritical undertone. Most of those who claim to have received the new religion do not behave right. This bias, in unequivocal terms, has to a great extent, affected the growth of the Christian faith in Igboland. This question would bring us to the idea of enculturation advocated by Vatican 11 Council of 1962, as whether it has made any difference in the accepting and living of the Christian message.

Africanization of the Christian values

Indigenization and cultural revival would make an interesting reading in our discussion in this book or research work. In the context of the African and Nigerian culture, some African and Nigerian scholars have suggested the term " Africanization and Odenigbo" as a way of making Christianity native or endemic to the African and Nigerian peoples in particular. Would this suggestion have any impact on the growth or decline of Christian faith among the Igbo? According to Peter Nlemadim Domnwachukwu in his book tagged "Authentic African Christianity: An inculturation model for the Igbo", said: " For Christianity to be authentic in Africa, African ways of life must replace Western ways of life, and that Africans must look at Christianity with the African "eye" and understand its tenets with the African " mind" (Nlemadim

Domnwachukwu, 2000). In as much as I agree with Nlemadim in making the Christian religion put on an African face, there is no way African ways of life must replace those of the west. Each culture is unique and has something to offer. By inculturation, we advocate a synthesis whereby; values that are of universal importance may have to be incorporated within each other's culture. There is bit of each other's ways of life that we need as Igbo people, and others need ours also.

Elements of tribalism and nepotism

Obviously, "tribalism and nepotism" have remained a cankerworm that has eaten deep into the fabric of Nigerians and Igbo generally. According to Chinua Achebe, nothing in Nigerian's political and socio - cultural history captures her problem of national integration more graphically than the chequered fortune of the word "tribe" in her vocabulary. The word "Tribe" has been accepted at one time as a friend, rejected as an enemy at another, and finally smuggled in through the back-door as an accomplice" (Achebe Chinua, 1983). This issue of tribe is found among some religious leaders who would find it hard if not impossible to accept a reassignment or transfer from one region, diocese to the other. This attitude is commonly known in Igboland as "sons of the soil syndrome" and it has destroyed the Church in a great way. The work, directly and indirectly examines the negative effect this monster has on the growth of the Christian faith in Igboland of Nigeria. Actually, when the work of God becomes a choice of chance, the net result will be a total decline of the growth of faith.

Elements and mentality of slave trading

Another area the book would look into is on the fact of secularism and materialism that have crippled the spread of the Christian religion in Igboland. Christianity has been secularized and commercialized to the point that many people are looking for magic powers, instant healings and here-and-now miracles. To complicate the whole issue, the ministers of the Gospel seem to have treated God as a commodity for the market place.

Eventually, the History of Igbo land of Nigeria as noted in this work and emphasized once again, has much to say about the dilemma in the growth of the Christian message. When religion instrumentally becomes a tool for commercialization, the growth of faith intrinsically suffers and the issue of dilemma remains un-addressed.

In the words of Lugard: "---the groups of the south-east have no history before the coming of the Europeans" (Margery Perham, Lugard, "The Years of Authority", 1898-1945, P. 459). This did not mean the people had no history or not existed as a people. Rather, the issue of 'no history' refers to a written document or history of the people. The traditional homeland of the Igbo people of south-eastern Nigeria lies between the Niger and the Cross Rivers, though substantial minority lives to the west of the Niger. Like other groups whose limits are not defined by obvious natural boundaries, they tend to merge into neighboring peoples.

Some western Igbo communities have much in common with their Ishan neighbors. Northern Igboland merges into the kingdom of Igala, and a number of border towns, such as Ogurugu, are equally at home in both languages. In the southeast, Arochukwu, historically one of the most important settlements of Igbo states, forms a peninsular in Ibibioland. In the Delta, no simple generalizations are possible. The general pattern is one of ever increasing Igbo infiltration, a process expanded, though probably not begun, under the impact of the trans-Atlantic slave trade. The trading cities of the Delta drew much of their population from the Igbo hinterland, and are one of the most important of them, Bonny, gradually adopted the Igbo language. The history of the Igbo people is inextricably entwined with that of the Delta, though because the Delta has already been the subject of intensive historical study, its history forms but a subordinate theme of enquiry

This study is primarily concerned with those of the Igbo people who remained in their ancestral homeland. Nevertheless, we must not forget the Igbos of the Diaspora, the thousands of men and women who went as involuntary emigrants to the New World in the era of the slave trade. A few of these victims were recaptured from the slave master ships and resettled in Sierra Leone, where they formed, in the nineteenth century, a flourishing community with a strong sense of it's Igbo identity. Those who reached the Americans were soon cut off, of necessity, from the memory of their origins, and their history becomes one with that of the Afro-Americans. Today, most of these African Americans do not accept fellow blacks for the simple fact that they were sold into slavery and can't understand why they have come there to disturb them.

Danger of natural habitat

Like many African peoples, the Igbo lived in a difficult and unpromising natural environment. The Delta is an infertile waste of tortuous creeks and mangrove swamps. Much of the Igbo interior consisted originally of dense tropical rainforest, making both agriculture and communications difficult. Its soils are highly leached and acid ---among the poorest of Nigeria soils. To the north, the forest merges into orchard bush, a region of rolling hills, grasslands and, scattered trees, which homesick Englishmen have sometimes compared with the Downs of southern England. In the long years of their history, the Igbo people went to cultivate the whole of the forest, and, with the other peoples of the Delta, transformed a watery and unproductive wilderness into a network of wealthy enter pot city-state. Having gone through all these problems and built their faith on what has worked for them, in the midst of their suffering and poverty, to tell them of a religion that has no bearing with their history, will always constitute a dilemma in its growth.

It was not until 1830 that Europeans discovered the course of the lower Niger, and thus set eyes for the first time on a few of the states of the Igbo interior. From then on, the world and other people have gradual and increasing knowledge of Igboland, and an increasing amount of documentation for its history, though it was not until the end of the century that they penetrated beyond the immediate hinterlands of the Delta and the Niger. Within the period that existed before the coming of the Europeans, the Igbo people of Nigeria had enjoyed a solidarity and community governed by the elders under the supervision of the ancestors. Any attempt to evangelize the people without first understanding the culture and nature of governance of the people will always lead to the dilemma in question.

Most of our discussions in this book deal with less than a hundred years of Igbo history. The history of the Igbo and their fore bearers go back four thousands years or more. But unfortunately, most of these historical facts are shrouded in obscurity, and is likely to remain so. We have three main sources of information about the Igbo past before the nineteenth century - the findings of archaeology, the oral traditions of the Igbo people themselves, and the observations of European visitors to the Delta. Each of these deals with a different time frame, and provides different kinds of information, so that it is difficult to combine them in a satisfactory synthesis. This inability to study the differences that have guided the people all these times constitutes obstacles for the growth of the Christian religion as well.

In this light, archaeological findings in Igboland go back as far as four thousand years. But archeology in the area is still in its infancy. Its flourishing growth was sadly disrupted by the events of recent years, as one of the lesser casualties of war. Only a few sites have been excavated, but these have yielded material of enormous significance, which has, in some respects, transformed our knowledge of the Igbo past. It seems likely that systematic archeological work in Igboland in the future will add greatly to our understanding of its history, though there are, of course, major limitations to the kind of information which the remains of material cultures can supply.

Elements of migration and language

Europeans began to visit the Delta towards the end of the fifteenth century. Their accounts are invaluable for the history of the Delta, and thus relevant to Igbo history, but they never visited the Igbo interior, and whatever they said about it was a generalized hearsay. The use of oral traditions presents special difficulties in the Igbo context, which are described more fully in the subsequent chapters. These issues spring largely from the fact that Igboland of Nigeria was not a centralized state, but consisted of a very large number of independent and relatively small political bodies. Their number makes the scientific study and collation of their traditions difficult, and their complicated and democratic systems of government were not particularly conducive to the systematic preservation of knowledge about the past that has equally infiltrated into the areas of religion.

There is one Christian faith or religion but practiced differently. The manner in which the Christian message was presented has led to religious bigotry whereas the Igbo traditional religion reflected holistically the faith of the people. However, perhaps the key difficulty is the near - impossibility of establishing a reliable chronology for each set of traditions - a necessary prelude to understanding their mutual relationship to external influences, such as the impact of the slave trade. Moreover, like all oral traditions they tend to preserve certain kinds of information only – such as the ones relating to the town's foundation, and its major wars.

Therefore, any piece of information based on these types of sources, forms, or the bases will differ from one another. The history of many people begins with a migration, and a founding father. The legacy of such founding fathers or original inhabitants affects the manners they perceive and practice their belief systems. But the available evidence suggests that the Igbo and their forbearers have lived much of their present homes from the dawn of human history. The fact that they and their neighbors speak differently but related languages points to this conclusion. Interpretation of language can also create religious dilemma in the growth of the Christian faith in Igboland. After all, most of the interpreters the westerners employed were not educated enough to understand what they were saying.

Consequently, as elaborately discussed within the cultural ambience of the people of Igboland, the missionary presence in Igboland of Nigeria, from 1885-1906 has great impact on the religious consciousness of the people of Igboland. Earlier to the period stated, Edmund Campion lamented: "We came but for souls, that was all our commission" (Edmund Campion at his trial, in 1581). The middle 1880s saw a radical change in the character and context of missionary activity in Igboland. For the past thirty years, it had been the preserve of Sierra Leonian agents of the Church Missionary Society, working within the framework, not of colonialism, but of autonomous African states. Now, both the agents of missionary work and the context of their endeavors were to change because of circumstances. They came for souls in Edmund Campion's words, but the after effect of their activities proved otherwise.

Two new missionary societies began work in Igboland. Both of them were Catholics - the Congregation of the Holy Ghost and the Society of African Missions on one side and the C.M.S, Niger Mission on the other. However, both of them were so challenged by troubles, which afflicted them that they became to all intents and purposes a new mission. Only the C.M.S churches in the Delta, which responded to these trials by creating an independent Pastorate, carried on the old tradition of Sirra Leonian missionary work. They were to consolidate the pioneering work of Igbo oil trader- missionaries, establishing catechists and churches in the southern Igbo oil markets. The cash oriented nature of establishment challenged the growth of the religion in question.

Elements of monopoly of the Christian mission in Africa

The history of the C.M.S Niger Mission in the nineties is one of slow and painful reconstruction from a state to utter ruin. The critics themselves soon left the mission. Some died or were invited back home, others were dismissed, or resigned in pique or disillusion, and for a time Archdeacon Dobinson was their only survivor on the Niger. More agents were sent from England, many of them were women, but high rate of turnover and frequent home leaves inevitably introduced an element of change and instability. As before, the mission was weakened by the absence of its Bishop. For the European who succeeded Crowther, Bishop Tugwell was based in Lagos, and the twin chimeras of Prohibition and the Conversion of Hausa-land deflected his energies.

The tragedies and injustice of the eighties have tended to obscure the achievements of those who came afterwards. This should not be so. The group included Dobinson himself, a marvel of self-control, patience, and love that won the confidence of the Igbo people to a singular degree, and Archdeacon Dennis, who continued the work of translation which Dobinson began, and whose achievements, affectionately embroidered with legend, are well preserved in oral tradition. Sidney Smith and George Basden, who also came at this time, were both destined to crown long years of work in Igboland by writing substantial studies of Igbo life. We quoted George Basden and his excellent contributions in this part of the globe – Igboland of Nigeria. Several West Indians of African decent also joined the mission – just as they had played a major role in the era of European leadership. Typically, they were men of little education, who had worked for the Royal Niger Company as gardeners, carpenters, or servants.

By 1907, there were seventy such Igbo agents in the mission. Their Catholic rivals claimed, doubtless with some exaggeration, that eight out of ten Protestant converts became polygamists. In Asaba, the mission gained accessions from slaves, who gladly attended church merely to please the Oyibos - who had delivered them from death. This attitude by which some people wanted to identify with the leaders of the Church, in a way, led to the dilemma of the growth of the Christian religion. In other words, hypocrisy does not advance religious practices. As it were, 1884 brought an end to the C.M.S's long monopoly of mission work on the lower Niger. Monopoly has never encouraged diversities, progress and division of labor. The Society of African Missions decided to establish a station there when the river was still an arena of Anglo-French commercial company, but when the first band of three reached Lokoja, towards the end of 1884, they found the French on the point of leaving. The more fundamental difficulty was the inherent one of obtaining converts to Christianity in a Muslim area. The presence of the Muslim in Nigeria created a big division among people, and eventually affected unity of belief in the true religion. This division has reached a high-water mark leading to killing of innocent souls.

The Holy Ghost Fathers, coming to the lower Niger a little later, in 1885, and established the first Catholic mission in Igboland. They, too, did so at the invitation of a French trading company. It was originally intended to settle at the confluence, but transport difficulties, created by the Royal Niger Company's hostility, defeated them, and they went no further than Onitsha. There, they obtained land through the good offices of the aged Bishop Crowther, to whom it was already credited to have said that: "I acquired this land for God's cause, take it". This pleasant and amicable relationship was to continue, though the C.M.S might well have resented their settlement at a well - established center of Protestant mission work, when so many towns lacked missionary activity altogether.

Both the Society of African Missions and the Congregation of the Holy Ghost Fathers were founded in France in the middle years of the nineteenth century. It was part of a sudden upsurge of interest in foreign missions. However, this has often been explained in terms of the growth of interest in colonies abroad, but which was in reality, like the Evangelical revival, a complex social phenomenon deserving more searching analysis from historians.

By 1906, there were probably, at the outside, 6,000 Igbo children at school. The numbers are large in comparison with the nineteenth century progress. But this insignificant number represents only a tiny minority of Igboland's children. We have examined the pattern of moving frontiers, by which colonial rule was established in Igboland, and the important variable of missionary influence. We shall turn to the question: "What extent did these actually affect the lives of the Igbo people in their religious perspectives".

Radical change from missionary activity

The white man brought Christianity to Igboland of Nigeria. They were white missionaries and not blacks. They came in with the Irish mentality and demeanor. Many Igbo people perceived them as ordinary men who carried out an extraordinary mission. They proposed and legislated on how the people should live, pray and govern. They also enshrined the radical notion that each human soul has intrinsic worth and values, a value not to be determined by inheritance or obtained after birth, but present from the very beginning. This radical notion brought a sense of concern to the traditional Igbo people/person who believed in the ancestral connection with their Chi – Obioma - God, or Chukwu - the Supreme Being who has endowed them with the potentials inherent in their being. It is the belief of the Igbos that every human being has equal worth and value, and therefore created equally, especially in terms of morality and righteousness. On the level of status, achievement and destiny, each person is different and unique. Hence, the Igbo say: "Nkpisi aka ise ahaghi out", meaning that the five fingers are not equal. We observed it already that "akaraka di icheiche" which means that peoples' destinies are different. That was the point Achebe argued in 'Things Fall Apart' that the determinant of individual achievement in life is a person's "chi" – the personal god. In his argument, if one's 'chi' says "yes", then all goes well for one, if not, one experiences bad fortune. The inequality of personal destiny and achievement is dramatized in the philosophy of "osu" caste system where the "diala" – the freeborn of the land are differentiated from those sacrificed to the gods.

Historically, the Igbo people are people of great culture and tradition before the advent of Christianity. This is the culture that deals with their religion and tradition. It is on this issue of equality between people of color that made the Igbo people to say that " Bekee- bu-agbara, and Igbo bu – muo", meaning that the white man is a deity, and the Igbo is a spirit. It is on this light, according to Nwachukwu, that the Igbo people see: "Religion in the indigenous Igbo culture is not an independent institution, but an integral and inseparable part of the entire Igbo culture and tradition" (Nwachukwu, 2002). One may likely ask the question: "Is there something that is 'created equal' we do not understand or know about?"

According to Huckabee in his book titled "Do the Right Thing Inside the movement that bring common sense back to America" stated: "We hold these truths to be self-evident that all men are created equal, that they are endowed by their creator with certain unalienable Rights, that among these are life, liberty and the pursuit of Happiness" (Huckabee, Mike, 2008, IR). With this phrase, we can argue that by nature we are created equal, but either by design or accident we find ourselves on these inequality among different races like the Irish missionaries who brought Christianity and colonization into Igboland of Nigeria.

Elements of colonization/ignorance

The first signs of colonization came to Igbo land when the first white man appeared at Onitsha town. Onitsha was prominent and comfortable for the white man because of her closeness to the ocean, the River Niger. When the first white man arrived, the elders of the town consulted the oracle and were told that others would soon follow the white man like him, and that he would destroy their way of life, culture and tradition, so the people got hold of him and killed him. It is possible to underline the role of ignorance in the belief system of a people, like that of the Igboland at that time. However, ignorance still plays major role in the dilemma of the growth of the Christian faith in Igboland today. Not long after the people killed the first white man that visited the Igbo territory, other white men arrived, and in revenge to the killing of their fellow white man, they massacred most of the people of the village, mainly their leaders. When the white men eventually settled, they instilled a religion that encouraged peace as the beginning stages of colonization. If they could change the fundamental beliefs of the tribe, they thought, then they could control the natives more easily. The initial seed of discord sown by these early missionaries was not meant to advance the growth of the Gospel message they brought to the people.

The introduction of a foreign element or religion seemed to tear the structural fabric of the Igbo society, her tradition and culture apart to a great extent. This new religion introduced by the missionaries brought a serious separation, division and war among the people. This division in question can be traced back or likened to the scriptures when Christ paradoxically said that he did not come to bring peace in the world, but sword and division (Mt 10: 34-38). This new religion introduced by the white men according to Chinua Achebe in his book called " Things Fall Apart" led to the separation of Okonkwo from his son Ikemefuna (Achebe, Chinua 1959). There was a weekly ritual that the entire Igbo community was supposed to observe before the arrival of the white men. Every morning, the head of every family before breakfast would do a libation with the palm wine or hot drink called 'snap'. The libation is in form of prayer, by which Chukwu - the Supreme Being is praised for guiding and bringing the entire family into a new day.

Also before the planting season begins, the head of the family must perform a ritual to the earth goddess for kindness, gentleness and peace of the village and for a bumper harvest. Anyone who breaks this law was forced to offer sacrifices to the earth goddess as sin offering and repentance. But with the introduction of the new religion, these important values began to be questioned. Yet, the white man did not follow the people from family to family or village to village as to know whether they practiced their traditional religion or not. That they taught the people a new religion due to ignorance of the prevailing one does not necessarily hold them accountable for the dilemma in the growth of the religion or faith they brought to Igboland. The people did not understand the missionary implication or why they should change a religion that has protected them for life.

Cultural conflicts, encounters/religious bigotry

The Igboland's confrontation with an alien culture and religion, its conquest, and the experience of alien rule that seemed to have created a spiritual and intellectual crisis among the Igbo were factors for which this topic was urgently necessitated. The missionary presence and the success of British arms, with which they were inevitably associated, challenged the inherited certainties and values of traditional religion. The spread of Christianity in Igboland and elsewhere, Islam, has been explained as a dimension of that enlargement of scale we have already had occasion to refer to. The remoteness of the traditional High God, and the active role of lesser spirits, reflected the essential local nature of traditional life. As the walls protecting the microcosm dissolve, local spirits lose their validity. Only the High God - the Supreme Being Chukwu remains.

The impact and presence of mutually seeming antagonistic missionary societies in Igboland at that time created its own problems, and consequently contributed to the decline of the Christian growth at the very beginning of Christianity in Igboland of Nigeria. An individual's denominational loyalties were usually decided by chance - the denomination of the school one attended, or the mission established in ones area and whether ones parents were Christians or not. Some were seriously troubled by the white man's criteria for accepting people based on religious bigotry or the religion they brought to the people.

We have a record of one village schoolmaster's adventures in comparative religion. There was a case reported by one of the early missionaries that brought a sharp division between the Catholics and Protestants. The report runs as follows:

> *When I was taking up my scholars in lesson there we read in history about Henry VIII. How he, on account of a wife established a new church on earth, which was known to be The C.M.S. After school I called the scholars to my house and said, that I "think" we have found out the true Church" (Internet resource).*

Denominationally, this statement angered the Non-Catholics but emboldened those who believe that the Catholic Church was the only true religion founded by Christ on earth. Not minding the conflict that surfaced, most of the scholars accepted what the teacher had instructed them. That misgiving still rears its ugly head in the relationship between the Catholics and the protestant.

Religion, as it were, became one of the causes of the dimensions of the uncertainties plaguing the growth of the Christian faith. Unlike the traditional religion, there are no doubts as if the ancestors and the Supreme God established their religion. The overthrow of Igboland's politics, the power of the Oyibo with his different values and irresistible technology, the rapid rise of skills which could be utilized in the new system - all these seemed to throw the entire inherited order of the Igboland into a question. Traditional society was based on a network of commonly accepted values, duties and expectations. There was no confusion as what constituted a crime or sin in Igbo traditional religion. Everybody knew the correct thing to do to please or offend the ancestors or the land.

Unfortunately, with the advent of the white man in Igboland of Nigeria, the fabric seemed to have been threatened. The first major novel by an Igbo man—Chinua Achebe's Things Fall Apart - derived both its title and its epigraph from the imagery of a European poet, "Things Fall apart; the center cannot hold" when mere anarchy is loosed upon the world. And if these intangibles of inner experience are more readily captured in the poet's or the novelist's imagery, they belong, nevertheless, as much as palm oil exports or road construction, to the realities of the historical past. For the people, religion meant life and stability.

This was precisely why the book looked into the derogatory use of the term Osu, Ume, Diala and other caste systems in Igboland of Nigeria. Everybody is a child of God, whether in the Christian context or the Igbo traditional set ups. Also the discriminatory impact against women, and the widowhood practices that have contributed immensely to the dilemma of the growth of Christian faith in Igboland need to be revisited by both religions. The Osu caste system, an indigenous religious belief system, practiced within the Igbo nation, it's discriminatory, dehumanizing and obnoxious practices as already noted here have really divided and alienated the Igbos from the tenets of the Christian religion. The people referred to by these names are regarded as sub-human being, the unclean class, or slaves in their own land. Until such matters condemned by Christianity are reflected in the lives of the people, Christianity will always remain a predicament in Igboland of Nigeria.

Elements of discrimination among citizens

In this book, I will employ the use of the term 'Osu' within the context of Ngor Okpala people to describe all the lower caste groups in Igboland. It should be noted that in their hierarchy of social status, the Ume (especially, in the author's community) belongs to the Osu class, while the Diala abhors any interactions or socialization with them. The story of the human race, from age to age, is full of the struggle to enjoy certain fundamental rights. These rights include freedom from inhuman treatment; freedom from slavery; freedom from discrimination, freedom of thought, assembly and association and other rights that are "reasonably justifiable in a democratic society" (Azikiwe 1965:455). Thus, any culture or tradition that bridges people's freedom or association violates their human and civil rights.

The discriminatory Osu caste system in Igboland of Nigeria is an example of such tradition and culture that bridges the people's rights to free association. This is an insult to human race, and it is disheartening to say the least. Besides some government laws and ecclesiastical efforts to give this ugly practice a mortal blow, these suspicions practices affect the growth of any religion, let alone Christianity that emphasizes unity and love of one's neighbors. It is sad to note that since 27 (Twenty-seven) years after the ratification of the Convention on the Elimination of Discrimination against Women (CEDAW) in 1985 without reservations, Nigerians are still practicing discrimination against the women and children of the Country. Pride and ignorance of the essence of life are parts of the major causes for these beliefs and practices. The worst form of this discrimination is the fact that a family of eight female children, without a male child, is still regarded as having no children or child. Thanks to the hard economy, things are changing and many women are becoming more relevant in families than some men.

Again, many women have made contributions towards the scope of religious influences in the progress and peace of any culture. In our own context, this book investigates and asks the basic questions as whether the Christian faith in Igbo land is actually in dilemma or not or whether nothing can be done to save it from such dilemma. Our research question has thrown some light in this regard as we shall see later on. There are no gainsaying that there are merits and demerits of Christianity in Igboland of Nigeria. Nevertheless, I will still insist that the Igbo people are learned and intelligent people. By now, they should have understood the main thrust of the Christian religion and stuck a balance or drew a spiritual map of their stand on the issue.

The book has shown that with the advent of Christianity, the traditional and religious sensibilities of the Igbo people were disrupted, no doubts, like in any situation where change is evident. The culture of the people seemed to have been swept away. The missionaries did not seem to see any values in the Igbo people's way of life. Commenting on these unhealthy missionary activities, Edmund Ilogu stated:

> *With the arrival of the missionaries and traders from 1857 onwards, the neat Pattern became disturbed. Plurality of religious and value concepts appeared for the first time to start the rapid change that has been going on in Igboland ever since then, although more rapid at some periods than others (Ilogu, Edmund, 1974:63).*

We have to look into the impact of Christianity in Igboland as it brought some sweeping changes in the religious beliefs of the people. With these changes, the idea of living in conformity with the laws of the land, which is an aspect of their religion and salvation, is equally affected.

Therefore, in this book, we attempted to find out whether the civilization and colonization of Igbo people is the same thing as their evangelization. As Odiegwu would describe it:

> *African traditional religion practiced by some Africans before the advent of Christianity in the continent has immense symbols, values that could enrich us as Christians today (Odiegwu, Donatus 1997:36).*

The question that strongly stares us in the face is: "Where are those African values and symbols?" What do we say of the Igbo people whose traditional and religious values had for a very long time, defined and formed vis-à-vis the Christian message? How far have the Igbo people completely abandoned their traditional religion to embrace Christianity?

Due to the syncretistic attitude of some of the people of Igbo towards their stand on both the Christian and traditional religions, it becomes difficult for somebody to properly understand how they appreciate the meaning of faith and belief in the Supreme Being - Chiukwu. This un-steadfastness in the religious consciousness of some of the people of Igboland and the lack of conviction to believe as salvific, in a particular religious tradition make this study difficult and here lies the dilemma in question. Has the Christian message changed the ways of Igbo people, their traditional belief in the ancestors, Chukwu, customs and mode of worship?

As a consequence, we are bound to investigate into the cause of this religious paradox and make attempts to proffer a solution. The main thrust of this book is the examination of the meaning and implication of the concept "Faith" in the African and Christian religious tradition in the light of the religious practices of the people of Igboland. This includes the study of the similarities and differences in the concept "faith" in various religious traditions of the world. We intend, by this analysis to enhance the knowledge of the word Christian faith among the Igbo in particular and world religions in general.

On the other hand, we shall examine to what extent the Christian faith has encouraged traditional beliefs and religion of the Igboland of Nigeria, especially as they affect the people of Ngor Okpala today. As such, we substantially borrowed some leaves from Nwachukwu's work on "Salvation in African context" and "Keeping Human Relationships Together" as already noted. Call this approach a critique or analysis; Nwachukwu's work is an invaluable tool in the investigation of the issue at hand.

Elements of Misrepresentation/Interpretation

Our primary reason for being systematic in handling this issue is to demonstrate the importance of religious values in the life of any Christian or believer. We cannot blame the missionaries who brought or introduced the Christian religion to the Igbo of Nigeria. From our investigation, they did not actually mean to destroy the people or plant seeds of discord among them. They introduced the Christian religion as a chief religion that had no equals. This religious bigotry blinded them from accepting the traditional religion and values of the Igbo for what they were. They thought they had brought light to a people who had been in darkness for ages. Unfortunately, the light of God had shown in the people's culture of hospitality, extended family systems, customs, and in such values as truth, unity, peace, and forgiveness, settlement of land disputes, native laws and ways of governance; convening a gathering in case something went wrong in the land before Christianity came.

The issue is that the Igbo of Nigeria had practised a religion that sustained and defined them as a people. If for no other reasons, the Igbo see themselves as religious people. To introduce another religion in their land needed to be done with uttermost care and diligence. But the missionaries did not see it that way. They thought they were bringing the original and real religion that could save people from their sins. This very method itself was against the people's spirit of solidarity in which the voices of one another were welcomed and heard. On the other hand, the implanters presumed that they did not need to listen to any other voice except what they wanted their interpreters to tell the people. Besides, most of those interpreters had no basic education and could not represent the white people properly. In a simple language, damages were unconsciously implemented instead of progress. The people were not dunces as the missionaries thought them to be.

The Igbo were very intelligent and in control of their culture. To have acted otherwise was brutal and misleading. Instead of dealing with the problems of the people, they unintentionally compounded them. That was the point Au, Wilkie meant when reiterating: "The failure to deal with problems of human growth weakens apostolic effectiveness" (Au, Wilkie, 1989:219). The apostolic zeal with which the early missionaries embarked upon in bringing the Christian faith to Igboland did not initially encourage religious advancement. In support of this line of argument, Emile Louis Victor de Lavelaye seemed to be referring to the situation at hand when he emphatically observed:

> *If Christianity were taught and understood comfortable to the spirit of its Founder, the existing social organism could not exist a day (Emile Louis Victor de Lavelaye, cited in Mead S. Frank, 1965:55).*

The simple interpretation judging from what Emile has noted is that Christianity is never introduced, presented or understood by the people due to the manner it was originally brought to the people.

The same problem has continued to rear its ugly head till tomorrow among the people themselves. For instance, when every religious group claims to be right and authentic in her teaching and practices, crimes remain unchecked. This is the big problem the book has to explain also. It was basically due to this missionary misnomer that an Indigenous African and Nigerian writer, Chinua Achebe made this elaborate statement:

Does the white man understand our custom about our land?
How can he when he does not even speak our tongue? But he
says that our customs are bad; and our own brothers who have
taken up his religion also say that our customs are bad. How
do you think we can fight when our own brothers have turned
against us? The white man is very clever. He came quietly and
peaceably with his religion. We were amused at his foolishness
and allowed him to stay. Now he has won our brothers, and
our clan can no longer act like one. He has put a knife on the
things that hold us together and we have fallen apart (Chinua,
Achebe. 1994:176).

There is no gainsaying that the sentiments Achebe articulated here best describes the situation at hand. The White man had no blames. That they did not understand us was not necessarily their fault. The only mistake they made in this regard was to enter into another man's territory without first studying their culture and likes and taboos. In this way, it is easy to determine how the missionary impacts in Igboland affected the growth of their religion there. Such missionary methodology can equally create a dilemma in interpersonal relationships.

A closer examination of the religious and traditional practices of the Igbo of Nigeria will be of immense asset to discover the various damaging effects the Christian religion has had on the growth of their religion and that of Christianity. This type of situation is not limited to Igboland alone. So many cultures of the world experience the same plight. For instance, the world has witnessed the effect of radical Moslem religion and its terrorist mission today. The Moslem religion per se is not bad; extremists have dragged the good values to the mud due to misinterpretation and wrong application of the tenets of the religion. Unlike in the African traditional setup, the people share certain universal values that go beyond any particular religion.

Practically, the people strongly hold to their belief in one Supreme Being and in such principles and values such as truth, justice, peace, hospitality, unity, love, honesty, humility, respect for the elderly, human life and dignity et cetera. These values are not measured by any one religion. They are such that could bring peace and harmony in any form of religion be it Hinduism, Buddhism, Islam, Christianity or African traditional religion. These values became thwarted and muddled because of human mismanagements and egocentric reasoning. If the missionaries had carried out some fieldwork or investigations and studies on the culture of the people, the matter could not have been what it is today.

Worse still, the whole evangelical mission seemed to have been presented within the context of civilization and development and not necessarily religious. That was the point Iluogu was making when he analyzed the arrival of the Missionaries and traders from 1857 onwards and how the neat pattern of the Igbo became disturbed. Also, plurality of religious and value concepts appeared for the first time to start the rapid change that has been going on in Igbo land ever since then till today.

In a more reflective manner, this work has raised serious theological questions as whether the Igbos would be better off without the Christian religion than experiencing the present dilemma of religious practices.

No religion could replace the values that have formed the people for ages, be it heavenly oriented or earthly. The people's values themselves are saving and eschatological too. In this light, Onwubiko, an indigenous Igbo writer maintained that:

> *In the traditional African societies, there were no atheists. This is because religion, in the indigenous African culture, is not an independent institution. It is an integral and inseparable part of the entire culture.... This is because social morality is dependent on religion" (Onwubiko, A. Oliver, 1991:23).*

Practically, if the Igbo of Nigeria have lacked anything in their lives as noted earlier, it was not in the area of religion or their belief in their God. What Elizabeth Isichei recorded about a German Missionary in Aboh in 1841 concerning the same Igbo people, is in strong support of our position in this work. Thus:

> *The Igbos are in their way a religious people - the word 'Tshukwu' (Chukwu-God) is continually heard. Tshukwu is supposed to do everything...Their notions of some attributes of the Supreme Being are, in many respects, correct, and their manner of experiencing striking. God made everything: He made both black and white is continually on their lips. Some of their parables are descriptive of the perfections of God (Isichei, Elizabeth, 1977:24).*

Surprisingly, the dilemma of the growth of the Christian message, faith and religion sprang up when some of the people who have been calling on the name of God saw him and refused to accept him fully in their hearts. That was the beginning of the problem. If the Christian message has been presented within the context of what the people already knew, the dilemma in question could not have been there. Even if elements of confusion crept up in the practice of the faith, as it is the situation today, it could have been minimal and relative.

In order to justify our enquiry, there is need to re-emphasize and have a comprehensive knowledge of the Igbo of Nigeria. As cited in Nwachukwu's book or survey on human relationships and incorporated in his work on Salvation in African Context, 2002, Nigeria is located in West Africa and shares land borders with the Republic of Benin in the West, Chad and Cameroon in the East, and Niger in the North. The territory of the Igbo land shares boundaries with Igala in the North, Isoko in the East, Ijawu/Itsekiri in the West and Urobhro in the South. The Igbo people of East-Southern Nigeria are generally homogenous – one language, one color, one belief system with slight dialectical differences, hence a bit heterogeneous. This was the situation before Christianity surfaced in Igboland. The people of Ngor Okpala in particular, share the same socio-religious, economic, political, ethical and moral principles.

The oneness of the Igbo people is something that should be encouraged in Christianity today. Their cosmology, epistemology, spirituality and anthropology are geared towards living in peace with God and humanity. Therefore, any religion that comes to them should encourage these basic values and not create confusions and problems. That was why Kinzer noted that:

The general shift in society from committed personal groupings [such as kinship and neighborhood groups] to more impersonal institutional settings has probably increased our modern problems with self-worth" (Kinzer, Mark. 1980:25).

The communal, collectivistic, interdependent structural lives of the people of Igboland distinguish and place them as unique from the rest of the western culture.

In the words of Ilogu, "Communality is the essence of the gods. They are the common possessions and guardians of all. No person alone sins against the gods. Punishment for one man is visited on all. The blessings of the gods are also shared by all" (Ilogu, Edmund C 1975:34-43). Unlike the Igbo, the westerners tend to emphasize individualistic and independent lifestyles. The impersonal institutional settings of the missionary activities in Igboland compounded some of the dilemma of the growth of the Christian faith there today. The Igbos are ontological people because whatever they do has remarkable reference to their future, abode with their God and ancestors. It was on this note that Basden made the following remarks about Igboland:

> *The ontological community denotes first and foremost ontological quality of human relations. It is ontological in so far as all members of the community are believed to descend from a common ancestor. Every man is linked to his parents on the natural level. His parents in turn are bound to their grand-parents, etc. This link which binds all members of the same family by propagation is broadened to include all members of the community or clan who are believed to be descendants of the same ancestor. Everyone considers himself as member of a definite community and as part of the whole, (Basden, 1966:122).*

Because the Igbos share a common cultural identity and vision, anything that happens to a member of the family or community is regarded and treated as affecting the rest of the people.

Their entire cosmology, ideology and belief systems are deeply "within the ambience of ancestral community life or in solidarity with the Umunna or community" (Nwachukwu, 2002:341). Goodness is praised as the basis of life and morality is synonymous with and the ingredient of this life. This is the way of life or pattern bequeathed to them by their God and ancestors. Based on these fundamentals, one can imagine how successful the Christian message will become in Igboland.

Consequently, to perceive any religion whether it is Christian or traditional that violates the ethical standards of Igboland is seen as a big threat to the ancestors who are the role models of religion and morality. (Nwachukwu, DLM, GTF, on the "Ethics of Aristotle", July 2007). In this light, Odiegwu was right to say that: "African Traditional religion practiced by some Africans before the advent of Christianity in the continent has immense symbols, values that could enrich us as Christians today (Odiegwu, Donatus 1997:36). The one million questions include: "Why has it not achieved this aim or enriched us?" As it were, there is every need to study some of those values of the Igbos that seem to have been neglected by the missionary and why the people considered them a dilemma in the growth of their faith.

Our suspicions are tantamount to what Ilo Chu observed in reference to the situation in Igboland. According to that observation: "There were obviously many things that the missionaries did, which in the light of today's thinking would be considered inappropriate. Whatever way of life or custom the missionaries did not understand, they often condemned in Africans as fetish and pagan" (Ilo Chu Stan, 2006:73). The big question that arises from what Ilo has noted is: "What are those things that the missionary did that if it were today would have been considered inappropriate and why they were taken that way in those days?"

On the same par, to this seeming predicament, Norman suggests that the human brain is not static but always in motion, undergoing or carrying a series of activities that shape the mind. In other words, once the mind is shaped, it discovers what is and makes decisions to act on a particular object or not. The people of Igboland could not have acted on what they did not understand initially. They welcomed the new religion which came in the form of civilization, bringing the opportunities of education, hospitals or health care, emphasizing hygiene of the physical environments, putting on of good wears etc. In a situation like that when the hungry were fed, the homeless given a place to rest, it was not proper or reasonable to begin to reject anything. It was later, as Norman noted, when the brain was fully activated to face the challenges of daily life that the people began to cry out. In the light of what we have just noted here, Norman has this to say:

> *The conventional answer of scientists has been that the human brain, from which all thought and action emanate, produces culture...Culture is not just produced by the brain; it is also by definition a series of activities that shape the mind... We become cultured through training in various activities, such as customs, arts, ways of interacting with people...learning of ideas, beliefs, shared philosophies, and religion (Norman, Doigde. 2007:287).*

Eventually, we are faced with the challenges of digging out the root cause of the predicaments of the growth of the Christian faith in Igboland as we have already observed some of them. Now, let us review most of the traditional values and beliefs of the Igbo people as Prof. Nwachukwu had already outlined in his book "Salvation in African Context" and "Keeping Human Relationships Together". I totally agree with the approach Nwachukwu employed in his analysis of the whole scenarios that took place between the missionaries and the Igbo people. The first one we have to consider here is:

"Symbol of Authority and Justice [Ofo na Ogu]"

The issue of *Ofo na Ogu or* authority and justice is a value shared by both Christianity and the traditional people of Igboland. Then how did this important value in the life of human beings become a problem? Can there be order or progress in human condition without these values? "Authority" according to Nwachukwu and the Igbo in general does not literally refer to political leadership or power to rule and control. It is understood in the context of integrity and truthfulness. The value of *Ofo na Ogu* stands for "justice" and "truthfulness" in the religious and day-to-day life of the people. They equally serve as the yardstick for measuring the truth of religious faith and practice. It is impossible to authentically practice any religion without [Ofo na Ogu] justice and truthfulness in it.

This is "justice" in a strict sense, by which eternity, our God or ancestors control human affairs and judge humanity at large. In line with what Ihuoma noted earlier, why do many Christians disregard their Bible when they want to carry out their obnoxious acts or evil intentions, but fear the value of *"Ofo na Ogu"* especially when it is invoked in settling cases in the land? Something is being revealed there. By simple implication, the "Ofo na Ogu" represents an undeniable value that cannot be joked with even by ardent Christians. As it were, when honest and good people observe how such traditional values as mentioned above are being respected more than those of the Christian values of "love and unity" the growth of the faith is hampered. Specifically speaking, the Traditional O*fo* is of three types. According to Nwachukwu:

> *The ancestral One (Ofo Ndichie); that of a medicine man or chief priest of a shrine (Ofo Nwadibia or Ezemmuo) and the One belonging to titled men (Nze na ozo). To hold an Ofo, which is in a form of carved object, is to hold Ogu. Any object or symbol could be used for it today. Ofo is the symbol of Authority and (na) Ogu means Justice or Truthfulness. The two can be used interchangeably. The Ofo is "the authority of the ancestors that is being handed down from one generation to the other"* *(Nwachukwu, 2002:129).*

Besides the traditional O*fo* there is *ofo* with small letter "*o*" which represents the staff of an office or the authority of the custodian who is the boss. As can be observed in many offices as in the government quarters, anybody, man or woman can handle it.

According to Emean, the "*Ofo Nwadibia, Nzenaozo, Ezemmuo*" can be thrown away at the death of the custodian, but that of *Ndichie* passes from one *Opara* to another for posterity, (Emean, 1998:22). The Ofo is a binding force between the spiritual world and the physical world. It unites the body and spirit of everybody in the community. In this understanding Uchendu said: "Community spirit is very strong among the Igbos. Almost from the first born, the individual is aware of his dependence on his kin group and his community" (Uchendu, V. C., 1965:34). This communal spirit and life are the forces that guide and bind the people of Igboland of Nigeria.

Today while some people, mainly the Christians kick against the use of "Ofo na Ogu" because the missionaries branded it fetish, why will any honest person not see reasons for living truthfully a life guided by justice and peace. This is where I disagreed with Nwachukwu. While Nwachukwu seemed to be shifting the blames on the missionaries, the people themselves who know the values of these principles should not leave any stone unturned in perpetuating them in their lives. Yes, the missionaries did what they had got to do out of ignorance. If the people actually value truthfulness and justice, should they ascribe their failures to practice them to other people? There are no doubts that the traditional and Christian values have been mixed up to the point that many people are confused as regards the basic religious values to emphasize. Yet, to live or die should not depend on the missionaries who came to show them the way to Christianity, whether their method was objective or not.

Again, if the people really value their culture and life styles, they should be able to see the significance of these values also in the Christian message and Gospel of peace, love, unity and forgiveness. These are values the people of Igboland of Nigeria are bound to accept as authentic. These Christian values are so much in line with the traditional "Ofo na Ogu" and should jointly condemn such immoral acts as incest, theft, fighting, slander, and disrespect of gray hairs, dishonesty etc. To neglect them because of the inroads of the missionaries in Igboland of Nigeria is a dilemma the people have to solve themselves. That some of the elders themselves who are meant to be the custodians of justice and order in the community have equally derailed, points to the dilemma of the growth of the Christian faith in Igboland as well. The missionaries made mistakes, which we should have corrected by now.

"Council of elders/associations of first sons"

In line with this discussion, the next value we need to touch here is "the Council of Elders/Association of First Sons *(Ndi Opara)*." This is a council of elders whose records have been proven by the community. What qualifies one to become a member of this council of elders or group is not by one's affluence, election, appointment or religious affiliation. It is solely by old age accompanied with sound moral standard. Unlike today, according to Nwachukwu, money seems to constitute the basis for belonging to this group. It has to be noted that this group meets every eight-market day to look into common problems that might affect the peace and progress of the community at large.

According to Meek: "The Council of elders were a body of mediators and referees than of prosecutors and judges, and the community was Republican in the true sense of the term, that is, a corporation in which government was the concern of all" (Meek, 1943:130) and "the elders have their practical effect in the maintenance of custom and tradition" (Onwubiko, 1999:23). The function of the elders was specified and clear. They are meant to be exemplary human beings in the midst of some unpredictable members of the community. According to Nwachukwu in this long statement:

The associations of the first sons" which means ndi opara play almost the same role as the council of elders. The expression ndi opara is always in the plural form. All the well-behaved elderly male children besides the first sons, ndi opara, are automatically members of the council. That is why each family has an "elder" who might be that way by age, sound moral life or divine. For instance, every first male among his siblings belongs to the group of ndi opara. A father who is the second or third son of his own parents might not enjoy the privileges and rights of ndi opara, which is available to his own first son. However, the father of that first son may enjoy the privilege of belonging to the council of elders by age or moral standard and holds the Ofo na Ogu, meaning "truth and justice" the symbol of authority of his family till death. At the death of a father, the first son eventually takes up the responsibility of looking after his father's compound and holds the Ofo na Ogu. The Ofo na Ogu is ancestral power of governance over the family or community and there has never been any confusion as who holds it for any period of time. Such a situation helps to ensure peaceful relationships among the community or compound concerned. It equally works well in many families when responsibilities and duties are clearly shared (Nwachukwu, Book on human relationships and culled from his work of Salvation in the African Context. 2002).

Unfortunately, according to Nwachukwu, confusion emerged into the soil of the Igbo land of Nigeria with the advent of Christianity and civilization. Just as a titled and retired teacher from Ezinihitte of Igbo land of Nigeria, Nze Ogonna, representing large opinion of his people described the situation in these words: "The community is now against itself. Today, the educated and the so-called Christians are trying to nip all our customs and traditions in the bud" (Nze Ogbonna, 70, April 20, 2001 in Nwachukwu). This is where I am worried, to whom is the confusion in question allotted to? What was wrong in doing the right thing? Who told the council of elders to stop practicing justice and integrity in their lives? How did the community begin to act against one another? Which traditions, customs and values did the missionaries try to nip in the bud? That Christian fanatics began to question the role of the elders has nothing to do with Christianity.

If the people at a point abandoned their God and began to fight each other is their own problem and not that of Christianity. The missionaries did not teach the people of Igboland to steal, quarrel with one another, kill each other or commit incest and murder or things like that. Rather, the dilemma of the growth of the Christian faith arose because the people were challenged to face a new life some of them were not able to accept. This is where I completely disagreed with Nwachukwu. Let the people of Igboland tell themselves the simple truth. The elders could have been better equipped to handle certain traditional matters than they thought they did, if they had harkened to some of the teachings of Christianity. This failure to keep in touch with the basic tenets of Christianity created the dilemma and predicament of the practice of the faith in question not necessarily the incarnation of the Christian message itself.

"Belief in God or Chukwu"

The Belief in God *[Chukwu]* of the Igbos is another important value, which I would want us to study in this research work. The fact that the Igbo people of Nigeria had worshipped the Supreme Being before the advent of the Christian religion is not debated. The word *"Chukw"* as Isichie Elizabeth observed regarding the testimony of one of the early German missionaries (1841) in Igbo land was heard, practiced and lived. In the light of Nwachukwu's position which I agree with in the following long remarks. :

> *The name "Chukwu stands for God Almighty" (Parrinder, 1969:26-36), which is etymologically derived from two Igbo words: 'Chi' and 'Ukwu'. Chi with the capital letter "C" stands for God – Who, not only gives life to the individual but also assures his marked relationship and identity to the community. When Chi goes with the small letter "c" it points*

to the destiny of men and women (Basden, 1966:147). The word Ukwu *means "great", God Almighty hence we speak of* Chukwu, *the Supreme God of creation and salvation. These are solid and spiritual values, which both the Christians and the Traditionalists agree to. In the Old Testament of the Christian Bible, for instance, Moses tells the Israelites that: "Your God is the God of gods, the Lord of lords" (Deuteronomy 10:17). The above statement seems to apply and speak of smaller gods that minister under the umbrella of the Great God of Christianity and the Igbo of Nigeria. In both Traditions, there is only one Supreme God. (Cf. Nwachukwu, 2002).*

In the sense as observed above, when *Chukwu* or God is considered strictly as the Creator, the people call him *Chineke*, the God who creates, *Onye-Okike* – He, who alone creates (Ikenga-Metuh, 1981:24), but as the controller of the Universe, he is called *Osebuluwa*, the sustainer of the world, for without him, the world would not exist. Within the context of prayer he is addressed as *Obasi-din'elu* (the sky God). For the Christians, *Chukwu* or *Chineke* is the only name of God they know today which implies life in itself. The peoples' strong belief in their God is manifested in the names they give to themselves -Theo-phoric names, (God-related names), which mean much to them and explain how deeply; religiously and faithfully they are committed to their identity with the Supernatural. They are their names in actions and behaviors. They believe and act their names in their entire lives. Such names include:

Nwa-chukwu (the child of God), Odinaka-Chi (one's destiny/ being is at God's hands), Chukwu–di (God is) Chi-Nonso, (God is present, especially when Chi-amaka (God is good), Olu-chi (God's handiwork), Chi- bu-ike or Ike-chi (God is power or

God's power), Chi-nedu (God leads), Ekechi (Destiny orthe life
derived from God) et cetera (Nwachukwu, 2002)

For Ilogu the word "*Ekechi* refers to God-given lot to man" (Ilogu, 1975:41). Unlike Nwachukwu in his analytical presentation, if there were dilemma and confusions in Igboland in the practice of the Christian religion, they are not completely traceable to the missionaries. The mistakes the missionaries made were common human factors that could be expected in every interpersonal relationship. The fact that the people accepted to be baptized by foreign names was part and parcel of the missionary evangelical program. It was not aimed to hurt the people as such, even if part of such missions were materially oriented. There was no way the missionaries could have employed the native names for God when they did not understand what they meant. The Igbo were introduced into the life wire of the Christian religion, period.

The problems that arose in the course of the implantation of the faith were as the results of inadequate or lack of communication on both sides – partly on the missionaries and partly on the people themselves. Blames should be shared among them. To condemn the terrific efforts the missionaries made to cross the Atlantic to bring the Christian message and civilization to Igboland is not proper. Whether they had other hidden agendas before or behind their missionary zeal or not, are immaterial here. They came, took some of the hosts' treasures and left them with their own. Some even died on account of bringing the message to Igboland. Comparatively, the people of Igboland have tremendously benefited from the missionary activities, which no Igbo man or woman can deny today. Therefore, the predicament and dilemma in the growth of the Christian religion have to be sought from the disposition of a people who were not ready for a change.

Moreover, it is hard to determine how the missionaries could be responsible for the dilemma of the growth of the Christian faith in Igboland when the people were surrendered by a litany of gods and belief systems in them? For instance:

> There are a host of other gods working in collaboration with Chukwu, the Supreme God in maintaining order in the relationship of the people. These gods include Ala [the Earth goddess, spirit or mother], Ogu [the god of justice], Ofo [the god of righteousness], Ahianj-oku-ukwu [the god of Agriculture], Amadioha [the god of Thunder, Lighting, and vengeance against evil doers], Ajala [the first Son of Ala], Umumiri [the god of the river], Igwe [the sky god], Emeregini [the first son of Ogu] et cetera (Interview with Nwachukwu, J. U., 59, February 4, 1989 in Nwachukwu 2002).

Among the pantheon of divinities that reign in Igboland are also Ogwugwu, Ekiri, Agwu [the god of might, courage and valor]. With this litany of gods, it becomes evident that the Igbo people of Nigeria, particularly Ngor Okpala people, have strong belief, not only, in the Supreme and Almighty God but also in His agents.

Again, with the involvement of the Igbo people of Nigeria with the colonial masters and other regions in Nigeria who traded on slaves, they came in contact with gods other than theirs. According to Edward Nwachukwu in Nwachukwu:

> Among those gods, are Amadioha-Ozuzu in Etche, Ojukwu in the Rivers State, Igwe-kala in Umunoha of Mbaitolu, Onyi Ora in Nri near Oba, Agbala at Awka all in Anambra State, Imo–miri Ochi and the long Juju of Aro-chukwu known as chukwu Abiayamah in Abia State. Some call it Chukwu

> *Abiama. This very Juju, Voodoo or Agbara of Aro-Chukwu was*
> *regarded as the most dreadful and powerful in the then Eastern*
> *Region, (Interview with Edward Nwachukwu, Retired School*
> *Teacher, 78, April 8, 2000 in Nwachukwu).*

The conclusion in this regard is that the people believed in these gods and had regards for them. Then, how can the failure to practise the faith authentically be completely apportioned to the missionaries? It is easy to ask of the success of Christianity in this part of the globe. The Christian message is straightforward and targeted. Thus, the new belief systems or syncretistic practices of the people are the major sources of socio-religious conflicts among the people today and why the Christian religion cannot be allowed to produce the fruit that lasts forever.

"Belief in spirits"

The people's tenacious belief in the spirits is another problem why the Christian faith seems to be stagnated in Igboland. It was Parrinder who rightly stated that: "The belief in spirits is one of the basic qualities of West African religion" (Parrinder, 1969:26-36). There is need to find out if the same concept of spirit in Christianity is the same with that of traditional belief of the people of Igboland. Nwachukwu rightly put it this way:

> *Among the Igbo in general spirits are called Ndi-Mmuo – the*
> *invisible beings that are not seen or perceived. They are primarily*
> *in the invisible world called Ala-Mmuo - land of the spirits.*
> *This is in sharp contrast to the 'home of the living'- Ala-Madu.*
> *In his own observation, using the criterion of habitation, Ejizu*
> *presents the universe into two hemispheres: "The world of man*
> *and the world of spirit–beings" (Ejizu, 2000:49). The most*

significant feature of this perception and ordering of reality in terms of space is that according to Uchendu, there is constant interaction between the world of man and the world of the dead; the visible and invisible forces (Uchendu, 1965:11-12). In lkenga-Metuh's view, there are two kinds of spirits, the non-human spirits and the human spirits (Ikenga-Metuh, 1981:60-82). The non-human spirits include "Chukwu (God), Ndi-Mmuo (the spirits created by God) the spirit forces (Ikenga-Metuh, 1981:60-82, Consult Nwachukwu, 2002).

Some other non-human classes of spirits in this analysis include the spirits of *Ndi-ichie*, (Ancestors), the invisible powers and principalities that are supernatural in nature but manifest in human situations. Many Igbo people in Ngor Okpala believe that witches, sorcerers, diviners, water spirits, *Ndi-otu* (secret societies), medicine men, et cetera, do possess supernatural powers in their every day to day activity.

At this point, it is possible to guess the root cause of the dilemma in question. Too much ingredient spoils the soup. It is true that the missionaries introduced a different concept of the spirit - the Holy Spirits and the Guarding Angels. They did not tell the people of Igboland to abandon their own knowledge of spirits. To say that the people's beliefs got entangled with the introduction of the new ones as Nwachukwu purported in his work is to say the least. The belief in the spirit of the Igbo ancestors should not have created any dilemma in believing in the Holy Spirit of Christianity. To accuse the missionaries for implanting the seed of discord and hindrance to the growth of the faith in Igboland is not appropriate. In the first place, the missionaries had no knowledge of what spirits the Igbo had as to understand their significance in the lives of the people.

Just as in the case of Belief in Self-God [*Chi*] of Igboland of Nigeria, that is the way Christians are associated with his personal spirit. It is true that every individual in Igboland is believed to possess a spirit, a transcendental 'self-god' or guardian angel known as *Chi* who guides and leads him or her through the course of life. This is what Idowu calls the "inner man", the "essential person" and this is usually conceived as something, which man obtains from deity himself and ultimately, the account of how man uses his talent must be rendered before deity (Idowu, 1976:60). In Azorji's own understanding: "Because God created human beings, each has its own *Chi* [divineness]" (Azorji, 1976:172). lkenga-Metuh agrees with Idowu and Azorji and presents the spirit in these words: "*Chi* is characterized as the immanent presence of God in man or man's guardian angel in life (Ikenga-Metuh, 1981:68-69). "*Chi* is man's spiritual self, the guardian spirit of each individual person through life (Ejizu, 2000:57). "*Chi*" simply means 'spirit'. In a simple language, spirit is that part of a person which he or she shares with the gods or God or the ancestors in the African context.

Our concern here is to determine how the missionaries were blamed for the introduction of a different spirit that has created problem for the people of Igboland. The issue of spirit or chi is well known and believed in Igboland and this reflects in the God-related names they give to their children such as "*Chi-ma* [God knows, that is, his or her self-god, knows], *Chi-kwe* [if his god permits), *Chi-jioke* [one's fortunes are at the hands of one's God], *Chiawuotu* (people's gods differ), *Chi-naaka* [only God decides], *Chi-nasa* [only God answers] et cetera (Nwachukwu, 2002). In other words, if the word "chi" or spirit stands for the individual self, how come that confusion emerged from it? If actually people can trust their spirit as their own values, they will be able to understand the need to appreciate the spirit of Christianity that talked of oneness and love.

"Belief in the ancestors"

The people's belief in the ancestors is another one that needs to be considered here. The ancestors are the role models of the Igbo. They guide and protect lives. Ejizu says that the ancestors represent another section of the same community in the spirit world and the concern of the living is equally their own concern (Ejizu in Azorji, 1976:177). The ancestors are properly called *Ndichie*, meaning the ancients or the first people. They are the first generation of founding fathers to which humanity and the Igbo owe their respect. The people emulate and consult them in prayers. The ancestors are almost placed on the same rating as God, except that the mighty-God or Chi-Ukwu has no comparison.

In Azorji's own view, "ancestors are those who died at a good old age and received grand funeral celebrations (rite of passage), those who were rightly buried by their community, *Umunna*" (Azorji, 1976:177). It was from this perspective that Basden remarked:

> *The Ibo will endure everything demanded of him in this life, will put up with hardships, the misbehavior of his children, indeed everything, in order to ensure that his burial will be properly performed. His whole future welfare depends upon this; hence it takes at all times almost prominent place in a man's calculation (Baseden, 1975:117).*

The sentiments and observations, which Baseden has raised here, are very striking for our society that does not care for anything – heaven or hell. The Igbos, or Ibos or Igbo will do all within their powers to emulate good lives, endure certain hardships without complaining to ensure that they join their ancestors in the land of the living. In this sense, the Ibos do not regard the present world as the land of living, but a passing one that leads one to the permanent place of peace and joy.

The issue of dilemma came within this belief when the missionaries failed to present their message in the context of the ancestors. The issue of ancestors was not unknown to the missionaries. For instance, in the Old Testament, Abraham, Isaac and Jacob are considered the ancestors of the Christian and Jewish religions. The missionaries are blamed for not introducing or presenting Jesus in that context may be as the Proto Ancestor of the Igbo people. However, it was impossible for the missionaries to understand what ancestors meant or could have done otherwise since they did not understand what the people regarded them to mean. Besides, language barrier was another factor that led to the dilemma of the growth of the Christian faith as we indicated earlier on. Obviously, if the missionaries had known what the ancestors meant in Igboland, they would not have condemned the practice or belief in them as fetish.

"Ritual worship"

The question of Ritual Worship among the Igbo seemed to have created another dilemma for the growth of the Christian message in question. In ritual worship, the people express their joy of being humans through sacrifices, dancing, praying in the form of incantations, symbolic presentation of items they regard as spiritual. As Mulago would put it, "Any group activity performed in the name of God falls within ritual worship" (Mulago, 1981:171-179). To offer sacrifices to *Chukwu* is to enter into his life style and presence. To enter God's presence is to be pure and holy. The traditionalists are well known in Igboland for honesty and trustworthiness. Like today, most Christians seem to be leading in most of the selfish happenings in the land. It was within such context that Gordon lamented that "it is a well-established fact in social science that on the average, churchgoers in our country harbor more racial, ethnic, and religious prejudices than the non-churchgoers" (Gordon, 1967:20). Ukpong on his own part, referring to the religious worships and sacrifices in general noted:

> *Cultic actions are not categorized in vertical terms of the higher and Lower but in qualitative terms of the more potent and less potent....sacrifice is conceived as a cultic action that is most potent in establishing communication with the spiritual beings (Ukpong, 1983:200).*

Even from what Ukpong has just said, the first face judgment on this matter is that the missionaries created the dilemma by introducing a religion where Churchgoers violate the laws of the land and do whatever they like. On the second consideration, it is clear that the missionaries did not teach the people to be dishonest or criminal-oriented. Their message was clear. For an Igbo Christian to go to Church and still steals and fights with neighbors are problems of the human nature and not that of Christianity.

In Nwachukwu's analysis, he insisted that the Igbo Traditional shrines for sacrifices of the native doctors and traditional priests (Ndi Ogo Mmuo) are highly revered and dreaded by everybody including Christians as sacred places. The remark is objective indeed. But, that the Christian places of sacrifice are not respected, as they should have been by the people, is not a dilemma created by missionaries. If the Igbo people did not understand the implication of what the missionaries taught them at that time, why can't they change today that their own sons and daughters are spiritual experts, ministers and evangelists? Camouflaging the Christian message in the name of being ministers has nothing to do with the missionaries. Moreover, to accuse the missionaries of not presenting the Christian places of worship in respectful contexts as the traditional shrines are to ask if the missionaries used them to play jokes other than to worship. That some of the present day ministers embezzle Church funds and create scandals is not to be blamed on Christianity. Christianity has never preached such or introduced that to the people.

"*The issue of village court or ala di mma*"

The Village Court [*Ala Di Mma*] of Igboland is essential to them. According to Nwachukwu:

> *Ala Di Mma literally means, "May the land be good or peaceful". It is a mandatory village court where different cases of fighting, bribery, land disputes, embezzlement of pubic funds, religious violations, sexual abuses et cetera are justified and settled by the leaders or eldest of the land. This village court is in accord with the legacy bequeathed to the Igbo people of Nigeria especially to Ezinihitte by their ancestors. The village court has link with the village gatherings and some social group systems, like Oku Umunna (Community summon or gathering), Iri mbata oke (a mandatory provision of food items to qualify as a member in the women group), nkwa ndomi [women dance], Igba mgba [wrestling], Otu ebiri [Age grade systems] et cetera (Nwachukwu, 2002).*

Having studied what Nwachukwu has enumerated above, I have my own observations to put across. In the first place, village court or Aladima is prominent and indispensable among the people of Igboland. This is the court in which different cases are settled. For instance the people had no civil courts in those days as today. The native law and custom guided the people throughout the governance of the community.

Today, accusing fingers seem to be pointing to the failure of the missionaries to do their job. This is not true. While I believe that, if the missionaries had understood what these courts meant at that time, they could not have disregarded them, I also maintain that they had no means available to them for such knowledge or information. Nobody abhors unity and peace except the present day terrorists. At least, if there is anything the Igbo person ever looks for; it is his unity with the rest of the community. The Igbo Catholic Priests, in support of the above view noted that the "Igbo man values... its unity and solidarity... places high premium on community loyalty...respect for age and elders (The Igbo Catholic priests, 2000:16).

The only problem envisaged is that the missionaries did not make any efforts to understand the people's customs and culture. But even if they tried, they had in mind that they were introducing a religion that could save the people from paganism. Even though there were no pagans in Igboland as noted already, the missionaries had no evil intention in bringing Christianity to the people. Therefore, the dilemma experienced today among the people of Igboland, calls for attention on both sides. The people have to re-examine themselves properly and admit if they actually need honesty, truth and justice in their lives. If they really do, how come there is much corruption in Igboland like many other western worlds that have Christian religion? In essence, the religious dilemma being discussed here might have its origin from human freedom, choice levels and character.

Consequently, if "the primary function of religion" according to Meek, "would seem to be the function of rites and standard of social behavior" (Meek, 1943:20), why then are there contradictions in religious practices today? The customary laws of the people help to unite the people together in their religious, moral and political life. They are not only the expressions of the dynamic spirit of co-responsibility among the people (Mozia, 1987:221), but also their solidarity with one another, God and the ancestors.

Lawlessness in the practice of Christian faith

Literally speaking, native laws (*Omenala*) for M.I. Mozia "means legitimate acts and reactions observed in the land" (Mozia, 1987:221). Native law or *Omenala* does not exclude westernization, civilization, science, technology, or modernization. In Osuji's own understanding, it includes "all provisions and prohibitions, traditional beliefs and practices, which are contained in the written or unwritten laws and customs and brought down from the ancestors to posterity" (Osuji, 1977:25). The big question that faces us is: who brought lawlessness among the people. Lawlessness is a factor in the dilemma of the growth of the Christian faith discussed here. For instance, a law that binds on Igboland can't be enforced on a person or a missionary who has no knowledge of its existence.

In this sense, supporting the importance of customs and native laws, Ilogu in Nwachukwu said:

> *Omenani, therefore becomes the means by which traditional Igbo society enforces conformity culturally speaking, Omenani is the means by which the ethos of the people is measured, the values of the society are contained from one generation to another...Because Omenani is derived from the guardian spirit of "Ala" and sanctified by the ancestors, it is religious in nature, although it fulfills social, moral and cultural sanctions" (Ilogu,*

*1974:23). From this eschatological viewpoint, the Ezinihitte
people regard their Omenala as a means of enjoying the beatific
vision of their God and ancestors. To be candid, if Christianity
had not succeeded in Ezinihitte soil today, it is practically due
to the peoples' irrevocable attitudes to Omenala. Even, when
certain aspects of the Omenala seem to go contrary to the Gospel
message or sounds negatively conceived, it has to be adhered to,
since the people see it as a legacy bequeathed to man by God or
the ancestors (Consult Nwachukwu, 2002 for details).*

The infallibility of the people's laws and customs and social
governance indicates the dilemma of the growth of the Christian
faith in Igboland. If nothing can be done to change the people's
customs and Omenala, then it means Christianity, which may not
accept all aspects of those customs, can never grow there. We can
now anticipate the reasons why the Christian religion has been
stagnated in Igboland. Therefore, pointing an accusing finger on the
missionary is not going to assist us in this enquiry. For instance, how
can any custom that relegates the position of women to the second
place be encouraged as a way of life of the Ibos? Such customs need
to be re-visited.

Religious insensitivity/greed of members

The danger of obstinacy in religious practices and hypocrisy
is another predicament that hinders the progress of the faith in
Igboland. Practically, the urgency and need for this research call
for self-supervision and commitment in representing the values of
Christianity in its practices. For instance, one writer, Raab, in his
fieldwork and survey carried out among religious groups, discovered
something that could be responsible for the dilemma of the growth
of the Christian faith among individuals including the people of

Igboland of Nigeria. If belief cannot influence action, what else will? A person who claims to be a medical doctor with no knowledge of medicine must be joking.

According to Raab, some Christian adherents maintain that despite the magnitude of religious practices and emphasis being laid on religion today, there are no changes in their behaviors and attitudes. Then, the big question that arises is: "What impact or of what significance is religion and its practices on society and the lives of such individuals?" Why have the records of crimes continued to be in the increase and disbelief in God multiplied? Excessive pursuit for material things, greed, avarice, egoistic, inordinate and insatiability in search of wealth regardless of what happens to religion are the foundations and reasons. No wonder Knitter cries out, stating that:

> *I would suggest that one of the major reasons why there is so much disunity and lack of peace in today's world is because the religions of the world have not done their job (Knitter, 1992:283).*

The emphasis on the point Knitter has raised here is not that religions of the world have no preachers, leaders and adherents. He is not even alluding that world religions do not have defined doctrines and belief systems. Rather, the emphasis today is that most of those religions that claim to bring peace and order to society perpetuate the crimes that abound in thousands in society. This is the height of hypocrisy when people who claim to represent Christ in their preaching turn around and practice a different thing.

To complicate matters, this is the age of fashion where many people seem to play 'hide and seek' games and put veils over their religious obligations and responsibilities. If society were to live by the values of Christianity, life would have been better than it is today. That was why St. Paul noted that: "For law abiders there was no law" (Rom. 6:10). In Pauline context, for law abiders, there should not have been any dichotomy in religious practices or the dilemma in the growth of the Gospel message. Until humanity identifies herself with her belief systems, the dilemma will always be there, extending to different cultures and ethnic groups. In this light, the admonition of Carl Anderson would have served humanity to realize the need to use our freedom deepen our faith in our source of being. In his own words: "If the history of the human race has taught us nothing else, it should at least have taught us that freedom in this instinctual sense is utterly illusory" (Carl, Anderson *2008:26).*

In other words, wrong use of freedom and the consequent bad choices we make equally affect the growth of the Christian faith, now, not only for people in Igboland of Nigeria, but also for every rational being. Good behavior is a grace. This is why, according to Whitson: "Sin is the refusal to believe...a refusal to accept truths revealed" (Whitson, 1995:60). Can there be any more truth revealed than the incarnation of Jesus Christ in human history, which many, especially from Igboland of Nigeria have refused to accept and practice? The story of the Good Samaritan teaches how those who claim to be deeply committed with the message of salvation fail at the point of execution of their duties (Luke 10:29-36).

That is to say, why is it hard for some ministers of the Gospel to emulate the good behaviors of so many lay people who are not Church leaders and practice the Christian religion as it is? Could it be as John's Gospel once expressed that: "Men have shown they prefer darkness to the light because their deeds are evil" (John 3:19)? What does life mean for a person who prefers darkness to the light of

God and neighbor, destruction to peace, sadness to happiness, and curse to blessing and so on? Belief systems and science should not be obstacles to authentic practice of the Christian faith.

In this light, the people of Igboland, should accept the Christian religion in the same spirit they have accepted education and western civilization today, even more so because God is the summary of their existence on earth. The admonition of his holiness, Pope Benedict XVI, during his papal visit to America is supportive of the above views: "There is no conflict between science, ethics and religion. It is a matter of choice between the sciences that dehumanize the human person and the sciences that uplift the human situation" (Papal Mass at National Stadium, USA, Thursday April 17, 2008 in Nwachukwu 2010).

Elements of Secularization

The greatest mistake of the century is for humanity to believe and accept "the death of God" theology brought about by secularism and worldly attractions. For instance, Dietrich Bonhoeffer had this to say:

> *Our coming to age forces us to a true recognition of our situation vis-à-vis God. God is teaching us that we must live as man who can get along very well without him. The God who is with us, is the God who forsakes us…before God and with him, we live without God. God allows himself to be edged out of the world and on the cross*" (Bonhoeffer, Dietrich. 1954:163).

The biggest question any sensible person could ask is whether science and technology have done more good than bad. Generally, it is impossible to blame science and technology for the ills of society.

Such mentality as expressed above indicates how an individual's life styles can affect his or her faith. Most people have no problem in what Bonhoeffer has said because they have not created any space for God in their hearts and programs. How can the God who is with us be the same God who has forsaken us? To nurture such feelings is to admit the reality of the dilemma in question, which the people of Igboland are experiencing in their religious practices today. It was in view of this ill that Dr. Josephine Nwachukwu Udaku sounds this seasonal warning:

> *It is good to encourage civilization but not to use civilization to backup evil things that manifest these days. Possibly you are among the parents who are concerned about the way our children are getting almost out of control behaviorally these days or do you belong to those who say it is a civilized world? The world is a global village so whatever is done in the United States is encouraged in our remote towns and villages. If you belong to this group, you are among those who fold their arms and watch values being misplaced. Or do you belong to those who are timelessly working to nip this current menace in the bud? (Dr. Nwachukwu Udaku, 2009:59 in Nwachukwu, 2010).*

In Harvey Cox's own subjective view, "life is a set of problems and not an unfathomable mystery…man perceives himself as the source of whatever significance the human enterprise holds" (Cox, Harvey. 1965:72). Life can only be a set of problem when one is not in touch with oneself and meaning. Passing judgment on a general issue based on one's subjective ideology may not be ideal to address reality as such. After all, in Prof. Nwachukwu's view, "Reality is the sum total of one's thoughts. Besides, we do not seem to perceive others/things as they are, but as we are". Let us be cautious in judging others, period.

Secularization is the product of human age, curiosity, and at times selfish invention. Friedrich Nietzsche, in his own cultural tendency made the following remarks: "God is dead! God stays dead! And it is we who have killed him" (Nietzsche, Friedrich. 1910:125). How can society that holds this ideology ever believe in the presence of God, let alone of Christianity? This same mentality has permeated the minds of most people in Igboland. These are the elements of dilemma facing this research work. In the light of Nietzsche's thought, how can man learn to live without God but claim to be a human problem solver himself? God gave man freedom and dominion over the earth, to be fruitful, multiply, fill the earth, subdue and conquer it (Gen.1: 28), to use it to fight God is human problem and not God's.

We cannot allow science and technology and the ugly monster of "secularization" (Keller Albert in Karl, Rahner. 1975:1554-1561) to paint the saving nature and capacity of Christian religion in particular. The Igbo people must learn to discover the presence of God in their lives. Christian faith must go beyond the bounds of worldly orientations. The experience of the Transcendence must not be allowed to shift to mundane and a "this – worldly faith" and thereby setting fire on the growth of the Christian faith in Igboland. In the spirit of these ugly scientific sentiments, V. M. Andrew said:

> *Lord, it is pretty difficult to believe in you now, when it is out of fashion. Science has usurped your place...Now-a-days...men have set foot on the moon and soon they will be in Mars. Test-tube babies will greet us soon. Artificial rains are on the way. Memory pills and such wonder drugs are in the market all speak of the wonders of science, and who is there who cares for you. Do you think Lord; these things will not have any influence on me? I am confused, Lord: I wonder if I still believe in you (V. M. Andrew. 1973:9-10, in Nwachukwu, 2010).*

.If it is pretty difficult to believe in God for whatever reason Andrew holds, the growth of Christianity is globally jeopardized and gradually stamped out of most cultures, including those of the Igboland of Nigeria. "Scientific knowledge is a process that demands the cooperation of others and development of the human mind for comprehension and practice. Therefore, turning around to attack the source of scientific knowledge is the highest display of affected ignorance. The modern man's consciousness of his greatness, achievements, power over himself and the universe alarmingly needs to be guided by spiritual psychology. These materialistic tendencies of "who cares or anything goes" are indications of moral emptiness of the age and signs of anti-clericalism also (Consult Nwachukwu, 2010).

Inhumanity to man is another factor of religious predicaments.

The rate the world experiences hatred, tale bearing, assassination of characters, hypocrisy of all forms, atrocities of all kinds et cetera even in God's vineyards, indicate why there is dilemma in religious growth in Igboland. How can the Gospel message be determined by materialistic tendencies and scientific age? How can material-oriented religion and ministry guarantee growth of the Christian religion anywhere? Today, many people flout both the natural and positive laws in their lives and nobody seems to be listening to the voice of reason. As long as society has gradually plunged into spiritual aridity and turns the joyous music of life into catastrophes, insensitivity remains the order of things. No wonder the Christian Bible asked:

> *Can people pick grapes from thorns, or figs from thistles? In the same way, a sound tree produces good fruit but a rotten tree*

> *bad fruit. A sound tree cannot bear bad fruit, nor a rotten tree*
> *bear good fruit .... I repeat, you will be able to tell them by*
> *their fruits (Mt. 7:16-20).*

To the biblical question if people can pick grapes from thorns, the answer is no. If people do not decide to live by the Christian message, it is wrong for the same people to turn around to blame it – the message if they run into trouble on account of their obstinacy and lack of listening ears. In other words, if the people of Igboland in Ngor Okpala could begin right now to integrate the values of Christianity in their culture and religion, definitely, the dilemma of religious growth will be given a different face.

Cafeteria religious practice/Anti-clericalism

Religion has to be perceived as a way of life that largely builds strong relationship with one's faith in oneself, neighbor and Supreme Being. The problem facing most religious people is to positively live up to the ideals of their message and radiate the moral principles of truth and openness to others. Failure to do so is to create predicaments for its growth. A psychologist, Gordon pointing the faces of religion noted:

> *There are two kinds of religion: Instrumental - which serves*
> *God for what you can get out of it; and the Intrinsic religion-*
> *which serves God regardless of what the consequences of that*
> *might be (Gordon, 1974:29-30).*

To serve God primarily for one's own end is instrumental and does not encourage the growth of Christian religion. But serving God regardless of personal gains is more inclusive and embracing. If the people of Igboland could appreciate religion in this spirit, they will begin to enjoy the growth of Christian and traditional religions in their lives. According to Raab as mentioned earlier:

> One study reports that 80% of members of religious groups indicate they are more concerned about comfortable life on earth than other-worldly considerations, and 54% admit that their religious beliefs do not have any effect on the way they conduct their daily affairs (Raab, 1964:15, cited in Nwachukwu, 2010).

The revelation of Raab indicates to a great extent why most Christians in Igboland of Nigeria have not allowed the Christian faith to grow in their land. If people's religious beliefs do not affect their ways of life, what justification has anybody to blame Christianity for creating chaos in Igboland or the dilemma in question? From the account Raab has given here, it is possible that the "human interests" implied in religion is as ambiguous and delicate as people assign different meanings to it. These are the problems that seem to create most of the hypocritical tendencies and the dilemma we encounter in religious practices in Igboland today. According to Cardinal Arinze: "Religion has three elements; truths to be believed (dogma), worship to be carried out (cult), and rules for guidance of conduct (morals)"(Arinze, A. Francis, 1970:31-32). These are the living expressions of the souls of vast group of people and all religious systems should be guided by these elements. Emphasizing one against the other does not assist any religious practices or the growth of the Christian religion in particular.

In a more elaborate observation, Arinze maintained that religion also consists of the following: "Objective' - body of truths, laws and rites by which man was sub – ordinate to the transcendent being and 'subjective' – the consciousness of ones dependence on transcendent being and the tendency to worship him" (Arinze, A. Francis, 1970:8). The body of truths, laws and rites are both accepted and encouraged in both Christianity and African traditional religion of the Igbo. As soon as people of Igboland realize the need for truth and justice in their lives, the Christian religion and faith will smoothly marry the traditional values for a holistic living and growth. It was in support of the religious values that Rear-Admiral Richard Byrd said that Christianity has not failed. It is simply that nations have failed to try it. There would be no war in a God-directed world (Richard Byrd cited in Mead S. Frank, 1965:62). The nations mentioned here, include Igboland and the people of Ngor Okpala. Religious practice is not a matter of pick and choose, it has a goal. People have got to know the God they worship.

To the question, according to Nwachukwu "why do they not know him?" Sweany provides answers in these words:

> *Christians are found almost everywhere...sometimes they are found in the church, but not all persons in churches are Christians..." because "What persons do outside the Churches is the test" (Sweaney E. James, Unity School of Christianity cited in Mead, 1965:67).*

Therefore, as long as people parade themselves everywhere as Christians without living the lives expected of them, the dilemma of religious hypocrisy will continue to frustrate its growth in Igboland of Nigeria. "The distortion of the word of God preached by the Church into human error, by a Christian who makes his own fancy and his own standard a measure of the word of God, and suits it to himself instead of himself to it, and so sets up his own Christianity against the Church's" (Rahner, Karl. 1964:64). If the ministers of Christian religion remain selfish and continue to set up their own

Christianity against the very way of life Christ preached is the beginning of Pseudo religious entities and failures of its growth generally.

As the Scriptures expressed it, "Can one blind man guide another? Surely both will fall into a pit" (Lk. 6:39). We need self-supervisions in the practice of Christianity because as James would put it: "Nobody must imagine that he is religious while he still goes on deceiving himself ...anyone who does this has the wrong idea of religion" James 1: 26-27. It is only reasonable that ministers preach to others from the wealth and riches of their beliefs, convictions and relationships with the one they represent, Jesus Christ. It was because of these hypocritical attitudes of the Christian ministers that the Catholic Prelate, Bishop Ezeonyia noted: "Religion is sold in the market place like everything else these days" (Ezeonyia, V.V., 1998:1). How can the Christian religion grow when it is sold like a commodity in the market? Ekweh, on his own side added these words: "A lot of people are so much concerned about personality, status, qualifications, without considering the wisdom of God in their lives (Ekweh, 2002:6-7).

Once personal importance is brought forward before the Gospel message, there will be no growth of the faith any more. Ministers of the word should not allow the spirit of wants or secularization get in the way of their primary needs, to lead themselves and others in the heavenly race as we noted already. In the light of these pseudo-religious paraphernalia and appearances of most ministers, Bishop Vincent Ezeonyia frowningly seemed to be referring to them when he described the various Christian sects in these words:

> *The Pentecostal type of religion seems to draw people who are highly emotional and long for spiritual "highs". The Liturgical*

types of religions appeal more to people who love order and drama. The Intellectual types of religions attract people who are looking for a cerebral faith. The Prosperity-religion has great appeal to those who seek wealth and health and power. The Fellowship type of religions draw people from who are looking for an experience of community" (Ezeonyia, V. Vincent, 1998: 34 in Nwachukwu 2010).

Today, it is no longer news, particularly in Nigeria that some armed robbers disguise themselves and operate as Rev. Gentlemen. Greed is part of the dilemma in question.

Reacting to this ugly situation, Joseph I. Omoregbe [as quoted in Nwachukwu 2010] remarkably stated that "If a person believes very strongly in making money, then money is his religion, if another person believes strongly in Marxism, then, Marxism is his religion and so on" (Omoregbe, I. Joseph, 1996: 1). According to Obiora, such earth bound, end-time or reward-on earth evangelists: "Dish out intriguing half-truths…. exaggerations, inarticulate premises, insinuations, distortion of facts, false testimonies…all geared towards the accumulation of wealth (Obiora K. Fidelis, 1998:79). These are practically the dilemma and cause of the hindrance of religious growth in Igboland. According to Nwachukwu:

It is timely to reflect and heed the words of Archbishop Okogie that "carrying the Bible is one of the quickest means of getting money today" (Okogie cited in Obiora, 1998:109) and for Obiora, "the Bible has become a deceptive tool" (Obiora, 1998: 191). What else can bring various relationships together than the Bible? How can "religion" be "blown out of proportion" (Obiora, 1998:119) because of greedy ministers? (Nwachukwu, 2010).

In order for the Christian message to bear fruit in Igboland, in Ekwuru's understanding, we cannot allow these signs of anti-clericalism to play any further roles in Christianity because of greedy ministers. As stated here: "The center of religious belief and practice has been variously tagged with commercial values.... The religious vision and mentality are obviously earth bound and totally mundane (Ekwuru, E. George, 1999:105). Each Ngor Okpala man and woman must begin to examine his traditional values in the light of the Christian message. That was the point Odoemene meant when he remarked:

> *Religion does not only serve the interest of the society but also of the individual, in that religion provides answers to the questions and the search for meaning, leads him into loving confrontation with the source of his being and integrates him into the society to enable him participate in the religious rituals of the community and values (Odoemene, N. Anacletus. 1993:54, cited in Nwachukwu).*

In this way, the growth of the Christian faith will be rapid and fast. Once people understand that religion has a powerful force and influence in their lives, nobody will tell them to approach it with resolute and convictions.

Need for dialogue in religious dilemma

We need to understand first, what dialogue is all about? In what Nwachukwu termed: "The possible starting point to religious dialogue" he stated: "This chapter, by its nature, must be seen to give detailed discussion or exposition of what dialogue is, touching all its ramifications so that the meeting of the two religions can be well understood" (Nwachukwu, 2002:245). Religious dialogue is so important, especially in our days that the world has become so sophisticated with technology and science. More especially, this is an age where some people want to subject faith to empirical verifications or an item for the laboratory. Continuing in this essential aspect of religious growth, Nwachukwu remarked:

> *The question, "what is one's attitude towards other peoples' religion" is fundamental in any religious dialogue. According to the figures calculated over many years by the staff of the world Christian Encyclopedia, Oxford, 1982, only 'one third [1.4 billion] of the world's population [4.8 billion] are nominally Christians" (Hans Kung, 1986: xiii). The calculation implies that there are so many other religions besides Christianity. In a world so closely knit together, both the geographical and historical horizons of our religious world are enormously expanding. However, our knowledge of other religions is still very limited. Therefore, there is need for inter-religious dialogue,and a call for global ecumenical consciousness (Ibid).*

The importance of this enquiry is predicated on the facts that the same Ngor Okpala person is also the Christian in question. As such, dialogue becomes inevitable since some Ngor Okpala people face different religious and ethical convictions, social interests and conflicting positions. According to Nwachukwu, "A way of dialogue will help to scatter confusions, doubts and interpersonal tensions among 'Ngor Okpala Christians" (Nwachukwu, 2002:246).

In an interesting note, Just as Kidd underlined in his observation on dialogue: "The tension which exists in dialogue shifts as participants become attuned to and understand one another" (J. W. Kidd, "Dialogue Modes of Universalism", Vol. XVII, No. 3, 1990, p. 109). From the above citation, the book is focused on diminishing such tensions as Kidd mentioned above. These tensions constitute major obstacles for the practice of the Christian religion by Ngor Okpala people. As Nwachukwu observed in his writing: "

> *Nobody solves a problem by running away from it. Peace is never achieved by imposition either. Thus, a clearer notion of concept "dialogue" is essential in this work. In dialogue we do not want to consider any of the religions as inconsequential but both can harbor the seed of salvation to our people. It is possible to say that Christianity has an upper hand, because it has mass fellowship. All the same, our last chapter shows how Christianity is responding and giving a wrong signal that [Ngor Okpala] people's religion should be phased out. Dialogue will enable Christianity to see why much should be accepted in Ngor Okpala religion for the purpose of salvation (Ibid).*

In a practical manner, we have noted that dialogue is an indispensable means of resolving tensions among people with conflicting religious beliefs and ideologies. Dialogue, "not only creates intimate inter-religious but also inter-confessional relationships, even at diametrically opposed positions for the purpose of peace and live-and-let-live" (Nwachukwu, 2002:247). In Mozia's own word, dialogue "possesses some 'magical force', which is capable of unifying persons and of strengthening the bonds among them" (M. I. Mozia, Solidarity in the Church and solidarity among the Igbos of Nigeria, 2nd ed., p. 1987:139).

From its etymology, "dialogue" comes from the Greek word 'dialogos' meaning conversation between two or more persons. According to The American Peoples' Encyclopedia: "Dialogue, from the Greek word 'dialogos' means the process of clarification of problems in the conversation between two or more people;

its essence is that participants alternately speak and listen" (Vol. 7, 1962:7-42). In Nwachukwu's own observation: "From this definition, dialogue involves the unfolding of a person's mind to another. In other words, there can be no fruitful dialogue unless there is an acceptance of one another's personalities" (Ibid). It was based on the same point Nwachukwu has raised here that Oyelade defines dialogue as 'a form of communication in the interest of better understanding of peoples' religious objectives... an involvement for honest pursuits of interests" (C. O. Oyelade, Muslim – 'Christian Dialogue' SHALOM Vol. IV, No. III, p.151).

On a different note, I believe that dialogue is a supportive presence to each other in the study of burning issues that lead to progress. Hastings in his own position, not only supported what Oyedale noted, but also insists that dialogue is "the passing across of ideas from one person or group of people to another" (A. Hastings, 1969:199). If I were to react to these views analytically, the concept and nature of dialogue propounded by both Oyedale and Hastings may be further qualified in order to find suitability in their applications to the Ngor Okpala people and their cosmological stand points. Agreeing with Oyedale to an extent, dialogue is a form of communication in the interests for better understanding. However, to limit this understanding to the people only to their religious objectives may create some quagmire between the people and Oyedale. To succeed in any inter-religious dialogue in Ngor Okpala if I may borrow from Nwachukwu, the peoples' entire cultural values in general, their political and social systems, traditional world-views et cetera, must be considered as well. We noted this already that the peoples' religion is inseparable from other cultural identities that make them a people.

Practically, Ngor Okpala peoples' life styles, their features and economies equally affect their religious beliefs. It is not just a belief in God or ancestors; religion is a way of life for them. As such, dialogue has to include all that. Regrettably, when the missionaries came first, we still remember, Christianity seemed not only to have destroyed the religious worldviews, but also almost every system that the people fashioned as sustaining them. This is why it will be hard for an Ngor Okpala man to accept wholeheartedly all that Hastings said here about dialogue that it is 'the passing across of ideas from one person to another". In the first place, for the people of Ngor Okpala, dialogue will involve life, their beliefs, and their persons as a people, including all the values that define them as a people. Anything short of that may not lead to any peaceful resolution.

As an indigenous writer, Mozia understands the people of Ngor Okpala more than the two experts we have examined and his position here will be better appreciated by the people. By saying that dialogue "is not just a communication of ideas, but also a communication of persons' he won the peoples' hearts. The people exist as a whole, integrally related to each other in an ontological level. Therefore, any discussion that concerns them will definitely include whatever makes them as a people and this makes the process of dialogue difficult among Ngor Okpala people. However, there is need to start one because it is through dialogue that a man can personally be present to another, both in words, deeds and actions. We do not just listen to words, but we must listen to the reactions of those we listen to. This is my own philosophy as a professional in this area. It is only when we listen to people that their words mean something to us.

In this light, we must understand, besides the Christian and traditional religions of the Igbo people, that there are so many other religions under the sun. That is, both the westerners [Christianity] and Africans should consider dialogue as one of their basic weapons and grounds for the pursuit of salvation in their lives and that of the world at large. Oblige me to quote the paper Cardinal Arinze presented to Catholic Institute of West Africa [C.I.W.A] staff and students, 23rd May 1986 as cited in Nwachukwu. He said: "Inter-religious dialogue helps each participant to grow in his own faith when he encounters another of a different religious persuasion and confronts his faith with that of other. Truth is often better reached, appreciated, understood and lived when met by other views" (Arinze, Francis, SHALOM, Vol. IV, No. III, 1970:125). Arinze has hammered on a note of warning to those who perpetuate indifference in accepting other peoples' religious worldviews. By what Arinze noted here, the need to be humble in discussing other peoples' values is being encouraged. In such a way, religious bigotry is being discouraged as well.

To this effect, the attempt to present Christian religion in dialogue with that of Ngor Okpala person will go a long way to bringing together the rich values inherent and common in them. That is why, in dialogue, the differences between people will be ignored and attention will be focused on matters that can advance their relationships. Rather, those differences will be utilized for a creative and healthier synthesis. In a developing point of view, Karol had this to say: "Dialogue, in fact, without evading the strains, the conflicts or the strives manifest in life of various human communities, takes up what is right and true in these differences, what may become a source of good for men" (K. Wojtyla, (Pope John Paul II), The Acting person, Holland: Reidel Publishing, 1979:287). In other words, dialogue is aimed at utilizing the values that could enrich both parties without minding more of the differences in them. In this sense, it means that dialogue has the power to unify the religion of Ngor Okpala people with Christianity without any manipulation of the people in any way.

Such encounters or confrontations, in which differences are kept aside and common values exchanged, will surely help Ngor Okpala people in the practice of the Christian religion in their land. Then, the big question would be, what are the common truth or value in the two religions that can be considered as a springboard for the growth of the Christian religion in Ngor Okpala? It is within the confines of such truths and values that lies the usefulness of dialogue in general. In such a situation, there is no radical appropriation of each other's religious tenets but what can benefit them as a whole. As cited in Nwachukwu, in this perspective, we can understand the point Cardinal Arinze meant when he said:

> *This dialogue is not aimed at converting the other to our faith although obviously it does not close the doors to that possibility. Dialogue and conversion are two aspects of the mission of the Church. There is however a sense in which every participant at dialogue should get converted. It is the sense of greater dedication to God (Arinze, Francis, Op.Cit. 1970:123, Nwachukwu, 2002:249).*

Actually, judging from what Arinze has observed above, conversion can occur in the process of dialogue. But any dialogue principally aimed at conversion might fail. Unfortunately, that was the case when the missionaries first came to Igboland of Nigeria. They came with the spirit of total change in the religion of the people and that is also part of the dilemma of the growth of the Christian religion in Igboland today.

On no grounds should conversion be encouraged in dialogue. If however it happens, then it is naturally accepted and welcomed. According to Nwachukwu, "As could be deduced from what Arinze said, dialogue is not primarily directed or aimed at conversion. It is related to conversion. Dialogue essentially promotes sincere search for the truth, greater obedience to God and openness to divine action" (Nwachukwu, 2002:250). This can only happen when the participants are open to each other. In a situation where some nurse a hidden agenda, there is always going to be a clash of interests and the goal of dialogue will not be achieved. "Consequently" according to Nwachukwu: "Dialogue is the participants' progressive movement to salvation. Dialogue may not end up in consensus, but it can create room for compromise and peace. Possibly this is true because in dialogue both Christians and African traditional religionists collaborate with one another as children of the same God" (Ibid).

In the situation of the missionaries and the Igbo people of Nigeria, if they had approached the implanting and welcoming of the new religion with some dialogue, it could have ameliorated the dilemma at hand. "Gracefully", according to Nwachukwu "once parties in dialogue collaborate in a search for a common meaning, in its historical, concrete situation, there could be total self-understanding and radical change of mind and acceptance of one another" and the new religion (Nwachukwu, 253). It should be noted that dialogue extends beyond religious circles to other important associations and companies where human interactions are necessary. Even in government quarters, there should be dialogue regarding how her finances and affairs should be run or administered. In dialogue, no one has absolute say or control. Each voice has to be heard and considered as well.

However, there is need for a distinction as regards dialogue and argument. In argument, the prevailing force is the aura of religious dominance, superiority and supremacy. This is a situation where the participants try to win their grounds or enforce others to believe them without minding how it affects their own positions. Scarcely does this situation lead to openness and conversion in Arinze's points of view. Rather, argument brings about strife and rancor. On the other hand, in Nwachuwku's view: "In any authentic dialogue, every one involved is as eager to receive what he intends to give, all try to be detached from the desire to impose their own opinions or view points. In this way, dialogue may remain personalistic because it unfolds the dignity and freedom which must be recognized and respected" (Nwachukwu, 2002:250, Mozia, 141).

Besides, as noted before, religious bigotry has no place in dialogue. Similarly, religious fanatics lose their grounds in any form of dialogue because while trying to maintain their religious preferences, they lose the trends of the event of the dialogue. Most often they lose their grounds because they are not broad-minded enough to accept reasons in other peoples' opinions. This happens because, having been influenced by ego-centric, self-centeredness, particularity, and in some cases, by ethnocentric mentality, cultural bias, superiority complex, they regard all other religions as inauthentic and misleading. Such people cannot advance any meaningful dialogue because they tend to privatize God as their own savior and disregard the importance of others even in going to heaven. To heal such prejudices that created part of the dilemma of the growth of the Christian religion in Igboland, dialogue must be seen as a 'sine qua non' for human progress and harmony.

Practically, truth of dialogue lies on the clear consciences of participants to search for that which promotes progress and deepens their faith. In this way, as cited in Nwachukwu, Mozia remarked:

> *Dialogue becomes an expression of the reciprocity of consciences which are united in the search for truth and valid solutions to problems that continually arise in the individual and in the communitarian life of the faithful (Mozia, 1987:160).*

This is where education becomes consequential. By education, each party learns something new from each other, and tries to maintain a common ground on certain issues and beliefs. Before the missionaries started on their evangelical movements, they had plans on what they intended to impart on the people as the target of the mission. On the other hand, the Igbo people of Nigeria had believed in themselves and their identity. They had and have a religion that has sustained them for posterity. For the incoming religion to succeed, a bit of education would have been necessary. There are certain issues that needed to be tabled for discussion before implementation becomes evident. Unfortunately, that was not the case. It was a sense and matter of superiority versus inferiority, which does not work out most of the time.

In another happy note, an indigenous writer, Omoregbe reacting to such ugly situation of religious superiority, has this to say as cited in Nwachukwu:

> *No culture is God's own culture, no race is his own race and no language is his own language. Similarly no religion is his own religion. It does not matter to God which culture a person comes from, of what nationality he is, which race he belongs to, which language he speaks or which religion he practices so long*

266

as he leads a good life and does His will. All religion are the
same to Him, all races are the same to Him and all languages
are the same to Him (Omoregbe, Joseph, 1999:xi, Nwachukwu,
2002:251).

Obviously, the above position may not be accepted by all religions
of the world especially those that claim orthodoxy and superiority.
On my part, I quite accept what Omoregbe has said here because
dialogue serves as a unifying factor of various religious groups.
It humbly invites and challenges different religions to a common
understanding and purpose. It is only through 'committed dialogue'
that the Christian message can enrich the people of Igboland,
especially Ngor Okpala citizens.

According to Justin Ekennia as cited in Nwachukwu: "Dialogue
is committed' in the sense that those who engage in such dialogue
consciously agreed to enter into it, and they would determine the
terms that would regulate their deliberations" (Ekennia, J. 2000:217,
Nwachukwu, Ibid). This is one thing that has to be borne in mind
today that we cannot successfully discuss ecumenical movement
without a dialogical process. Ecumenism from its etymological
viewpoint as cited in Nwachukwu, derives from:

'Oikumeni' has its root in antiquity. The Greeks used it to
designate the whole 'inhabited world'. But for the Romans,
ecumenism meant the Roman Empire, whereby ecumenical
council referred to the council convoked by the emperors. Unlike
the Roman application of the term, Christians fundamentally
conceive of it as a movement to peace, salvation, unity and love
for all the children of God. In this way, ecumenical council
refers to the universal meeting of the leaders of the Church,
with the Pope presiding. Such meetings take into account what

> *may hinder all other religious bodies from sharing in the light*
> *of a close union with God (Nwachukwu, 2002:252; Ekennia,*
> *Justin, Ibid).*

Therefore, the primary objective of ecumenism is to examine all the varied religious beliefs in the same spirit of love and friendship. To examine these different religious beliefs, dialogue becomes a necessity. In an unmistakable terms, as cited in Nwachukwu, the Second Vatican (Ecumenical) Council declared: "There can be no ecumenism, worthy of the name without interior conversion for it is from newness of attitude of mind, from self-denial and unstinted love, that desires for unity take their rise and develop in a mature way" (Vatican Council II, Conciliar Documents Decree on Ecumenism, Unifatis Redin tegratio, No. 7, Ed. By A. Flannery, Minnesota: The Liturgical Press, 1975, Nwachukwu, Ibid).

Actually, education of the mind "leads to a meaningful dialogical relationship by which the individuals become inter-dependent and co-responsible within the same mystery [divine-orientated] of human relationships. They can now appreciate the limit and ability of one another and be best disposed to listen and respond adequately to the truth presented to each of them in that dialogue" (Nwachukwu, Ibid). In this perspective, there are different forms of education, formal and informal. But in the case of the introduction of the Christian message into Igboland, formal education was not necessary at that time. Care should have been taken for each other to listen properly to their differences and areas of unity. If that approach had been taken, the dilemma in question would have remarkably been removed.

This is the education that would have taken the culture, values, feelings, and belief systems of the people into consideration, building up a dialogical relationship. Time would be devoted for this important aspect of the evangelization process. In Nwachukwu's own words:

> *Dialogue is a lubricating factor in any situation of doubts, confusions and divergent opinions. Through dialogue, people discover more areas of progress in their relationships and easily eradicate or resolve conflicts and disagreements. Thus, when a person tells his or her partner, "let us talk", it means there is a problem or something to be fixed or addressed, which every partner is bound to get involved (Ibid).*

According to the above quotation, dialogue lubricates tensions between two opposing groups and clarifies doubts and elements of confusion. A situation where a new religion was introduced without any form of dialogue will always leave some imprint of confusion and disagreement, hence the dilemma of the growth of the Christian religion in Igboland, especially among Ngor Okpala people who believed tenaciously in their God.

Issue of Religious Indifferentism/Pluralism

We need to note right away that dialogue and ecumenism cannot compromise the basic tenets and identity of a people. In other words, ecumenism is not the same thing as religious indifferentism. To think otherwise leads to an unavoidable risk which religious dialogue must encounter. According to Nwachukwu:

> *These risks had always sprung up from the point of view of the ideas expressed and exchanged in dialogue. Every religion has some beliefs that explicitly mark it out from other religions. These basic facts or beliefs, which define every religion, cannot be bought at the price of ecumenism or dialogue. Okoro in Nwachukwu*

has quoted Cardinal Arinze as saying: Inter-religious dialogue is not simply peaceful co-existence or mutual tolerance. Nor is it a merely academic study of religions; it is not simply exchange of information about different religions. While it is not opposed to conversion, inter-religious dialogue in its general nature is not exactly the same thing as proclamation of the Gospel message (Nwachukwu, 2002:253; K. C. Okoro, 2000:4-5).

In his understanding, dialogue is a meeting of hearts and minds as noted already. It is a communication between two or more believers of different religious faith, walking together towards the common truth. It is a religious partnership without complexes and without hidden agenda or motives so that everyone else sees the end and benefits of the discussion.

Eventually, differences of religious beliefs are essentially important in any dialogical encounter. "Most often, according to Nwachukwu:

Religious indifferentism places all its emphasis on conduct, and not necessarily on doctrines. But the question has always been: how can we correctly say that an action is good or bad unless there is a doctrine or moral order to back it up? It becomes unthinkable for certain religious groups to play down on their doctrines in the name of ecumenical movement. In Cardinal Arinze's word as quoted by Okoro, inter-religious dialogue cannot be identified as an effort toward a synthetic union of several religions. All the official teachings of the Catholic faith, for instance, which seem to have been guaranteed against error by Christ himself are kept to the letters (Nwachukwu, 2002:254).

Differences in religious beliefs may not be an excuse to any form of dialogue. Even among Ngor Okpala people, there are certain beliefs that cannot be compromised under any pretence whatsoever. The differences in religion must always be there irrespective of dialogue and ecumenism. It was on this note that Arinze as cited in Nwachukwu lamented, thus:

> *To regard the difference in doctrine between religious groups as 'much ado about nothing' is to involve oneself in muddled thinking, obvious contradictions, sentimental over flow, negation of the first principles of logic and the dictates of common sense, and implicit denial of the validity of objective criteria to truth and error* (Nwachukwu, 2002:255).

Based on what Arinze noted in Nwachukwu, Christ himself instituted the Church primarily for human salvation. There is no one way of entering the Church. The institution does not mean any use of force or obligation. Through dialogue, and in the spirit of oneness or ecumenism, the Ngor Okpala people will see reasons to accept the Christian religion, not as foreign but part of their culture and religion. When this happens, the issues of indifferentism and superiority become instruments for greater reunion and love. That is why the parties in dialogue are as important as the dialogue itself. Such people must have the willingness and preparedness to engage in the dialogue. For Ekennia as cited in Nwachukwu: "Who can really discern what their interests, goals, and true needs are?" The parties are to have certain things in common and possess equal bargaining power, which involves equal and free participation in dialogue (Nwachukwu, 2002:259).

On the other hand *Religious pluralism* has got to do with the various common issues that must be accepted by each party. As a matter of fact, pluralism operates under the principles of acceptance and diversity, unity in diversity. It is a system that emphasizes the common good of all. As far as religion is concerned, it is coming together of religious bodies with common recognition and credence to all beliefs systems. This is not always possible. On this note, Wikipdia observes: "For pluralism to function and be successful in achieving the common good, all groups have to agree to a minimal consensus regarding both shared values, which tie the different groups to society, and shared rules...This sounds good but is impractical and can we dare to say impossible when there will always be certain truths that are non-compromising" (Wikipedia, Internet Encyclopedia). Continuing in this standpoint of pluralism, Wikipedia says:

> *Religious pluralism is a set of worldviews that stands on the premise that one religion is not the sole exclusive source of values, truths, and supreme deity. It therefore must recognize that at least 'some' truth must exist in other belief systems. This is one example of 'they can't all be right"* (Ibid).

As long as some religious values are not compromised despite ecumenism – indifferentism, and some are relative and comprised – pluralism, we are bound to discuss some of the principles that guide dialogue. To maintain a fruitful and effective dialogue, these principles must be observed. We considered a few among them as culled from Prof. Nwachukwu, 2002:269-274).

Five Principles for Effective Dialogue

1. The capacity to listen:

Listening is everyday occurrence. Because of that, many have taken it for granted. Yet, this art or quality in human life has acquired an academic attention. In the first place, listening is not the same thing as hearing. Most often, we hear practically everything that is happening in our noisy world. At times, we hear and do not listen and some other times, we listen and do not hear the electricity of feelings implied in the activity. It has become so important that I decided to treat and include this session in this book for the purpose of edification and didactics. If only the world would understand the implication of listening to one another especially in moments of distress, pains, and needs, the world would have been a better place than it is today. No wonder Jesus told his disciples:

> *I still have many things to say to you but they would be too much for you now. But when the Spirit of truth comes he will lead you to complete truth, since he will not be speaking as from himself but will say only what he has learnt from me; and he will tell you of the things to come (John 16: 12-13).*

From what Jesus told his disciples, it is easy to discover basically five things:

1. Jesus was convinced he had said all he needed to tell them but they did not seem to be listening.
2. The Holy Spirit he would send in his name was not going to say anything new except what he heard Jesus say.
3. What Spirit of truth was Jesus referring to? Was he telling them any lie all these days?
4. The borderline is that, each of us needs to listen carefully to what people tell us. By listening, we understand people and become part of what we listen to.
5. People are their stories and values. To listen is to recognize and to respect.

In dialogue, listening is the number one key. At times, people jump into arguments without listening to the issue at hand only to discover that they have been fighting themselves. For instance, assuming your wife tells you, now that the government is giving scholarship, is it not time or proper to send our maid to school? The emphatic word here is "send our maid to school" and without even listening or taking note that the government has offered scholarship, the man may become angry and continue to argue why they should send a maid to school in these words: "What are you saying, to send the Maid to school? Why did her parents fail to do so? Was that our agreement with her parents? More especially where are you going to get the money for such an undertaking? You know I am no longer working, and we depend on your pensions alone. That will not happen in this house..." The power to possess others lies in listening to them. As noted already, the failure of the missionaries to listen to the people of Igboland of Nigeria was the major factor in the dilemma of the growth of the Christian religion.

The skill to listen is as important as the people engaged in any conversation or communication especially on one-on-one basis. There can be no committed dialogue where the participants do not possess the ability and capacity to listen attentively to each other. Patience is an aspect of listening capacity. It is also a virtue as we saw already in this book. Even in any form of human relationship, the ability or preparedness to listen is so important. Most often, it is failure to listen that creates crisis in human interactions and the dilemma of the growth of the Christian religion of Igboland. Had the missionaries engaged the Igbo people in any form of dialogue first, the rapport would have been easily built than forcing each other to listen to their voices. When we are forced to listen to what concerns us, we cannot hear anything. When we listen, we hear. Attention has to be given to whomever that is speaking to us, whether it is nonsensical or meaningful, we are bound to listen. When a conversation fails, it means there is no patience and prudence exercised in that communication.

According to Mozia as cited in Nwachukwu, "An authentic dialogue demands an obedient listening, from the parties participating in it. This means a rapt listening, a hearkening with all our being so that we can totally respond" (Mozia, I. Michael. Solidarity in the Church and Solidarity among the Ibos [2nd Ed.] Ibadan: Claverianum Press, 1987:162). Again, Mozia has pointed out an important factor that underlies listening and that is obedient. To listen to others is to be obedient to them too. The world is in turmoil and conflicts today because nobody wants to listen to the voice of reason. Even in many Congresses of the wing of the government, the ability to listen to good argument is lacking. When everybody is talking sense and no one is listening, it means all the people involved are simply making noise or wasting their time. For religion to grow in Igboland, especially in Ngor Okpala, the people must listen to the implications of the Christian message and decide whether or not to accept it fully and avoid the dilemma in question.

The importance of listening is such that it hinges on human care, regard and respect. I strongly believe that without it, there can be no effective human communication and interactions. The aim of dialogue is to enrich each other's side or views without taking rigid positions. Whenever, we try to listen to others in dialogue or in communication, we simply tell them that we are happy and ready to benefit from them and share with them what we have. It is a process of cooperation in building values that will enrich each party for effective results in the matter or issue being discussed. To act otherwise is to fail in the understanding process or education that dialogue brings to both parties. To listen is to enrich self, benefit from the dialogue. One may begin to ask: "Must I listen to annoying words or conversations?" No conversation is annoying till you have listened to the teller. It might be possible that what sounds like annoying words might turn out to be for your own progress, development and advantages. To listen is to reason along with whomever that is talking to us. It is to accord the other some space and dignity that a human person deserves.

2. The need for Self-awareness:

Today, I have discovered from research that 80% of quarrels that happen in families result from misunderstanding. Most often, misunderstanding comes from failure to grasp our status quo or positions. The need for self-awareness cannot be overemphasized in our time. It is appalling that many people do not even know their personality types and temperaments. These are important steps of mastering who we are. For instance, when a hot-tempered personality relates with a psycho-pathetic personality, definitely there is going to be war every day. What of when the introverted marry the extroverted – that is, the schizothymic and the cyclothymic personalities? This is where emotional intelligence and education of the human person become urgent. In a situation where a schizothymic – an introverted person marries the cyclothymic – extroverted partner, only magic or miracle will make them live harmoniously. That is why pastoral psychology is designed to assist people in different levels of their family or group problems.

There is always a problem when people engage with others without proper study of who they are. Each person is supposed to have a clear knowledge of the person he or she is before any meaningful dialogue or relationship is possible. This is part of the education we talked about in which each party remains flexible to accept any possible points of agreements. If a party makes up its mind on what to accept and what not to accept, there can be no effective dialogue. The sequence and procedure employed in dialogue or the way one presents one's points in any dialogue matters a lot because what one communicates in dialogue is not only words or ideas but also one's personality, belief systems within the level of their acceptability. According to Allport's observation: "Personality is the dynamic organization within the individual of those psycho-physical systems that determine his characteristic behavior and thought" Allport, G. Pattern and Growth in Personality. NY: Holt Rinehart & Winston, 1961:28). This self-consciousness of the various traits of personality types creates self-confidence in dialogue where one can freely share one's ideas in a friendly atmosphere and manner.

3. Elements of Revolution:

It has to be noted that, often, change is synonymous with controversy because a lot of people are opposed to it. As it were, every committed dialogue is revolutionary but not confrontational because of the change it is about to bring. That is why the language of dialogue has to be understood by all. We shall come back to this important factor. The manner in which a participant presents his points may create disagreements and repulsions. It is always anticipated in any form of dialogue. That was why we discussed and hammered about religious indifferentism in which, despite the fact that we want to achieve a common consensus, parties are obliged to maintain certain positions that are particularly peculiar to them. Religious dialogue does not mean all issues are going to be compromised by both parties. Each party has the right to retain what they consider the untouchables. However, revolution in this context should be understood in terms of a peaceful movement, a radical change to something better and not to violence.

Most people associate revolution with the types we have at Iraq and other war zones. Revolution exists in different categories. There is revolution in the homes, at work places, in individual lives, practically everywhere in the globe. In dialogue, revolution only refers to the points being considered with no specific reference to individual personalities or culture. Dialogical revolution is momentary, ephemeral and lasts as long as the discussion that creates change is in session. The participants in dialogue may encounter some initial problems in their bid to arrive at the truth. That is all the revolution in question and as soon as the problem is resolved, there is order. Partners of different industries are called upon to exercise the same spirit of determination in arriving at a peaceful conclusion of any point. In a sincere dialogue, antithesis will always lead to synthesis. According to Vatican II, "Dialogue can... achieve cooperation between individuals, groups or communities who may at times differ in ideology" (Op. cit. page, 1010). This is why education is very important in any effective dialogue.

4. Openness and the spirit of Sincerity:

The issue of openness and spirit of sincerity is one of the factors that create progress and advancement in life, whether in the family circle or elsewhere. It is one thing to speak of openness and another to be one actually. Openness is an indispensable prerequisite for any meaningful dialogue. Openness begins from self and not necessarily from the other. As Nwachukwu indicated in his book in Spiritual Psychology, we tell people how to treat us. If we want our partners to be open to us, we must show them one first. You cannot expect your partner to be honest when you are greedy and selfish (Nwachukwu, 2010). The spirit of sincerity is not forced into anybody. It is just there as spiritual beings to be proactively employed in whatever we do. But unfortunately this is what is lacking in most human communications today. Once this same spirit goes into dialogue that demands sincerity, nothing can be achieved in the process.

In this manner, participants in dialogue should try as much as they can, to avoid deceit, suspicion, arguments to win, and apathy, self-interests, bigotry, partisan, from their thoughts and build the spirit of truth, mutual respect, tolerance, confidence and flexibility. It was on this note that the Second Vatican Council defined dialogue as: "Every form of dialogue, insofar as the participants are involved in mutual give and take, involves a certain reciprocity...For the object of dialogue is that one side should come closer to the other side and should understand it better" (Vatican II, Counciliar Documents Humane Personae Dignitatem, 28 August 1968, page 1006). This is what it means to be open to others. To be open does not mean complacence – a feeling of secure self-satisfaction. It is being reasonable and actively involved in one's committed goals. It is only within this magnitude that dialogue will be fruitful and progressive.

5. History of Dialogue:

Any authentic dialogue should be historical in nature. We carry our histories from birth to death. That reminds me. We emphasis much on our birthdays and accompany them with specific songs, but nothing is said about our death days. Could it be that, the only histories we have of ourselves are those we could record ourselves? Yet, every body's birthday is a reported speech. No one is sure of one's birthday just as no one is aware of one's death day. When we celebrate birthdays, we trust and believe that the records of our births as handed to us by our associates are true and because we are alive to do so. It is necessary to note that the ways we lead our lives determine the nature of birthdays we celebrate and what people will say at our back when we are no more living in the body. Thus, our histories are as important as how we present ourselves in dialogue.

This implies that the subject matter to be presented in such a dialogue should be weighed and seen from its historical perspective to avoid and guide participants from being biased and judgmental. There is nothing we know of ourselves, or our world that has no imprint of history in it. Therefore, to hold effective dialogue, it has to do with its historical backgrounds and values. Whether any dialogue is verbal or dialogue of action, it "can produce a greater incentive that urges people to collaborate in the common search for the meaning of life in their historical adventure through life" (Op.cit.165). For instance, if the subject matter of the dialogue is on religious doctrine, while parties guide against religious indifferentism, the need to trace the historical background of such a doctrine that has a common value agreement is very important.

Interestingly, the need for dialogue cannot be overemphasized in the life of rational beings. Dialogue encourages mutuality and solidarity in relationships. It creates order, unity and peace. It is inconceivable to have human interactions and interpersonal transactions without some sort of understanding and agreement between people, individuals and nations. In dialogue we clear our differences and accept the truth of each other. For instance, in religious circles, dialogue will surely make various religions and denominations come together and appreciate themselves as systems and people in search for the same meaning and goal. It was because the missionaries had no such agenda to engage the people in dialogue despite the poor language barriers that led to the initial dilemma of the growth of the Christian religion in Igboland. The dilemma will continue as long as religious leaders, groups and individuals do not find time to come together and discuss their difference on a wider note. Having extensively studied the various minds on this dilemma, we have to state how we got to our conclusion and research in chapter three. This does not mean there are no more reasons for the decline of the Christian religion or faith in Igboland especially as it affects the people of Ngor Okpala.

CHAPTER THREE

༺༒༻

METHODOLOGY

Methodology guided the development of this book. The technical and scientific supervision of Nwachukwu tremendously assisted us in this academic venture. We are going to approach the chapter under the following parameters or items:

- ➤ The design of the study
- ➤ The area of the research or study
- ➤ Our population
- ➤ Sampling approach
- ➤ The instrument for collecting the data for this research
- ➤ Developing and validating of the instrument employed
- ➤ Reliability of the instrument
- ➤ Manner of collecting the data
- ➤ The method and technique of analyzing the data

1. The major design of this work is the efforts we made to contact the teachers who confidentially gave us their perceptions on the problems at hand. They equally know that there is real problem

concerning the growth of the Christian faith in Igboland especially among Ngor Okpala people. Their responses were the main data that guided us in this investigation.

2. The area of study concerns mainly the dilemma, the predicament and the harm that the Christian religion seems to have done on the people of Igboland in general and Ngor Okpala in particular. This part of the research raised these questions: "Is it true that there is dilemma in the growth of the Christian faith among these people? What are the factors responsible for the dilemma and can anything be done to assist its growth? In this light, all the aspects of literature, fieldwork, interviews, which could guide us to arrive at an answer become parts of our area of study as already seen.

3. The population of this work includes the various religious groups in society. Our emphasis was on the Christian religion that was presented to the people of Igboland. In this sense, we tried to concentrate our investigation on the dilemma of the growth of the Christian religion in Igboland with greater attention on the people of Ngor Okpala.

Practically, our population singled out 244 teachers in Ngor Okpala who assisted in the collection of our data for this research work. The choice of these teachers was that they have comprehensive knowledge of what is going on around Igboland concerning the dilemma of the growth of the Christian faith in Nigeria and beyond.

4. Sampling technique involved a sample of 124 teachers whom we chose from the whole population of 244 teachers. We adopted a random selection technique with stratified or representative sampling procedure to include different levels and gender of the teachers. Each

of the teachers was considered as important as any of them and their responses were critically examined.

5. The instrument for data collection is the "TPDGCF" Questionnaire, meaning "The perception of the dilemma of the growth of the Christian faith". The questionnaire comprised of 16 questions, which each teacher had to comment on and furnish us with what he or she thinks of the matter or concern raised. Like in many research works, this section is two in number – A and B.

Section 'A' seeks information concerning the teachers' demographic and ideographic positions. Section "B" has the 16 contents of the questionnaire. These 16 questions are shared into 5 other sections and each of them has a box of questions from which the teachers select and rate his or her scores. These scores are later analyzed in chapter four of the book as indicated in the various research questions.

6. The development and validation of the instrument were done be professionals who understood the problem at hand. The rigorous tasks of visiting most of these teachers and collecting their responses were not easy. These teachers in both secondary schools and Universities seriously examined the initial construction of the instrument. They equally weighed its capability to measure such a major issue of faith crisis in Igboland. After some corrections were made, the questionnaire came from 40 questions to this 16. All these procedures took the researcher several weeks of intensive hard work to accomplish and both the researcher and respondents unanimously agreed that the instrument was valid enough for the work at hand.

7. Reliability of instrument was a process that took technical means. For us to choose the 124 respondents, we had already distributed our questionnaire to the 244 tipped for the population. After their responses, we re-administered the same instrument to other group of teachers who were not fundamentally and initially chosen for this research. They equally gave professional responses that helped us to compare and contrast what options and individuals are most competent to handle our enquiry. From this method, we were able to arrive at the number and reliability index of 124 by the process of choice and elimination.

8. The method of our data collection equally took rigorous steps. The researcher had to visit the teachers on personal basis, gave them some lectures on the dilemma at hand and asked them to air their opinions from their own perspectives and findings. There was no delay in distributing and collecting of the questions. They simply ticked the options that best suited their own views and the researcher had to collect them on the spot to avoid loss of materials and guide against revealing confidentiality.

9. The technique for data analysis was simply based on the information the teachers gave us. By employing a simple percentage, we multiplied each response by 100 and divided by the total respondents or number of teachers. After this fieldwork, in chapter four of the book, we presented, analyzed and interpreted our data for the development of the book.

CHAPTER FOUR

⁓

DATA PRESENTATION, ANALYSIS AND INTERPRETATION OF RESULTS

This chapter has two main sections, namely:

    i.   Presentation and analysis of the data collected
   ii.   The interpretation of the data

i. Presentation and analysis of the data collected

As we saw in chapter three, the presentation of the teachers is being analyzed here - question by question. We tried to present each result of the analysis in a table from which the teachers made their selections. From the results we drew few conclusions.

Research Question I: The nature and level of the dilemma of the growth of the Christian faith in Igboland?

Table 4.1 Responses on the nature and level of religious crisis as seen among the people

Question	Mode of Response	
Among which category or group have you observed some dilemma in the practice of the Christian faith among the people?	Frequency (No)	%
i. Among the Catholics	28	22.58
ii. Among the Protestants	30	24.19
iii. Among traditional religionists	24	19.35
iv. Among Christian Fanatics	42	33.87
Total	124	100

From table 4.1, 28 (22.58%) of the teachers indicate that serious lack of faith comes from Catholics. 30 of them representing 24.19% shift the blame on Protestants. While the Traditionalists hold 24 (19.35%), the Christian have 42 (33.87%) of the responses.

Research Question II: The Sources (causes) of Faith Dilemma in the growth of the Christian Religion?

Table 4.2: Responses to determine the cause of the religious predicaments and dilemma among the people of Igboland.

Question	Mode of Response	
Which of the items below is the cause and source of religious dilemma in the growth of the Christian faith in Igboland?	Frequency of Responses (No)	Percentage of Responses
i. Poor catechesis and lack of proper direction	26	20.96
ii. Lack of self-conviction and interests in religious matters	44	35.48
iii. Personal choices and materialistic tendencies	32	25.80
iv. Role of religious ministers and bigotry	22	17.74
Total	124	100

The respondents in table 4.2 hold that poor catechesis and lack of proper direction score 26 (20.96%) of the analysis. In their evaluations, 44 (35.48) of their responses point accusing fingers to lack of self-conviction and interests in religious matters. The issue of personal choices and materialistic tendencies scored 32 or 25.80% of the analysis. The number that maintains that the role of religious ministers and bigotry is responsible for the dilemma is 22 (17.74%).

<u>Research Question III:</u> The possibility of totally eradicating religious predicaments in the growth of the Christian faith in Igboland of Nigeria?

Table 4.3: Responses to ascertain whether or not the religious dilemma can completely be wiped out from the practice of the Christian religion in Igboland.

Question	Mode of Response	
In your own opinion, do you think religious dilemma can totally be stamped out among the people of Nigeria?	Frequency of responses	Percentage
i. Yes ii. No	48 76	38.70 61.29
Total	124	100

Table 4.3 has shown that 48 of the respondents or teachers representing 38.70% of the sample say that religious dilemma can totally be crushed from Igboland. On the other hand, 76 of them, that is, 61.29% frankly hold that it is impossible to wipe out hypocrisy or predicaments in the growth of Christian faith from Igboland.

Research Question IV: Management of religious crisis in the growth of the Christian faith in Igboland?

Table 4.4: Responses to elicit possible measures by which the religious dilemma in the growth of Christian faith in Igboland can be handled.

Question	Mode of Response	
By which of these measures do you suggest can best assist in determining the control of religious crisis in Igboland?	Frequency (No)	Percentage - %
i. People to live by examples	44	35.48
ii. The Church to become in practice truly the human face of Christ	32	25.80
iii. Enculturation of both religious values for holistic enhancement of the practice of religion	22	17.74
iv. Need for flexibility and readiness for change	26	20.96
Total	124	100

As could be ascertained from table 4.4 of our response, 44(35.48%) agree that religious growth can only come about when people, ministers and members live by example. In this account, 32(25.80) say that the only way to move the Christian faith forward is when the Church becomes indeed, the human face of Christ. However, while 22(17.74%) of them maintain that enculturation of both religious values for holistic enhancement of the Christian faith will do it, 26(20.96%) suggest that the people of Igboland, especially those from Ngor Okpala must be flexible in their belief systems and ready to accept changes.

Research Question V: Effects of religious dilemma in the progress of society in general?

Table 4.5: Responses to elicit from the respondents if religious crisis and dilemma can affect or hamper the progress of society generally.

Question	Mode of Response	
In your own opinion, do you think religious predicaments and crisis can affect the progress of society in any way?	Frequency (No)	%
i. Yes ii. No	124 0	100 0
Total	124	100

The above table 4.5 of response, 124 (100%) of the teachers unanimously agree that dilemma in religious matters will always affect society in a very drastic manner. But none of the respondents agreed that religious disorder and dilemma would not affect the society in general.

ii. The Interpretation of the analysis

Interpretations are based on and determined by the figures or scores each teacher or respondent assigned to the variables or questions from the instrument or questionnaire. This is always a context analysis in that each interpretation is brought about by the responses from the context being analyzed.

For instance, the result we obtained from table 4.1 has shown that Christian fanatics are responsible for serious lack of the Christian faith and religion in Ngor Okpala of the Igboland of Nigeria. The simple interpretation is that their behaviors are not compatible with the Christian principles and values because they scored the highest in the analysis - of 34%. The Protestants are second with 24% in this process of the evaluation of those who have shown great lack of practice in the pursuit of Christian faith in Igboland. In line with this interpretation, it is clear that Protestants are not living up to their expectations. However, the Catholics scored the 3rd place with 23% showing serious lack of practice in their Christian belief. It is also possible from this interpretation, that most of the respondents are Catholics.

That evaluation of serious lack of faith in the Christian religion among the traditional religionists came to 19% has a lot to say in this interpretation. In the first place, the traditionalists do not care much about what the Christians are doing. Again, there is every indication that the traditionalists are faithful to their religion. In other words, the hypocrisy of saying one thing and doing another is not traceable to them. This is food for thought for the Christians to examine themselves and how they hold their religious beliefs and practices in Igboland.

On the other hand, the results we got from table 4.2 indicate that poor catechesis and lack of proper spiritual direction are responsible for the dilemma of the growth of the Christian faith in Igboland. The 26 (20.96%) of respondents supported it. From the analysis, that is the 3rd position out of the variables we conclude that the missionaries were not necessarily the cause of the religious predicaments in Igboland. 44(35.48%) of them, taking the first position, hold that the major cause of this religious dilemma is lack of self-conviction and interest in religious matters. In other words, it has been revealed that most of the people have no interest in religious matters, either owing to selfishness and materialism or self-conviction in believing that the supernatural will solve their problems on earth. This is in line with the 32(25.80%) of the respondents who point out that the cause of religious hindrance in Igboland is personal choices and materialistic tendencies.

The simple face interpretation is that many people, mainly Christians, in Igboland are no longer interested in listening to the promptings of the Christian message but prefer to live by the age of science and technology. Again, 22(17.74%) showed that the role of religious ministers and rivalries or bigotry is the cause and source of religious predicament in Igboland. The interpretation is that, even though there are many factors responsible for it, the ministers have been doing their best. As to whether they live by what they preach or teach is a different point as our interpretation has indicated.

As we could discover from table 4.3 of our analysis, 48(38.70%) of the respondents agree that religious dilemma can totally be wiped out of society and Igboland of Nigeria once the people begin to do things right and follow the values of Christianity. But, it is shocking that a total number of 76(61.29%) believed that religious dilemma could not be wiped out of Igboland. The simple interpretation for those in this position could be that the minorities, who are doing whatever it takes to live by good examples, have no intention of violating the basic tenets of Christianity. In this sense, those in this camp have no problems with the traditional religions as being an obstacle for the practice of their faith. But those who insist that religious dilemma cannot be crushed have shown a strong disbelief in what Christ could do in their lives. They maintain this position, either based on the nature of man that is frail and corrupt or his inability to cope with the Christian principles and regulations.

From our table 4.4, 44(35.48%) of the respondents, being the highest, hold that there is always a way to check this predicament of religious growth and that once people begin to live by examples, the problem could be contended with. The Church took the second position with 32(25.80%) of the respondents implying that the Church has big work to do in this regard. Besides personal life examples, the Church has also to live by example and teach the Christian message in practice and words. As it were, emphasis seems to have been laid more on words than doing of the words today.

Enculturation of both religious values are necessary for the enhancement of the practice of the Christian religion in Igboland. 22(17.74%) agreed on that point. The missionaries had done their work; the people themselves can decide to live by the principles and values that encourage their faith instead of division. On the same par, 26(20.96%) of them are of the opinion that the people need to be flexible in their belief system and begin to appreciate the values of other religions that encourage peace and unity and accept change when necessary.

In our final table 4.5, the respondents unanimously agreed that if nothing is done and convince people of the need to accept the Christian message for what it is and integrate the traditional values that are compatible with Christianity; society would always suffer at large. In other words, the whole 124 (100%) teachers maintain that religious dilemma will always affect the progress and peace of the people. The simple face interpretation is that people have got to sit up and think of the meaning of this life and try to appreciate their source as such.

CHAPTER FIVE

~

SUMMARY OF WORK AND FINDIGS

This book began by establishing what faith means in our context. We tried to give a synopsis of the various chapters the work embarked upon as a scientific approach to the problem at hand – the dilemma of the growth of the Christian faith in Igboland, a psycho-pastoral approach. However, we equally employed simple words and symbolic expressions to make clearer our stand on the issue of faith and religion as understood by the Igbos of Nigeria. Nevertheless, our conclusion will solely depend on the position and contributions of the researcher and results of our findings in this book.

Also, it has to be borne in mind that in a course such as this, where every Dick and Harry claims to have some knowledge, it would be impossible for any researcher to exhaust the topic. In this light, we are not going to regard this work as final, though there is the projection that this write-up can form a springboard from which more research and scholarly works on the issue can emerge. Our voices, through research, have been heard. The matter has been made public. There is dilemma in the growth of the Christian religion in

Ngor Okpala because those who should have guided society in the ways to sound moral lives and peace are hiding under the carpet of religious indifferentism. Religion is part of us and we need to show it in our lives and actions.

As such, we generally traced the background of the study, which pointed to the fact that many religious and anthropologists in Igboland tend to give conflicting interpretations for the word "faith" and religion. The background also threw much light on the problem that has necessitated this psycho-socio pastoral enquiry, eliciting the question: "what do we do?" The issue of faith and religion dates as far back as the creation of man. Faith and believing have been part and parcel of the human story. While the westerners generally believe in God, the Igbo of Nigeria, not only believe but they also relate with their ancestors/God and tend to communicate with them on their daily lives. It is impossible to achieve any progress in one's life where there is no belief and faith in it. No wonder in the creation account, it was said that God forbade Adam and Eve, regarding the tree of the knowledge of good and evil in the garden (Gen 2: 17). No epoch in the history of mankind, including the people of Igboland has passed without raising the questions concerning the ultimate end of man and the best ways one can attempt to arrive at meaningful ends.

Experience has shown that man's life on earth is shrouded with uncertainties and some mysteries. The question that stares us in the face is if man has any final destiny? If man has destiny, we believe, the research has posited the challenge why has he consistently neglected to acknowledge the gifts of his creation or God and appreciate them in lively and meaningful worship that lacks philosophical debates. Nonetheless, it is a platitude that man has a creator who cares for him. But who that creator is, remains a mystery to so many people including some Igbo. Hence, man is continually in a struggle for a lasting security and in a search for his creator. This continuous struggle for meaning seemed to have been confused by the new religion that did not seem to understand that of the traditional one.

The Christian revelation presented God as the all-embracing and loving father, the creator of heaven and earth. But, contrary to the above qualifications, man is faced with the stark reality of suffering in his world. Thus, we are constrained to ask further questions. Why is man created at all? God created all things in the world, then what of the problem of evil? Most often, we argue that, if God is infinitely perfect he ought not to have created such a world. Or, is suffering part of God's plan for creating man? The Igbo man sees suffering as part of God's punishment on humanity. In essence, man is not supposed to suffer. But it is because man is not living according to God's directions that he has to suffer and die young. That is precisely why, in Igboland, early death is seen as evil, bad omen for the community and the affected family.

According to Mozia, this moral responsibility among the members of the Igbo community does not result solely from the ontological dimension (Mozia, I. Michael 1987). The Igbo, especially in the eastern part of Nigeria, strongly believe that faith is a gratuitous gift from God and that it comes from hearing and hearing comes from the word of God. The Igbo man sees faith as the beginning of a Christian man and woman, and the foundation of all righteousness. By faith, we hold many truths about God, which the philosophers were unable to discover by natural reason. For instance, his providence and omnipotence, and that he alone is to be worshiped. It is through this faith, that is supernatural in essence and virtue and by which [through the help of God and through the assistance of his grace] we believe what he has revealed himself to be true that the Igbos of Nigeria try to uphold his supremacy in their tradition.

Finally, we attempted to analyze the situation that has kept the Christian faith in Igboland of Nigeria in its dangling stage since the arrival of the white man. It revealed the people's ignorance of what the Christian religion was all about, the effects of colonialism, nepotism, hypocrisy, Cultural crisis, selfishness of religious leaders etc. Our findings suggested possible areas of prospective research on the topic at hand. The research exposed some of the ills, and the syndrome of prosperity preachers that are negating the true message of Christ today. When Christ categorically stated that those who should worship him must do so in spirit and in truth, with humility and simplicity of hearts but the reverse is the case today.

The work equally noted that before the advent of western education, colonialism and Christianity, traditional religion had laid the basis of the behavior of the Igbo people of Nigeria that did not seem to accommodate other religions. The survey suggested that people should be flexible to accommodate change in their life. Social and cultural identifications, principles of socialization from one generation to the other were highly respected. The new religion has only come to perfect them if the people of Igboland would understand the implications. The expressions of the sense of the sacred of the Igbo were rather encouraged by Christianity and did not intend to destroy them, as some Africans seem to claim.

The Igbo people had scared places, objects, persons, and periods and so does Christianity. The enculturation the work spoke about is best fitted here. Thanks to the shrines of the traditional religion of the people of Igboland, which were even used for oaths and appeasing God, the gods or ancestors, or as means of socio-cultural and political control. The same exists in Christianity but in different contexts and appellations. We said it already, according to Rtd. Councilor Okere: "The gods were interested in the moral probity and improbity of individual members of the society" (Interview with Councilor Francis Okere, aged 80, a traditional Ezeji in Ngor Okpala, July 6, 2003).

For the people of Igboland, ever before Christianity arrived, their religion was their life, their culture, and their identity as a people. For the westerners religion is a subject to be studied but for the people of Ngor Okpala, religion is part and parcel of the people's culture and life style. It was just normal for every Igbo person to live in conformity with the norms and morality of the land, in order, not only to offend the gods, but also to have peace and to prosper. From our findings, these norms, which are in conformity and compatible with the Christian faith, should complement each other to avoid syncretistic practices but growth in one's faith and belief.

As outlined in the summary account of the book in our introductory section, discussions in this book were designed, presented, measured and analyzed. Our limitations and educational implications were equally spelt out and prospective researchers, challenged to do more work on the related topic at hand. The next chapter, "work yet to be done" is the highest mark of academic honesty. The 'dilemma of the growth of the Christian religion in Nigeria, a psycho-pastoral approach' is an open ended-project that can be tackled from various perspectives. These other aspects not tackled here are what we expect in the following chapter. It is a form of self-evaluation and sign of scholarship that needs to be emulated by individuals in their relationships with other people. This is the summary of the book. Our findings will be incorporated into the recommendations for further research work.

CHAPTER SIX

꧁

WORK YET TO BE DONE

We noted it already that in a research work or book of this magnitude, there is no researcher or author that can exhaust the areas of study to the point that nothing more can be done on it. Such a topic like "The dilemma of the growth of the Christian faith in Igboland: A Psycho-pastoral perspective" is so wide that it will be difficult for any researcher to justify all it demands. In view of this handicap, we shall discuss this chapter under the following headings:

1. The limitation of the study

The limitation of this book is summarized along these areas, scope, content, methodology, language and population. With reference to scope, the work was limited to Igboland of Nigeria with particular emphasis on the people of Ngor Okpala. The question is, why was it that the researcher did not, in actual fact, include various ethnic and dialectical groups like the people of Ohafia, Afikpo, Ngwa, Mbaise, Orlu and part of Umuahia metropolitan in his work? Then, how can a research based on Igboland that excludes these areas be validated? That is part of the limitation. As we have noted in this book, Nigeria is famous for her huge population of about 150 million people. She is the largest national population on the African continent and the most populated black nation in the universe, made up of a population of about 374 different ethnic groups. With her multi- ethnic, multi-cultural, and multi- religious nature, and so many other factors in this thickly populated and complex nation on the globe, we could only go as far as our investigation allowed. Even the professionals we approached for data collection and analysis of the problems on the ground, could not have exhausted the areas to be covered. These also add to the limitation of the book.

In content, the book is not as exhaustive as already noted in the scope. Why was the emphasis laid on the Christian faith, when in Igboland there are various groups who don't believe in Christianity like the traditionalists and others who don't worship any god or force? Again, it is claiming too much discussing the Christian religion without concentrating on one particular denomination since there are so many Christian faith groups in Igboland. A study based only on the psychological and pastoral aspect of man that does not touch his social, economic, political components, is not complete. This overgeneralization is a limitation too.

The methodology employed here seemed to have emphasized only percentages. Why did the author avoid using "mean and mode" systems and other mathematical formulae to analyze his book? Whatever reasons the researcher may have for this procedure, without any explanation is also a limitation. The language of the work is English, which means that this work is designed for only the English-speaking people. Then, there are many Christians in Igboland who speak other languages, including their native tongue. In other words, how is this work going to be relevant to the majority of them? Actually, the problems encountered in the course of Christian religious growth in Ngor Okpala have indicated serious constraints and dilemma to effective educational achievement. As part of the limitations, the constraints include:

a. There is lack of qualified and experienced teachers for the Christian religion.
b. There is lack of instructional materials and facilities that aid the teaching and learning of Christian religion in Ngor Okpala.
c. There is a serious lack of interest in religion generally, hence the dilemma.

On the same point, the research employed investigators from Igboland of Nigeria as the main instrument and population, with particular reference to Ngor Okpala people. Why did the author not include teachers from other schools from Igboland and some from other countries? To have employed only teachers from Igboland to study and report a matter that involved westerners is to say the least, also a limitation.

2. The educational implication of our enquiry

There are a lot of implications that this research has revealed both for individual, self and communal assessments. After reading this book or research work, few things may come to mind such as: "What is the purpose of the book?" Whatever reason that is given here points to its educational implication. For instance, as stated in chapter one, the primary focus of the book is to suggest ways in which the Christian faith will be accepted for what it is and bear fruit among the people of Igboland, especially Ngor Okpala. Therefore, the creation of this consciousness that something is wrong with the practice of Christianity has great implication for educational attainment. The issue is once more considered from a wider spectrum for educational enhancement.

As long as children are the future of tomorrow, much emphasis should be placed on teaching and imparting religious values to them. Unfortunately, the elders of most of these children do not give them any good examples and this makes it impossible for them to pick interest in it. The implication of these lacks is that the moral dimension of Christian religion, which should be the motivating force in the practice of religion, is not there. In order to have religion back on track, the ministers and teachers or catechists who are essentially the instructional materials for this religious growth must claim their responsibility and lead society to the right direction. According to Dr. John Okoro, writing on the evaluation of possible constraints to effective Christian religious education in secondary schools, the Nigerian experience, noted:

> *No meaningful teaching and learning of [religious education or growth - mine] can take place under non-conducive environment. This researcher therefore seeks the impact such environmental factors, such as the role of government and other relevant agencies, such as the education board and the ministry of education; influence of families and parents; the influence of churches, would play in Christian religious education of students as very vital for effectiveness. Students themselves must be up and doing and play their own part for there to be a success in that regard. The students must cultivate moral virtues and imbibe discipline as part of their educational agenda (Dr. John Okoro, GTF/Oxford, 2010).*

The Agencies Dr. Okoro have indicated above need to be involved in the education and upbringing of the youth to start appreciating the values of religion in their lives. However, the best teaching and education they need is good examples from these formators and religious leaders. Not much can be achieved when society is not disciplined and focused on doing the right things. "Days of kneeling theology are over. We need doers of the words" (Nwachukwu, 2011). The net results of the dilemma are the inadequacy of both human and material resources for imparting of Christian Religion.

As a way of recapitulation and emphasis, the suggestions Dr. John Okoro made here are pertinent for the growth of the Christian religion in Igboland and Ngor Okpala. These invaluable points will be included in our final recommendations for the educational implications of this book. According to Okoro's recommendations:

- ✓ The government and all the educational agencies responsible for the posting and assignment of teachers should make available Christian Religious Knowledge teachers in secondary schools.
- ✓ Every Christian Religious teacher has the responsibility of transmission of the faith, and work to foster the student's faith, so that it may be living, conscious, and active as they examine their lives. And as Christians they follow Christ more closely and so embrace the truth, contribute to the good, and build a more just society with and for others. It is important to have in mind that teachers of Christian religion are transmitters of the faith, as they help young people to be "clothed in Christ" and become "salt of the earth and light for the world". This role is more specific to those who teach a classroom course in Religious education, for its purpose is two –fold. The first is to impart knowledge about the Christian faith tradition; that is to bring revelation to bear on their lives.

✓ The second is to encourage young people to follow in the footsteps of Christ; that is to act on God's behalf for the good of all creation. By virtue of his profession, the teacher is to educate the young to their faith, and the content and meaning of their faith. They are to mentor young people in their journey, to accompany them as they struggle with this knowledge and seek to integrate it in their daily lives. They are also to witness to the gospel and speak on behalf of the faith community. The Government therefore should employ qualified and experienced Christian Religious Knowledge teachers and post them to schools in the more badly affected areas in order to facilitate effective teaching and learning in Christian religious education.

✓ Learning occurs through the skilful use of many learning strategies such as research, comparative essay writing, reading, presentation, and newspaper search, to name but a few. The skilled teacher relies on a variety of learning strategies to present new information so as to capture the interest of all students. It is important to adopt a methodology that serves to accomplish the purpose of religious education, while giving pride of place to the power of the word and work of the Holy Spirit, who functions through revelation to affect conversion.

✓ In-service training programs therefore should always be organized for Christian Religious Education teachers in order to update their knowledge of the subject and foster new educational technology in them. Also, workshops, lectures and seminars should be organized for teachers of Christian Religious Education. If properly done, it will go a long way to improve the standard and help for effective learning and teaching of the subject.

✓ It is through the application of new learning to real life situations that students are moved towards acquisition and application of knowledge necessary for living lives as light and salt of the earth. Understanding is not fully realized until the students have been able to appropriate what they have read, researched, discovered and learnt with the very concrete things around them. There is need for adequate instructional materials and facilities to be provided to enhance thorough and effective teaching of their subject. The application and proper utilization of these materials will reduce the problems associated with Effective Christian religious education. The students are also motivated to learn with some ease.

✓ There is need for the establishment of resource centers in different areas, followed by establishment of standard libraries where reading texts, commentaries are available for students to lay hands on outside the classroom.

✓ Adequate human and material resources are always needed to help with effective Christian religious education. None should be under estimated. With or without Government intervention of supporting them with teaching aids, schools should also consider having their own make-shift arrangements so that teachers and students can always lay hands on something, in and outside the classroom.

✓ Students come to school from various cultural frame works, backgrounds, family structures, value systems, intellectual stories and limitations. Exploring these prior experiences need to be addressed as part of the teaching process for transformation and growth. As a School program, Christian religious education should be pursued with sensitivity to the freedom and responsibility of students, to the practical and social conditions in which students live. The teacher must teach the student to narrate his or her own lived experience in this regard, so as to accept the invitation of the Holy spirit to conversion, to commitment, to hope, and to discover more and more in his [or her] life, God's plan for their life.

✓ It is with such sensitivity that the teachers recognize the various effects of Christian religious education on the life of students who have different backgrounds regarding their Christian faith. When students are already strong in their Christian faith, Christian religious education assists them to understand better the Christian message, by relating it to their great existential concerns common to every human being, to the various visions of life particularly evident in their cultures, and to those moral questions, which confront them and humanity today.

✓ Those students who have doubts, or who are searching for a faith, can also find in Christian religious education the possibility of discovering what exactly faith in Jesus Christ is, what response Christianity makes to their questions, and gives them the opportunity to examine their own choices more deeply.

✓ In the case of students who are non-believers, Christian religious education assumes the character of a missionary proclamation of the gospel and is ordered to a decision of faith, which may eventually mature or be nurtured. Thus, the need for teachers to be vigilant and sensitive in the classroom with students who listen to them in the classroom. Hence, the teacher ought to rely on the movement of the Holy Spirit and trust in the teaching process to transform the students over time and space.

✓ Curriculum requirements need to identify the intrinsic connection between the content of Religious Education courses and the life experience of students. What this means is that students should be given the opportunity to recognize the various ways Christian religious education can affect human growth, development and understanding. Within the Christian faith, such integration of religious learning with its appropriate knowledge, attitudes and skills are placed within a response to life centered on the person of Jesus Christ.

✓ Student assessment is an integral part of the teaching-learning cycle. If the learning process within the Christian Religious education in the classroom is to be effective, a variety of assessment and evaluation strategies must be planned alongside learning activities. The criteria by which performance is to be measured must be clearly stated and known by students. Clear outcomes and criteria allow students to be part of the evaluation process. In this way, students develop a sense of standards and criteria for their own work.

✓ This researcher would recommend the need for Family life education of students and the need for parents to work together with teachers for effective Christian religious education. Adolescence is a time of struggle and difficulty concerning issues related to personal growth, relationships, and sexuality. For this reason, Christian Religious education curriculum ought to include materials and resources for family life education for each grade level of secondary school. As the primary educators of their children, parents entrust their children to schools to complement their growth, though in the academic domain, but also in the moral domain. When parents show interest in the Christian religious education of their children, by raising questions and engaging in discussions, educational growth becomes more meaningful. This cooperative relationship is of particular value in the family life strand of secondary school Christian religious education courses. School-based learning should assist and complete the work of parents, furnishing adolescents, for instance, with an evaluation of sexuality as value and task of the whole person, created male and female in the image of God. A mutually supportive role between teachers and parents in this area of human formation will positively influence the maturity of young people.

✓ Finally, Christian religious education must be taught in such a way as to stimulate the students towards new expressions of the gospel. Students and teachers should not be afraid to use traditional formulae and the technical language of the faith, but it must express its meaning and demonstrate its existential importance. It is necessary for the education to embrace the forms and terms proper to the culture of those students that are taught (Culled from Dr. John Okoro's unpublished work, GTF/Oxford, 2010).

Moreover, the people of Igboland, Ngor Okpala have been educated through this work that rigidity to their cultural beliefs will not assist them move forward in religious objectivity. Religion is meant to assist people live better lives and not create confusion and bigotry among them. The book in effect, has alerted the people of the need to welcome Christianity in the spirit of their culture. Christianity can only remain foreign in any culture that does not accept it. To accept Christianity is to accept Christ as the Son of God. The people should see Christ as their Proto-ancestor and not as a competitor. Both the people's culture and Christianity can be married to produce such values the people can always count on. In view of this line of thoughts, the educational implication of this book includes human relationship and changes, which require that:

❖ Christians should avoid rivalries among themselves;

❖ Christian fanatics have to see reasons in their culture and native customs also;

❖ Ministers of the Christian religion must try and teach and explain to the people the meanings of the mystery they preach to them;

❖ Religious dilemma is not a child of Christianity, but human problem;

❖ Hypocrisy has to be avoided by both Christians and the traditional religionists;

❖ The Church or Churches in Igboland should see it as their primary function to organize some conferences among themselves as ways of dialogue and enculturation;

❖ People should understand that the greatest calamity that can befall a people is the feeling that there is no God and that each person has the powers to do whatever he or she wants without any regard to nature and the supernatural;

❖ The religious crisis or dilemma in question is the fruit of human selfishness and greed; then, the need to avoid them is important;

❖ The book has called each person, whether Christian or not to lead by examples.

Based on the foregoing, the book recommends what prospective researchers on the growth of Christian religion should do or not do. It was on this basis that Dr. Okoro made the following statements:

Education courses invite students to build their relationship with the person of Jesus Christ as witnessed to by the Christian faith, which recognizes the centrality of God, the dignity of the human person, and the importance of ethical norms. This witness takes many forms, but essential to its self-understanding is the place of Sacred Scripture, Christian teachings, and its moral foundations for Christian living and Family Life Education. Course content and learning requirements are shaped by this self-understanding and opportunities are provided to integrate the foundations of faith and life in a manner conducive to both human and religious identity. Christian Religious Education is therefore more than teaching life skills or sharing information. Religious Education seeks to form, inform, and transform the human person (Okoro J, GTF/Oxford, 2010).

Practically, many people are not in touch with themselves for lots of reasons. There is much going on in individual lives; society appears polluted by all forms of atrocities. In a situation like this, religion suffers. Thus, the Ngor Okpala people and prospective researchers on this area should consider the following:

i. The progress the Christian faith has made in Igboland and not always from the negative aspects;

ii. Review the culture of other groups in Igboland and not to draw a conclusion from what happens in Ngor Opkala to judge the whole Igboland;

iii. Christianity and the African traditional religions are possible research topics;

iv. Effects of pride and pomposity in religious practice;

v. Role of Christian ministers in Igboland of Nigeria;

vi. Have the Igbo accepted the Christian message is also a researchable concern, question or inquiry?

vii. Who is a Christian or traditionalist in the face of corruption in Igboland?

CONCLUSION

Researching on the above topic has been an interesting one. The book has given some insights to the psychological and pastoral perspectives of the people in question. Anybody reading this book will automatically perceive that the Igbo people of Nigeria love themselves? Love in this context is not the opposite of hate, but the abiding presence of peace, openness, truth, justice, sincerity, and sensitivity – the embodiment of Christ. As Nwachukwu remarked, "You cannot love the person you deceive". Their religion is part of their culture. To infringe upon their belief system is to attack their sacredness.

Eventually, the book has challenged the people to begin to accept others as they really are. Missionaries did not bring Christianity to destroy their land, but to teach them a new way of life that might have sounded foreign to them. In this light, the book has created the awareness that, despite the differences in people's cultures, they can still live together once they take to the road of flexibility and change. The book has touched on a variety of points, thereby bringing out the rich culture of the people of Igboland, their cosmology, and psychology – what affects a member of the community is considered as affecting everybody. The collegiality and solidarity of the Igbo have been high lightened in this book. Christianity can only be meaningful in Igboland of Nigeria when taught and introduced in the spirit of the founder. Hypocrisy is not a term in the divine equation. The Igbo need ministers who will tell the truth at all times and lead them by example.

Consequently, the research adopted a unique position by involving teachers, who are indigenous to Igboland, in the development and analysis of the book. This book, "The Dilemma of the growth of the Christian faith in Igboland – Psychological and Pastoral Perspective," should be a reference manual where, not only Christians can draw some spiritual maps, but the traditionalists may as well. Having come a long way in this discussion, there is also the need to acknowledge our sources in chapter seven of this book.

CHAPTER SEVEN

⟨⟨

RESOURCES AND BIBLIOGRAPHY

Achebe, Chinua. 1994. Things fall apart. New York: Anchor Books.

Achebe, Chinua, 1983. The trouble with Nigeria, Fourth Dimension publishing co. Ltd.

Alexander, J. (ed). 1966. The Jerusalem Bible. Darton: Longman & Todd Ltd. Altizir, T., 1966. *The Gospel of Christian Atheism,* Philadelphia: Bobbs Merill Press,

Agwulonu, Fedelis, I. The Creative Intelligence, 2001

Arinze, Francis A. 1970. Sacrifice in Ibo Religion. Ibadan: University Press.

Aristotle – Biography, The Philosopher's Lighthouse, Aristotle's Life. Don Asselin, Anozie I. Peter, *The Religious Import of Igbo Names,* Rome: Urban University, 1982.

Anscombe, G. E. M, Modern Moral Philosophy, 1958, Philosophy 33: 1 – 19.

Aumann, Jordan. 1985. Christian Spirituality. Wipf and Stock Publishers

Austin, F. (ed). 1975. Vatican Council II, the Conciliar and Post Councilliar Documents. Dublin: Fowler Wright Book Ltd.

Ayandele, Emmanuel A. 1988. The Missionary Impact on Modern Nigeria 1842-1914. London: Longman.

Azorji, Eugene E. 1986. The Concept of the Sacred in Igbo Traditional Religion. Rome: Urban University.

Baunoch, Joseph (ed). 2006. Foundation Theology 2006. South Bend, Indiana: Cloverdale Book Publishers.

Bellow, J. 1981. Basic Principles of Teaching Education in Africa. Ibadan: Spectrum Books Ltd.

Benedict XVI. Pope. 2009. THE PRIESTHOOD Spiritual Thoughts Series. Vatican: Libreria Editrice Vaticana.

Benedict XVI, Pope, His Visit to Africa, Arkansas Catholic, Volume 97, Number 39, October 3, 2009.

Benson, Herbert, 1996. (With Marg Stark), *Timeless Healing; the Power and Biology of Belief,* New York: Simon & Schuster Publishers,

Bradbury, R.E. 1959. The Benin Kingdom and the Edo-speaking peoples of South –Western Nigeria: Ethnographic Survey of Africa, London

Buchanna, K. M and Pugh, J.C, 1964, land and people in Nigeria, London

Castrovilla, Mari. (Ed.). 2000. A Guide to Religious Ministries For Catholic Men and Women 21ˢᵗ Edition. New York: Catholic News

Publishing Company. Chantilly, VA: The Teaching Company, 2001.

Chcethan J.N, 1901. Works in the Igbo Country , Niger and Yoruba Notes.

Childe Gordon, 1942. What Happened in History, Harmondsworth Publishers.

Clayton, A. E, 1900. The parting of the ways, Niger and Yoruba Notes

David, Daniel; Lynn, Steven Jay (2009). Rational and irrational belief, research, theory and clinical practice, Ellis, Albert book New York US Oxford University press Binghamton, NY.

Dike, Victor, E. 1999. "The Caste System in Nigeria, Democratization and Culture: Socio- political and Civil Rights Implications" Online publication: www.afbis.com, June 13, 1999

Douglas, J. D. & Hillyer, N. (eds). 1992. New Bible Dictionary Second Edition. Wheaton: Intervarsity Press.

Eamon, Tobin. 1993. How to Forgive Yourself and Others: Steps to Reconciliation. Revised and Expanded. MO: Liguori Publications.

Ejizu, Christopher I. 1984. "Continuity and Discontinuity in African Traditional Religion" in Cahiers des Religions Africaines. Vol.18. No. 1.

Ekejiuba. F, 1967. Preliminary Notes on Brasswork of Eastern Nigeria, African Notes, IV, No 2, 11-15.

Ekennia, N. Justin, 2003. *Bio-Medical Ethics, Issues, Trends & Problems,* Owerri, Nigeria: Barloz Publishers Inc.

Ekweh, Christian I. 2002. Righteousness: An Insightful Commentary on Proverbs Ch. 3. Jos: Deka Publishers.

Ekpunobi, E. 1982. A handbook for the Teaching of Religious and Moral in Schools and Colleges. Kaduna: Baraka Publishers.

Ellis, Albert (1957). Rational psychotherapy and individual psychology. Journal of individual psychology.

Ellis, Albert (2003). Early theories and practices of rational emotive behavior, Journal of rational-emotive and cognitive-behavior therapy.

Ejizu, I. Christopher, "Continuity and Discontinuity in African Traditional Religion" *in Cahiers des Religions Africaines.* Vol.18. No. 1, 1984

Ezeoke, E. Aiphonsus, 2011. Dying Education: Necessary Reformation, The Nigerian Case. Indiana: iUniverse Publications.

Ezeonyia, Vincent V. 1998.Tears of Misfortune, Pastoral Letter. Ehi: Sibros Printing Press.

Fagothey, A. 1963. *Right and Reason,* London: The C. V. Mosby Company Flannery, Austin, (ed.) 1975. *Vatican Council 11, The Conciliar and Post Conciliar Documents,* Dublin: Fowler Wright Books

Frick, B. Willar, 1989. Humanistic Psychology: Conversations with; Abraham Maslow, Gardner Murphy, Carl Rogers, Wyndham Hall Press.Goot, Vander Mary, 1987. Narrating Psychology or How Psychology gets made, USA, Wyndham Hall Press.

George, Harris, 1999. *Agent-Centered Morality, An Aristotelian Alternative to Kantian Internalism,* Berkeley, California: Univ. of California press.

Haring, B. 1964. Christian Renewal in a changing world. New York: Desclee Company, Inc.

Haring, B. 1964. *Christian Renewal in a changing World,* New York: Desclee Company, Inc.

Hannah Arendt, 1958. *The Human Condition,* Chicago: Univ. of Chicago Press

Hartle D, Bronze, 1966. Objects from Ezira, Eastern Nigeria, The West African Archaeological Newsletter, (No 4)

Hellwig, K. Monika. 1981. Understanding Catholicism. New York: Paulist Press.

Idowu, Bolaji E. 1976. African Traditional Religion, A Definition. London: SCM press.

Henry B. Veatch, *Aristotle: A Contemporary Appreciation,* Bloomington: Indiana Univ. Press, 1974.

Heraclitus, Talk: Heraclitus Wikiquote, July 2, 2009

Heraclitus, Internet Encyclopedia of Philosophy (IEP)

Heraclitus, Wikipedia, the free Encyclopedia

Higgins T. S., *Man As Man,* Milwaukee: The Bruce Publishers, 1948.

Hollander, R., Sugrue, M. & Thurn, D. *The Bible and Western Culture, Parts 11 – 111, Springfield, VA:* The Teaching Company, LP, 1999.

Iheoma, Eugene E, 1990. The Bible in Christian life. Nigeria

Ilega, Daniel I. (ed). 2000. West African Religious Traditions, Ado-Ekiti: Hamaz Global Ventures.

Ilogu Edmund C, 1974. Christianity and Igbo Culture, London: Nok Publishers Ltd.

Ilo, C. Stan. 2006. The Face of Africa: Looking Beyond The *Shadows,* Bloomington, IN, USA: AuthorHouse Publishers.

Isichei, Elizabeth. 1977. A History of the Igbo People. London: Macmillan Press.

John Paul 11. 1995. Evangelium Vitae. Vatican: Vatican Press.

Johnson K. Timothy, 1999. *The Writings of the New Testament, An Interpretation, Revised Edition,* Minneapolis: Fortress Press,

Josef Pieper, *The Four Cardinal Virtues; Prudence, Justice, Fortitude, Temperance,* tr. Richard and Clara Winston, NY: Harcourt, Brace, and World, 1965.

Kant I., Foundations of the Metaphysics of Morals, J. Ellingen edition, Indianapolis: Hacket, 1992.

Karol Wojtyla, Pope John Paul 11, 1981. Love and Responsibility, tr. H. T. Willetts, NY: Farrar, Straus, Giroux.

Kelly, Eugene, 2006. The Basics of Western Philosophy, Greenwood Press. Kilani, R. Abdul, 2000. "Structural Adjustment Program and Religious Consciousness in Nigeria" *in the Journal of Religion and Culture Vol. 1,* Port Harcourt: University Press

Knight, Kevin. 2007. The Advent. The Catholic Encyclopedia.

Koterski, W. Joseph, 2001. *The Ethics of Aristotle, Video Series, Tapes 1-111,* VA: The Teaching Company

Koterski, W. Joseph, S.J., 2001. Philosophy & Intellectual History: The Ethics of Aristotle, Chantilly, VA: The Teaching Company.

Kraut, R. 2005. Aristotle's Ethics in Stanford Encyclopedia of Philosophy, Lawrence, J. P. 1972. *Individual Instruction,* London: McGraw Hill Book Company,

Lennox G. James, 2001. *Aristotle's Philosophy of Biology: Studies in the Origin of the Life Sciences,* Cambridge: Cambridge Univ. press.

Lindesmith, A. R. & Strauss, A. L. 1956. Social Psychology. New York: Holt, Rinehart & Winston, Inc.

Lucas, C. J. 1976. What is Philosophy of Education? London: The Macmillan Co.

Mackie, J. L., 1990. Ethics: Investing Right and Wrong. London: Penguin Books,.

MacNutt, Francis. 1992. The Power to Heal. Indiana: Ave Maria Press. McKenzie, J. L. 1966. Dictionary of the Bible. London: Cassoll & Co. Ltd.

Meliaender, Gilbert, 1981. *Friendship,* Notre Dame: Univ. of Notre Dame Press.

Michael, De La Bedoyere, 1966. The Future of Catholic Christianity. London: Garden City Press.

Morgan, John H. 2003. Unfinished Business. The Terminal All-But-Dissertation Phenomenon in American Higher Education. Bristol Indiana: Cloverdale Corporation.

Morgan, John H. & Neitzke, Russell. 2007. From Beginning to End. Internet Research and the Writing Process: An author's guide with CD-Rom. South Bend, IN: Clover Books.

Morgan, John H. (Ed.) 2009. Foundation Theology 2009 Student Essays for Ministry Professionals. Mishawaka, Indiana: The Victoria Press.

Mozia, Michael I, 1987. Solidarity in the Church and Solidarity among the Igbos of Nigeria. Ibadan: Claverianum press

Murray, M. V., 1960. Problems in Ethics, New York: Holt & Company, Inc.

Murphy, Stephen A. Poker Sites Matching Player's Donations to Haiti

Nwachukwu, Anthony O. 2002. Salvation in African Context. Owerri, Nigeria: Barloz Publishers.

Nwachukwu, Anthony O. 2010. Keeping Human Relationships Together: Self Guide to Healthy Living [Studies in Spiritual Psychology vis-à-vis Human Values], IN, USA: iUniverse Publications

Nwigwe, L. 1983, A Patriotic Invitation for a Moral Renaissance of fresh. Enugu: Snap press

Nwigwe, B. E. 2001. Elements of Philosophy. Port Harcourt: PAM Unique Publishing Company Ltd.

Obiora, Fidelis K. 1998. The Devine Deceit Business in Religion. Enugu: Rex Charles & Patrick.

Odiegwu, Donatus, 1997. Evangelization and Inculturation in Africa Yesterday and Today, Enugu : Center News Magazine.

Okeke, C.C. 1989. Philosophy of Education, Concepts, Analysis and applications. Owerri: Totan Publishers.

Olson, Robert G. 1967 Deontological Ethics, In Paul Edwards (ed.) The Encyclopedia of Philosophy, London: Collier Macmillan

Omoregbe, Joseph I. 1996. A Philosophical Look at Religion. London: Joja Press.

Omoregbe, Joseph I. 1999. Comparative Religion Christianity and Other World Religions in Dialogue. Lagos: Joja Press.

Onwubiko, Oliver A. 1999. African Thought, Religion and Culture. *Vol.1.* Enugu: Snaap Press.

Owen, A. N., 1928. Ethics: General and Special, New York: Macmillan Company.

Philips Simpson, L. Peter, *The Politics of Aristotle, tr. with introduction, analysis, and notes,* Chapel Hill, NC: Univ. of North Carolina Press, 1997.

Paulin, C. H. 1992. Salvific Invitation and Loving Response: The Fundamental Christian Dialogue. Lagos, Academy Press PLC.

Rahner, Karl. 1982. Encyclopedia of Theology, The Concise Sacramentum Mundi. (ed). New York: Crossroad Publishing Company.

Robinson, N. Daniel (Prof.) 1997. The Great Ideas of Psychology. By [Part 1 of 4 to Part 4 of 4.] Printed in United States of America, The Teaching Company Limited Partnership.

Robley E. Whitson, *The Center Scriptures,* IN: The United Institute, 1995.

Romero, A. Anna & Kemp, M. Steven, 2007. *Psychology Demystified, A Self- Teaching Guide,* New York, NY: McGraw-Hill.

Ross W. D. tr. Nicomachean Ethics by Aristotle 350 BC, Books 1-10. Schollimeier, Paul, 1994. *Other Selves: Aristotle on Personal and political Friendships,* Albany: SUNY Press,

Sherman, Nancy, 1997. *Making a Necessity of Virtues: Aristotle and Kant on Virtue,* Cambridge: Cambridge Univ. Press,

Shaw J. & Morgan John H. 2006. Religion and Society, Summer Programme in Theology 2006. Indiana: Cloverdale Corporation.

Shaw, Thurstan, Igbo-Ukwu, 1970. An Account of Archaeological Discoveries in Eastern Nigeria, London, 2 Vols.

Singer, P., 1979. Practical Ethics, Cambridge: Cambridge University Press

Sugrue, M. & Ford, A., 1999. *The Bible and Western Culture, Part 1*, Springfield, VA: The Teaching Company Limited Partnership,

Sugrue, A., Hollander, R., & Thurn, D., 1999. *The Bible and the Western Culture, Video Series, Parts 1-111*, VA: The Teaching Company,

Talbot, P.A. 1969. The peoples of Southern Nigeria; Vol, 11, London

Trimpey, Jack (1974), The Small Book, Rational recovery system, 1st Ed. Published by Delacorte Press Bantam Doubleday Dell Publishing group Inc. 666 fifth Avenue, New York, NY 10103.

Uchedu, Victor C. 1965. The Igbo of Southeast Nigeria Chicago: Holt, Rinehart and Winston Publishers

Velten, Emmett & Penn, Patricia E. 2010. REBT for people with co-occurring

problems; professional resources press/professional resources exchange.

Webster, M. 1979. Webster's New Collegiate Dictionary, Massachusetts: G. & C. Merriam Company. W. F. R. Hardie, *Aristotle's Ethical Theory*, Oxford: Oxford University Press, 1980.

William, T. 1929. History of Philosophy. New York: Ginn & Co. Inc.

William K. Frankena, 1980. *Thinking of Morality,* Ann Arbor: Univ. of Michigan.

Wolman, B. B., ed., 1973. *Dictionary of Behavioral Science,* New York: Litlon Educational Publishers

Yves, Simon. 1992. The Tradition of Natural Law. Bronx, NY: Fordham Univ. Press.

Members of the Catholic (Trans) 1970. Biblical Association of America, *The New American Bible,* Kansas: Catholic Bible publishers.

The Jerusalem Bible, Darton, Longman & Todd, London: 1968 Edition.

The Catholic Bishop's Conference of Nigeria. 2004. I Chose You-The Nigerian in the Third Millennium. A publication of the Catholic Secretariat of Nigeria.

The Catholic Encyclopedia, Vol. IV. 1908. NY: Robert Appleton Company.

The Catechism of the Catholic Church. 1994. Vatican: Paulist Press.

Britannica, Internet Guide Selection, 1997-2002. *Aristotle: Ethics and the Virtues.* Garth Kemerling.

The population of the Igbos is more than that of Norway, Switzerland, Denmark, Belgium, and Luxembourg combined (Igbo Studies Association (not dated) www.igbostudies.com/ information. htm

Arkansas Catholic, Conference of African Bishop's Synod in Rome, Volume 98, Number 40, November 7, 2009.

The Account, which follows of the Igbo- Ukwu investigations, and their significance is bound on Thurstan Shaw, Igbo- Ukwu. An account of archaeological discoveries in eastern Nigeria (Vol 3, London), 1970.

Interview with Councilor FRANCIS Nwanjiziaka, 80, a traditional Ezeji in Ngor Okpala, on 6th July 2008.

Wikipedia, *the Free Encyclopedia* – launched as the English Wikipedia on January 15, 2001, (Internet accessible Materials).

2010 Haiti Earthquake News and Media at Open Directory Project

Haiti earthquake aid pledged by country, *DataBlog* at The Guardian

ICT4Peace Foudation Wiki on Haiti Earthquake

The Internet Encyclopedia of Philosophy, Aristotle (384-322 BCE.): Ethics.

Human Nature and Eudaimonia in Aristotle, NY: Peter Lang, 1989.

National Reference Center for Bioethics Literature, World's Largest Library for ethical issues in medicine and biomedical research

CHAPTER EIGHT

⟨℘⟩

APPENDICES AND GLOSSARY OF TERMS

APPENDICES

APPENDIX I: The 'TPDGCF' Questionnaire

The 'TPDGCF' Questionnaire is designed to elicit information from the Teachers on their Perception of the Dilemma of the Growth of the Christian Faith in Igboland of Nigeria. This is not a pass or fail assessment instrument. It is a research instrument or tool that would help to determine the psychological and pastoral implications and effects of the Christian faith on the Ibo people of Nigeria. The instrument could equally be used to guide hypocritical ways and lapses in the practice of the Christian faith generally. You, as a respondent, are therefore requested to respond to the questions as clearly, distinctively and honestly as possible. Whatever answer or response you give will be treated with utmost confidentiality and privacy.

Section A: Personal Data

Name (optional)...

Age.................................... Sex..............

Nationality...

Type of Profession and Marital status (1) Retired ---------------

(2) Current ---------------- (3) Single -----------------

(4) Married -----------------------------------

Length of time in your Profession................................

Highest Qualification/Position in your area of

specialty...

Indicate your State/Country/Autonomous

Community/Village............................. ....

Section B: Main body of TPDGCF

B.1: The nature and level of the dilemma of the growth of the Christian faith in Igboland

Kindly indicate your opinion(s) from the items below, among which category or group of people you have observed serious lack of real faith in religion

1. Among the Catholics
2. The Protestants
3. Traditional religionists
4. Christian Fanatics

B.2: Sources (causes) of Fatih Dilemma in the growth of the Christian Religion

From the items, numbered 9 – 12, kindly choose what could be the possible source(s) or cause(s) of the dilemma of the growth the Christian faith among the Ibos.

5. Poor Catechesis and lack of proper direction
6. Lack of self-convictions and interests in religious matters
7. Personal choices and materialistic tendencies
8. Role of religious ministers and bigotry

B.3: The possibility of totally eradicating religious predicaments in the growth of the Christian faith

From the two options given below, kindly indicate your opinion. Is it possible to completely eradicate religious dilemma and hypocrisy from its practice?

9. Religious dilemma and confusion can totally be crushed among the people
10. Such eradication would completely be impossible in the practice of Christian faith

B.4: Management of religious crisis in the growth of the Christian faith

In like manners, kindly indicate, which of these is the most plausible option(s) in the management of religious crisis among the people of Igboland?

11. People to live by examples
12. The Church to become in practice truly the human face of Christ

13. Enculturation of both religious values for holistic enhancement of the practice
14. Need for flexibility and ready for change

B.5:   Effects of Disorder and crisis on the progress of society

In your own opinion, do you think that lack of coherence and order in religious matters has any effect on the progress of society at large?

15. Disorder in religious matters can always hamper the progress of society
16. Disorder and faith crisis have no effect at all on the progress and unity of society

APPENDIX II: Glossary of Terms

Homo ------------------------------ Latin word for man

Ubiquitious ------------------------ Adjective, meaning – to be everywhere at the same point in time

Abrakataba ------------------------- Igbo expression for man-made magic

CBCN ------------------------------ Catholic Bishops' Conference of Nigeria

Umunna ---------------------------- Igbo word for one's community member/s

Endemic --------------------------- Referring to what is particular for the Africans

Oyibo ------------------------------ Oyibo is an Igbo word for the
white man/woman

Bekee-bu-agbara -------------------- The white people are seen as the
diety

Muo -------------------------------- Spirit ie, Igbo people are spirit

IR ---------------------------------- Internet Resource/s

CEDAW ---------------------------- Convention on the Elimination
of Discrimination Against
Women (1985)

DLM ------------------------------- Distance Learning Module/s

GTF -------------------------------- Graduate Theological
Foundation, in Indiana

Ndi Ogo Muo --------------------- Worshippers of the gods other
than God

TPDGCF -------------------------- Teachers' Perceptions of the
Dilemma of the Growth of
the Christian Faith (Research
Instrument)

Author Biography

Bartholomew N. Okere was born in the family of Okere Asonye in Umuaku-Ntu, Ngor Okpala Local Government Area. He was ordained a Catholic Priest in 1990. As a dedicated Priest, he travelled to Jerusalem on Pilgrimage (JP), as an effort to deepen the growth of the Nigerian Faith. Dr. Okere is Nigerian and has served as Pastor and Zonal Vicar for eighteen years in Nigeria, during which time he published two scholarly books. He founded many organizations that emphasize and encourage the study of the Bible as a weapon to put into practice the teachings of the Catholic faith. Once a youth Leader, he always emphasized that discipline and values of right choices and behaviors are the keys to success. He has worked in many Parishes in the Archdiocese of Owerri, Nigeria. In addition to his Priestly Ministry on different levels, Dr. Okere has held many ecclesiastical and public positions in the Catholic Church. He was Assistant Administrator of Assumpta Cathedral Church, Owerri, Nigeria and a Fourth Degree Faithful Friar, and Honorary Life membership of the Knights of St. Columbus International.

His primary and post primary education distinguished him among his colleagues and acquaintances. Educated and schooled at Sacred Heart Seminary, Nsude Enugu and St.John Cross Nsukka, he came out in flying colors. He holds the B.A. Honors in Philosophy and M.A in Divinity from the St. Joseph's Major Seminary, Ikot Ekpene and Bigard Memorial Seminary, Enugu respectively, (affiliated Institutions of the Urbanian University, Rome). Dr. Okere, as a Counselor and Psychologist, had Post Graduate Diploma in Drug and Alcohol Counseling, Clinical Pastoral Education, Certificate for Resolve through Sharing (RTS), Bereavement Training in Early Pregnancy Loss, Stillbirth and Newborn Death. He is a Board Certified Chaplain (BCC) and member of the National Association of Catholic Chaplains (NACC) and has served over six years in the Hospital Ministry. He holds a PhD in Pastoral Psychology from the Graduate Theological Foundation (GTF), an affiliate of Oxford University, London.

REV. DR. BARTHOLOMEW N. OKERE
Barthnneji07@gmail.com